ETERNAL WARRIOR

DAYS OF STEEL

PETER MILLIGAN | CARY NORD | BRIAN REBER | DAVE SHARPE

D1223633

CONTENTS

Collection Cover Art: Bryan Hitch with David Baron

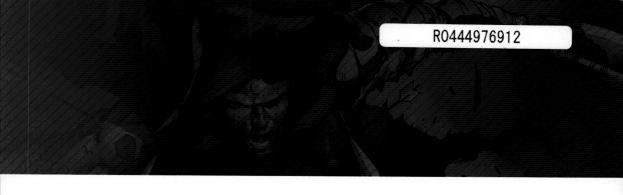

Editor: Alejandro Arbona
Editor-in-Chief: Warren Simons

VALIANT.

Peter Cuneo
Chairman

Dinesh Shamdasani
CEO & Chief Creative Officer

Gavin Cuneo
Chief Operating Officer & CFO

Fred Pierce
Publisher

Warren Simons
VP Editor-in-Chief

Walter Black
VP Operations

Hunter Gorinson
Director of Marketing, Communications
& Digital Media

Atom! Freeman
Matthew Klein
Andy Liegl
Sales Managers

Josh Johns
Digital Sales & Special Projects Manager

Travis Escarfullery
Jeff Walker
Production & Design Managers

Alejandro Arbona
Editor

Tom Brennan
Kyle Andrukiewicz
Associate Editors

Peter Stern
Publishing & Operations Manager

Chris Daniels
Marketing Coordinator

Ivan Cohen
Collection Editor

Steve Blackwell
Collection Designer

Rian Hughes/Device
Trade Dress & Book Design

Russell Brown
President, Consumer Products,
Promotions and Ad Sales

Jason Kothari
Vice Chairman

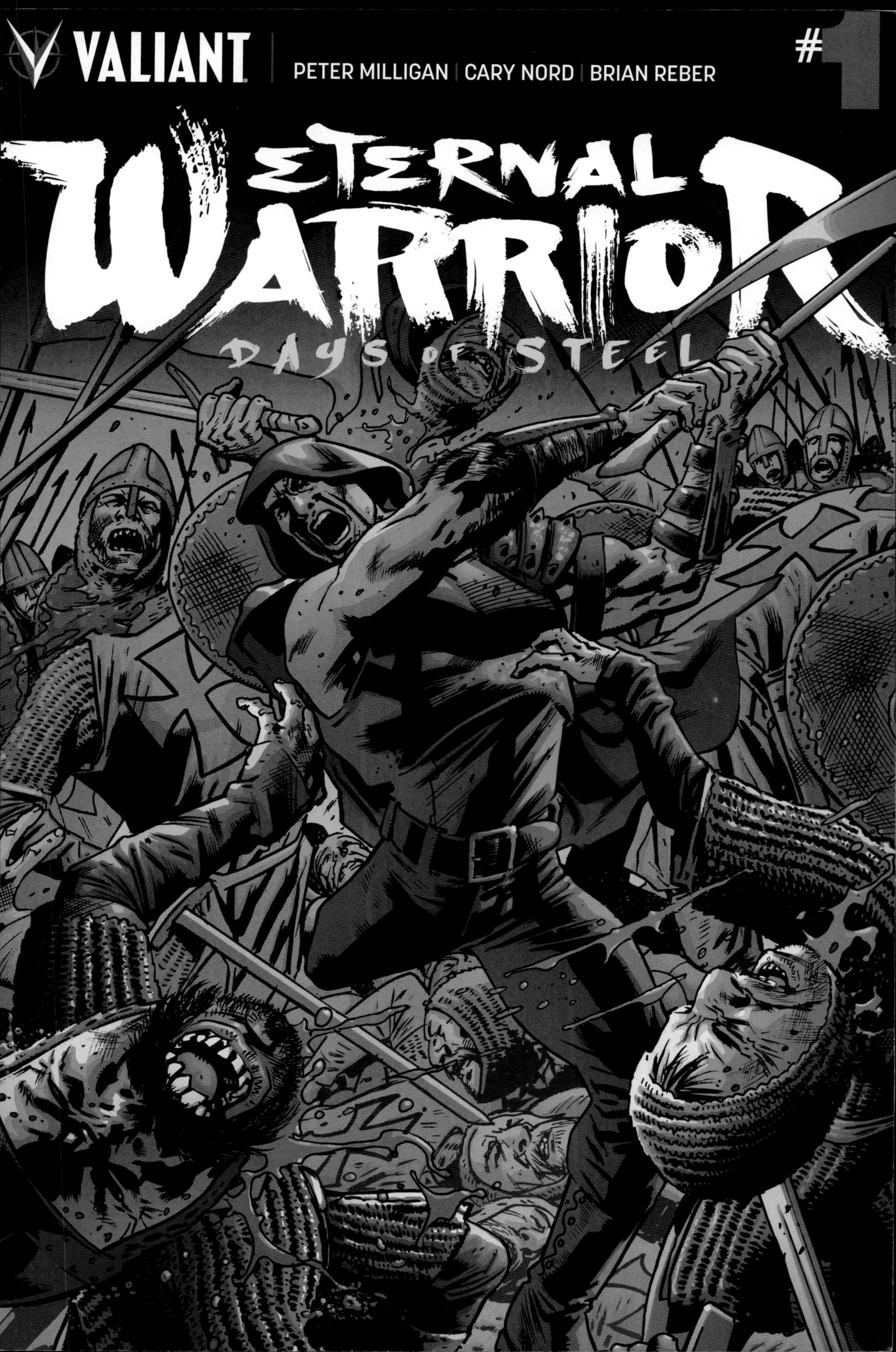
VALIANT
PETER MILLIGAN | CARY NORD | BRIAN REBER
#1
ETERNAL WARRIOR
DAYS OF STEEL

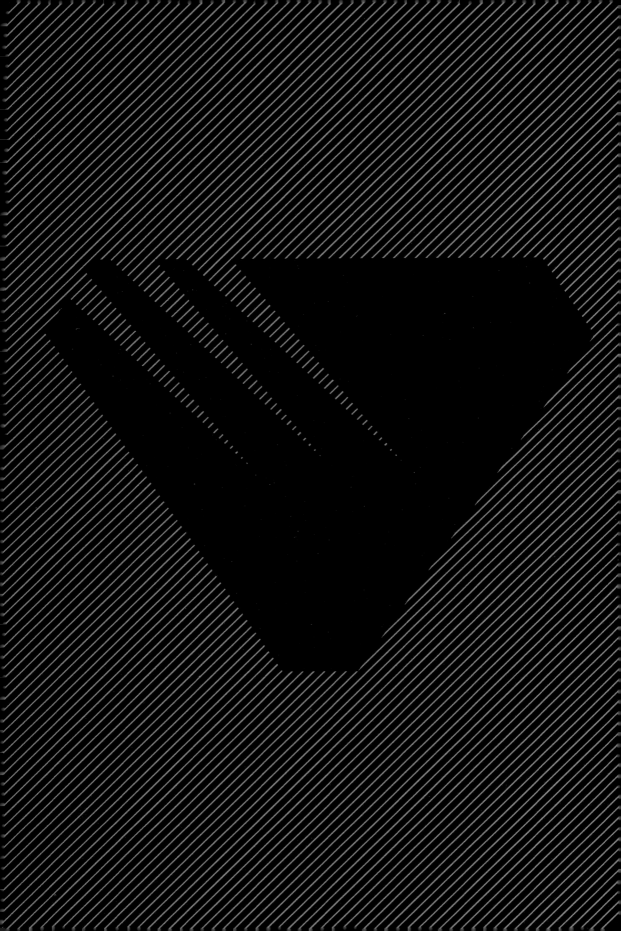

ETERNAL WARRIOR: DAYS OF STEEL

The story so far...

Gilad Anni-Padda is an immortal...and he has spent millennia in combat.

Serving at the behest of the Geomancer–who hears the voice of the Earth, and relays its commands–Gilad is the Eternal Warrior.

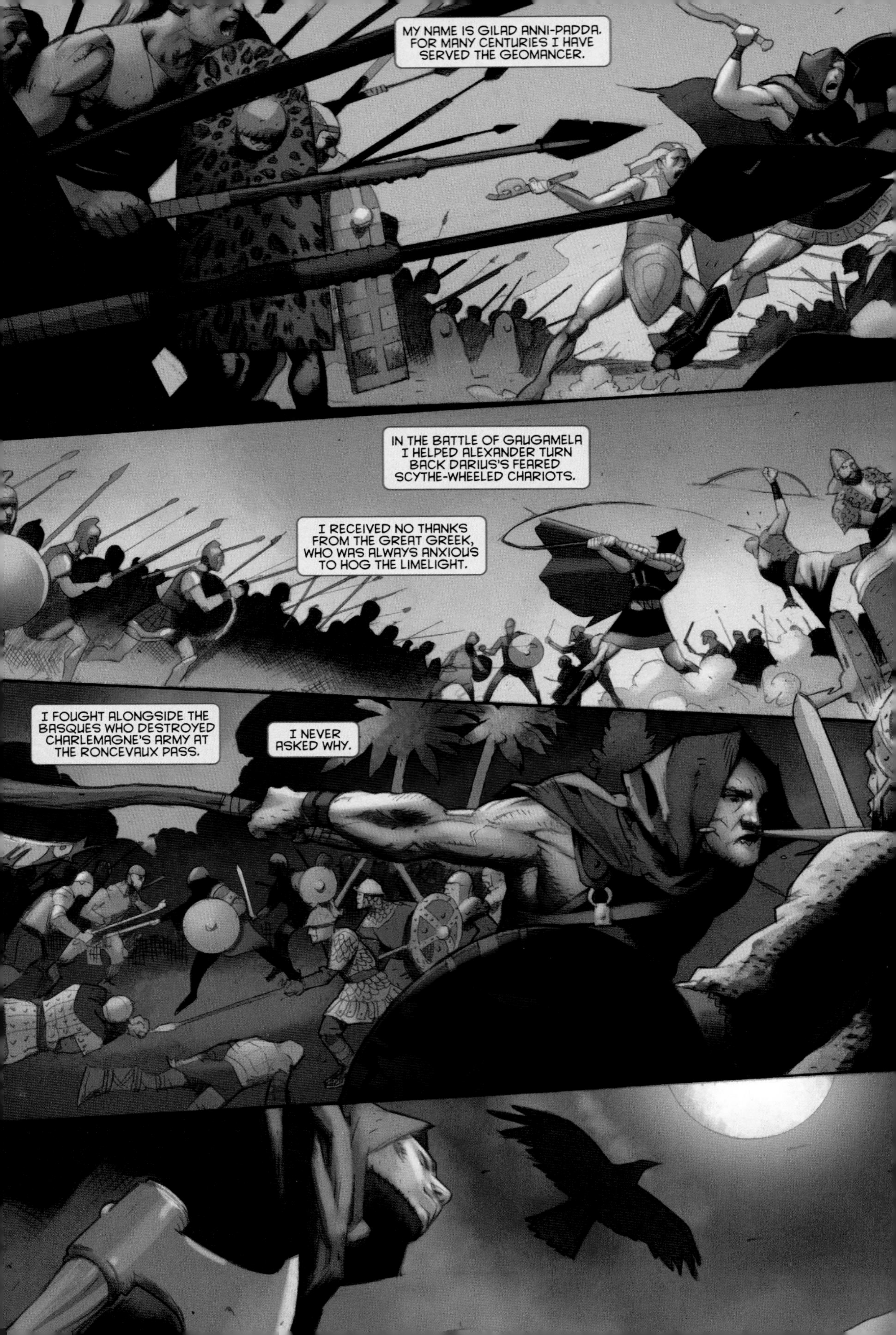
MY NAME IS GILAD ANNI-PADDA. FOR MANY CENTURIES I HAVE SERVED THE GEOMANCER.
IN THE BATTLE OF GAUGAMELA I HELPED ALEXANDER TURN BACK DARIUS'S FEARED SCYTHE-WHEELED CHARIOTS.
I RECEIVED NO THANKS FROM THE GREAT GREEK, WHO WAS ALWAYS ANXIOUS TO HOG THE LIMELIGHT.
I FOUGHT ALONGSIDE THE BASQUES WHO DESTROYED CHARLEMAGNE'S ARMY AT THE RONCEVAUX PASS.
I NEVER ASKED WHY.

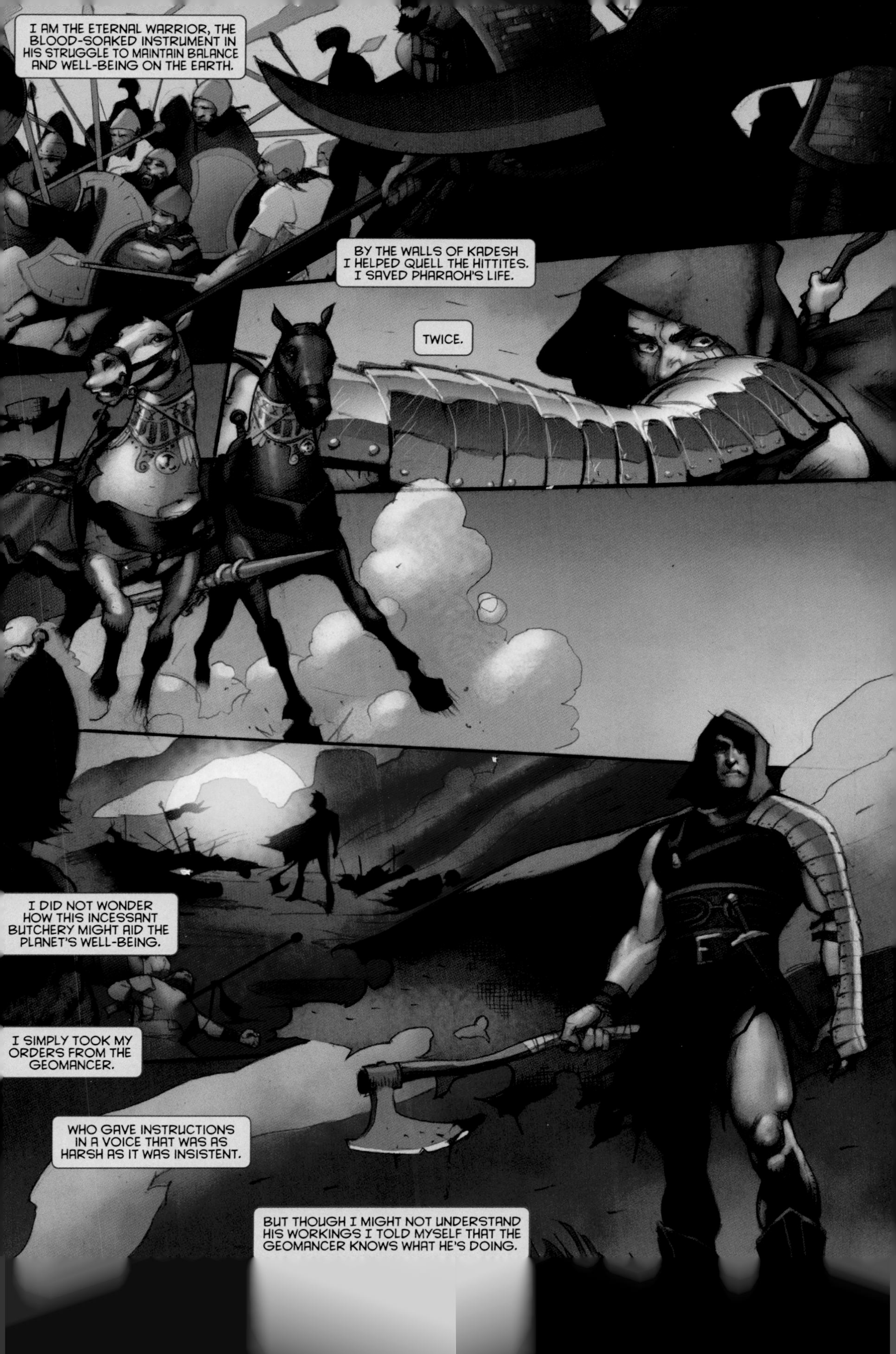
I AM THE ETERNAL WARRIOR, THE BLOOD-SOAKED INSTRUMENT IN HIS STRUGGLE TO MAINTAIN BALANCE AND WELL-BEING ON THE EARTH.
BY THE WALLS OF KADESH I HELPED QUELL THE HITTITES. I SAVED PHARAOH'S LIFE.
TWICE.
I DID NOT WONDER HOW THIS INCESSANT BUTCHERY MIGHT AID THE PLANET'S WELL-BEING.
I SIMPLY TOOK MY ORDERS FROM THE GEOMANCER.
WHO GAVE INSTRUCTIONS IN A VOICE THAT WAS AS HARSH AS IT WAS INSISTENT.
BUT THOUGH I MIGHT NOT UNDERSTAND HIS WORKINGS I TOLD MYSELF THAT THE GEOMANCER KNOWS WHAT HE'S DOING.

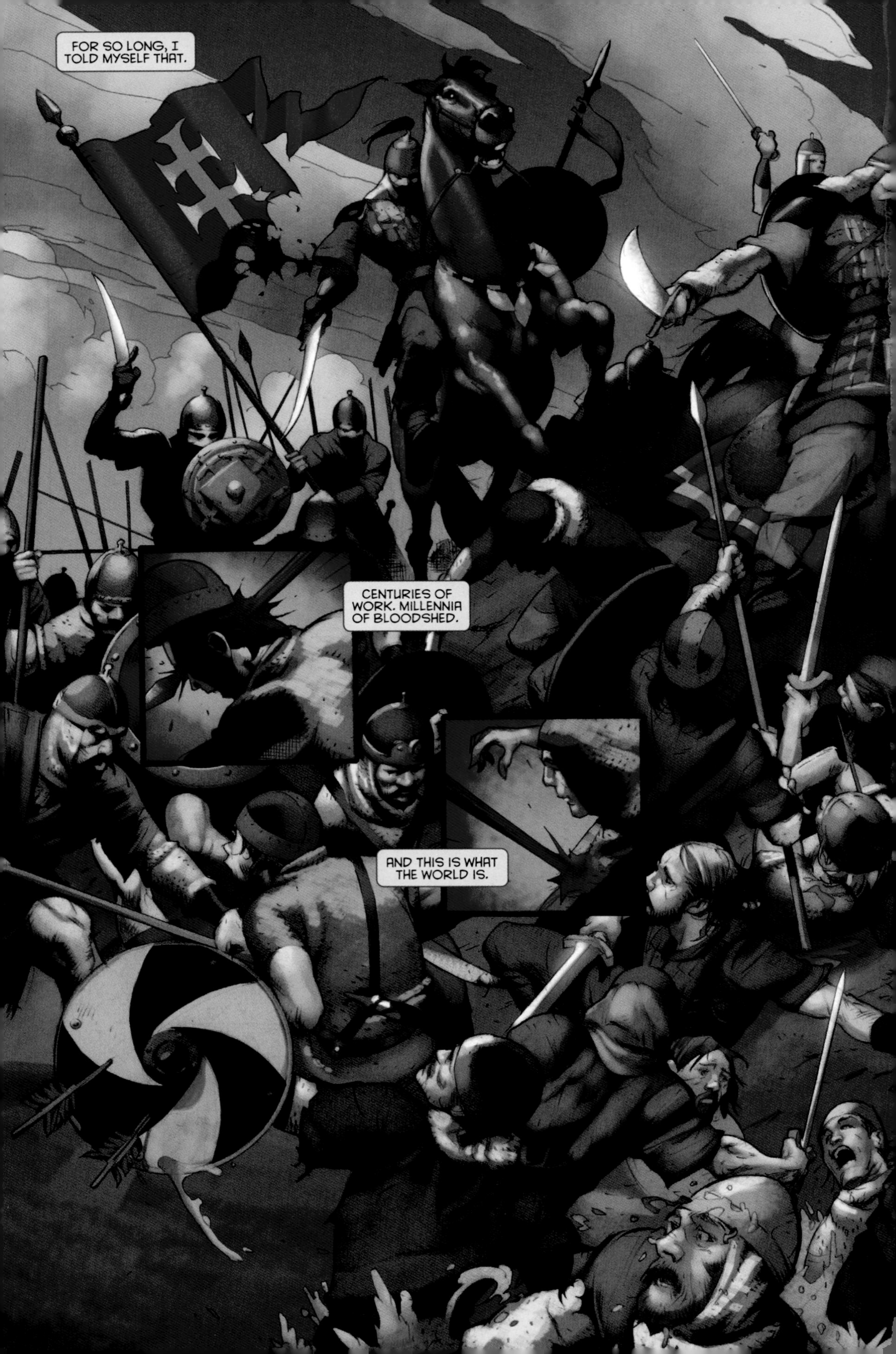
FOR SO LONG, I TOLD MYSELF THAT.
CENTURIES OF WORK. MILLENNIA OF BLOODSHED.
AND THIS IS WHAT THE WORLD IS.

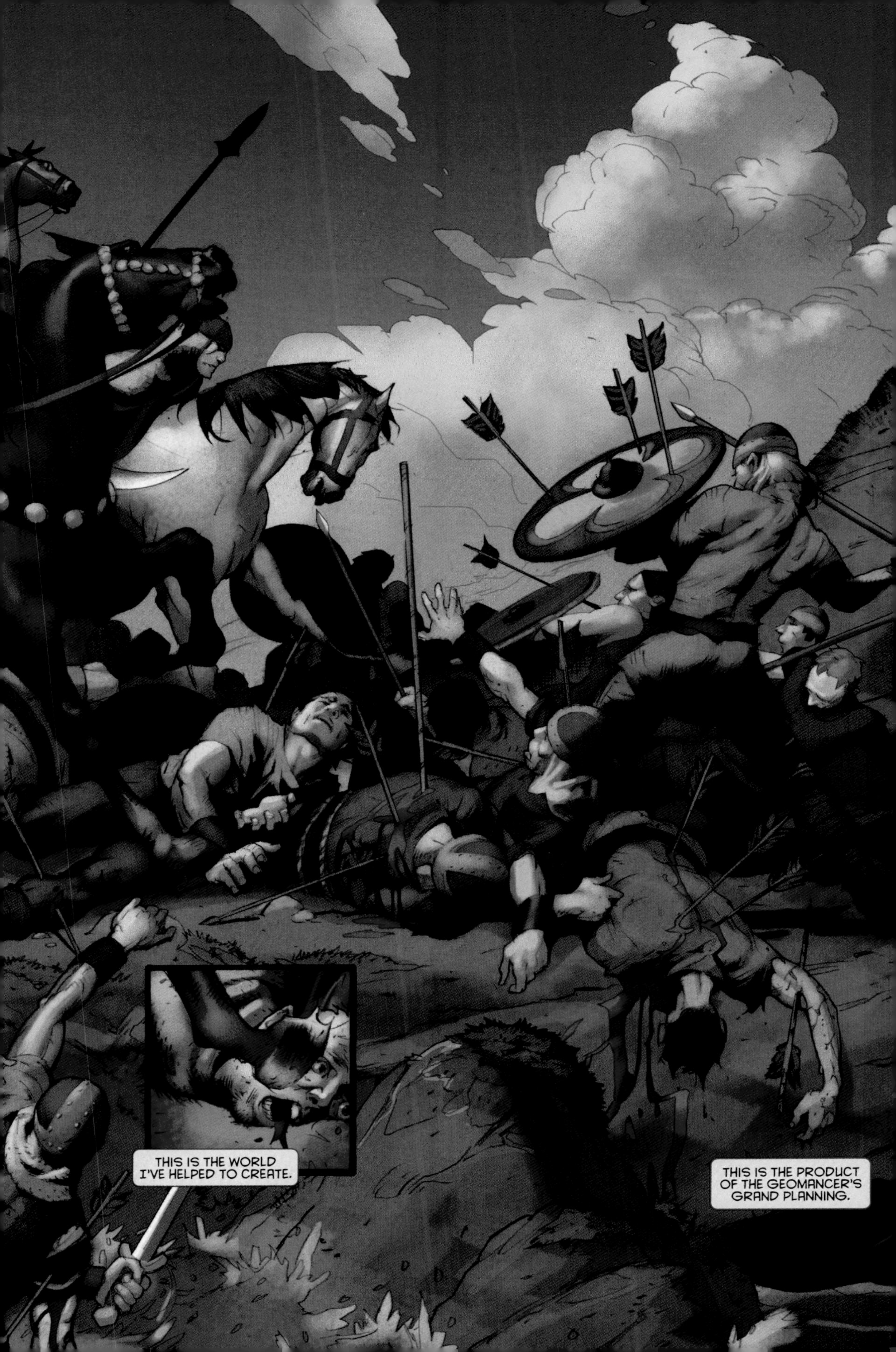
THIS IS THE WORLD
I'VE HELPED TO CREATE.
THIS IS THE PRODUCT
OF THE GEOMANCER'S
GRAND PLANNING.

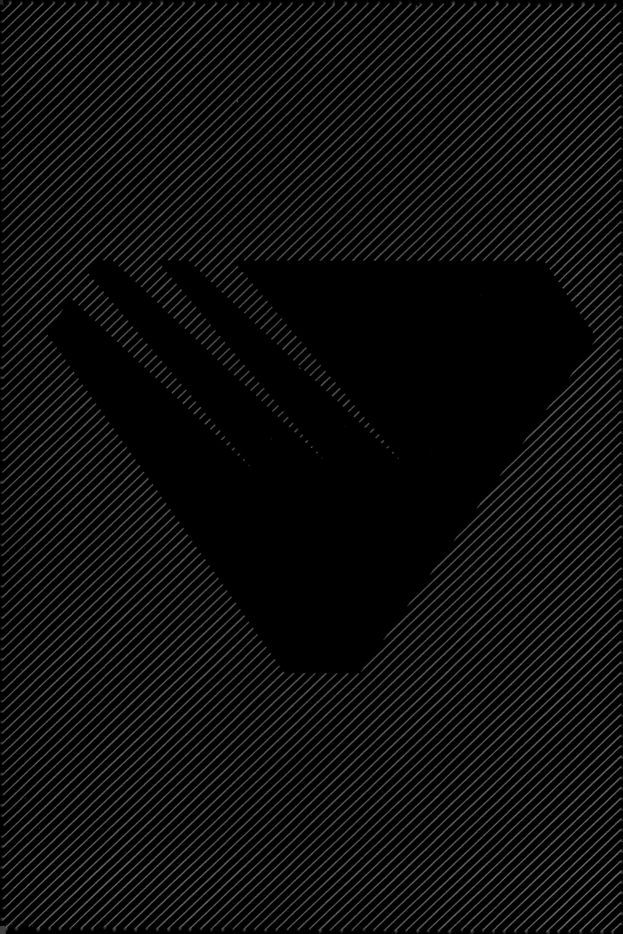

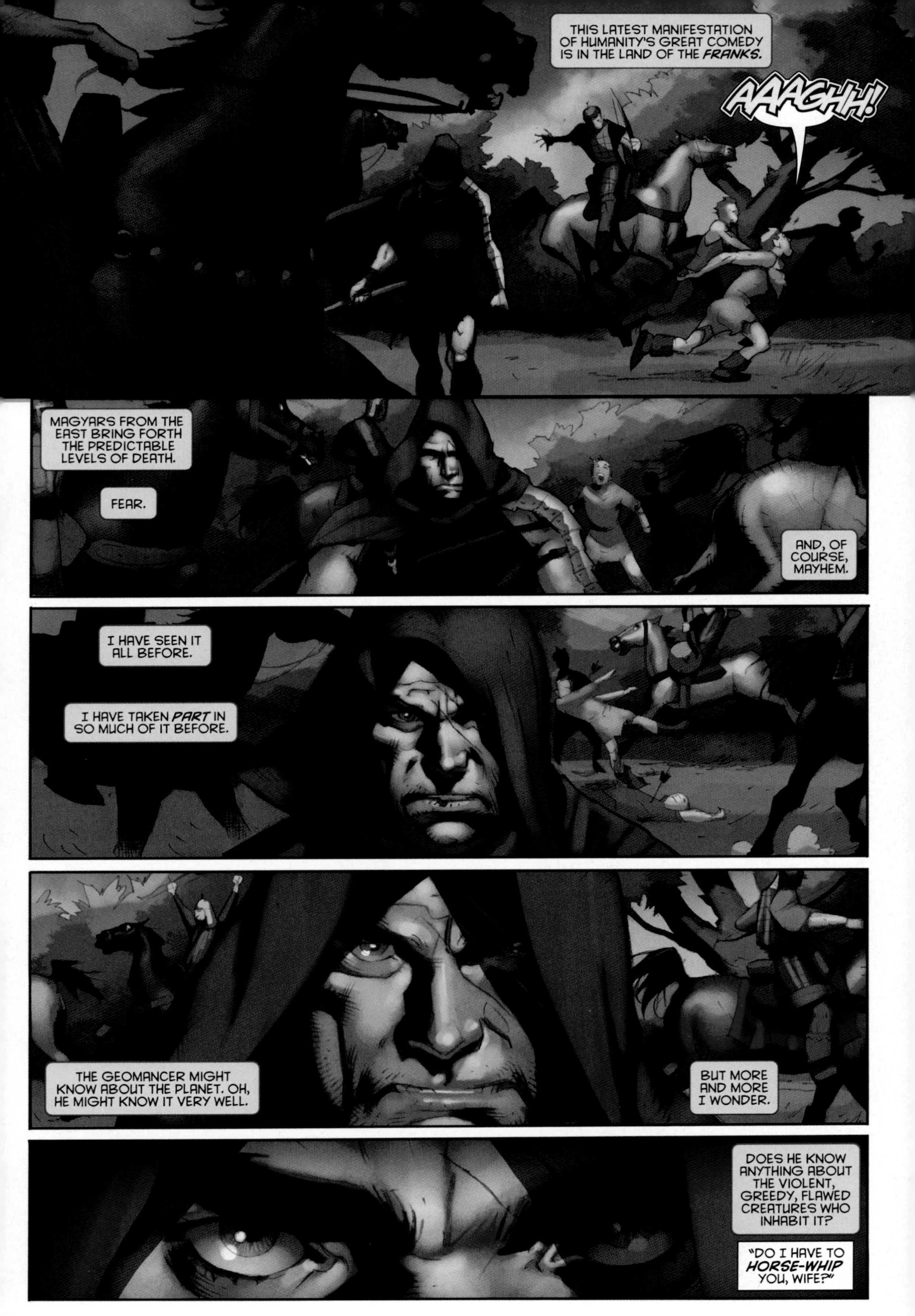
THIS LATEST MANIFESTATION OF HUMANITY'S GREAT COMEDY IS IN THE LAND OF THE *FRANKS.*
AAAGHH!
MAGYARS FROM THE EAST BRING FORTH THE PREDICTABLE LEVELS OF DEATH.
FEAR.
AND, OF COURSE, MAYHEM.
I HAVE SEEN IT ALL BEFORE.
I HAVE TAKEN *PART* IN SO MUCH OF IT BEFORE.
THE GEOMANCER MIGHT KNOW ABOUT THE PLANET. OH, HE MIGHT KNOW IT VERY WELL.
BUT MORE AND MORE I WONDER.
DOES HE KNOW ANYTHING ABOUT THE VIOLENT, GREEDY, FLAWED CREATURES WHO INHABIT IT?
"DO I HAVE TO ***HORSE-WHIP*** YOU, WIFE?"

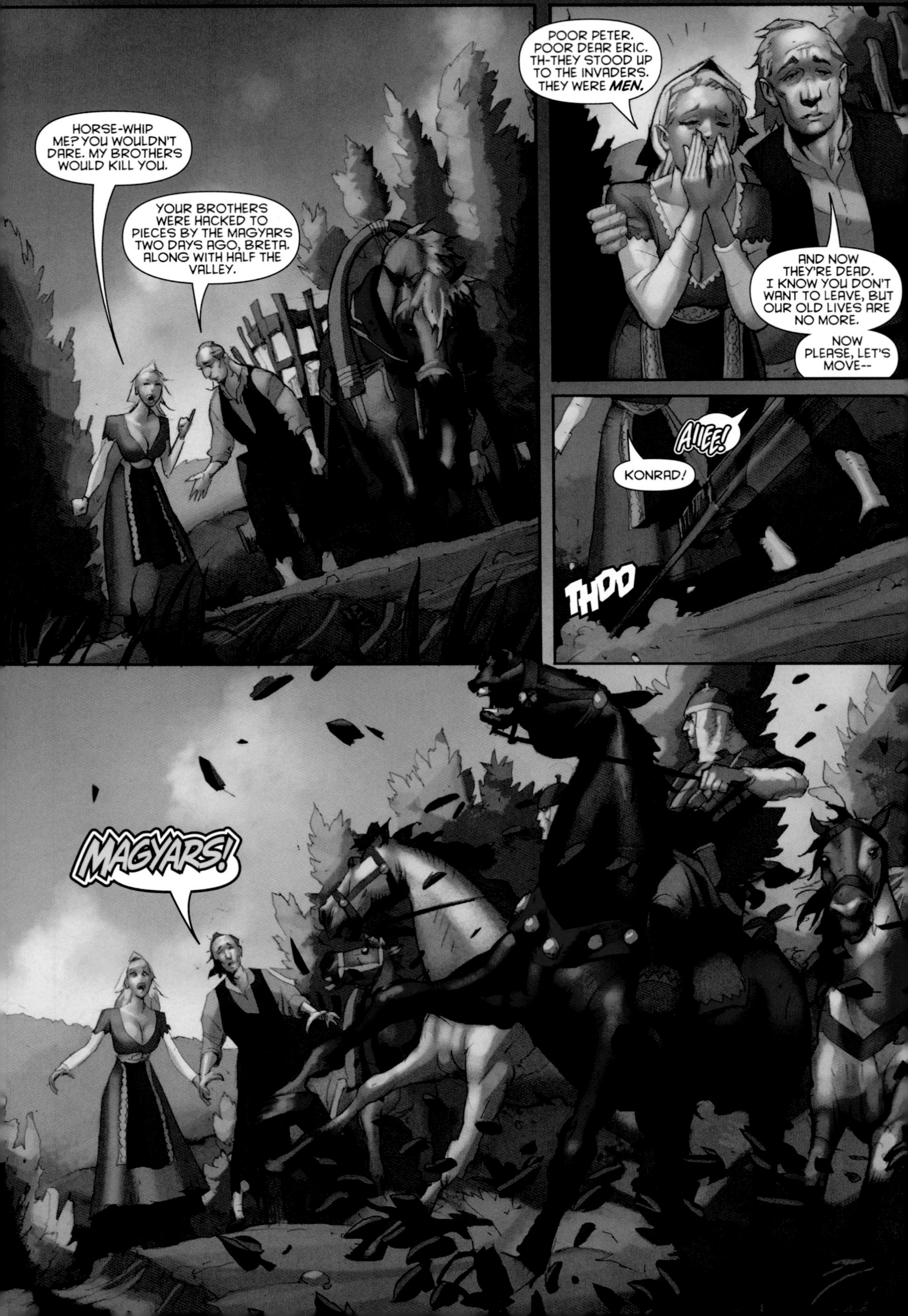
HORSE-WHIP ME? YOU WOULDN'T DARE. MY BROTHERS WOULD KILL YOU.
YOUR BROTHERS WERE HACKED TO PIECES BY THE MAGYARS TWO DAYS AGO, BRETA. ALONG WITH HALF THE VALLEY.
POOR PETER. POOR DEAR ERIC. TH-THEY STOOD UP TO THE INVADERS. THEY WERE *MEN.*
AND NOW THEY'RE DEAD. I KNOW YOU DON'T WANT TO LEAVE, BUT OUR OLD LIVES ARE NO MORE.
NOW PLEASE, LET'S MOVE--
AIIEE!
KONRAD!
THDD
MAGYARS!

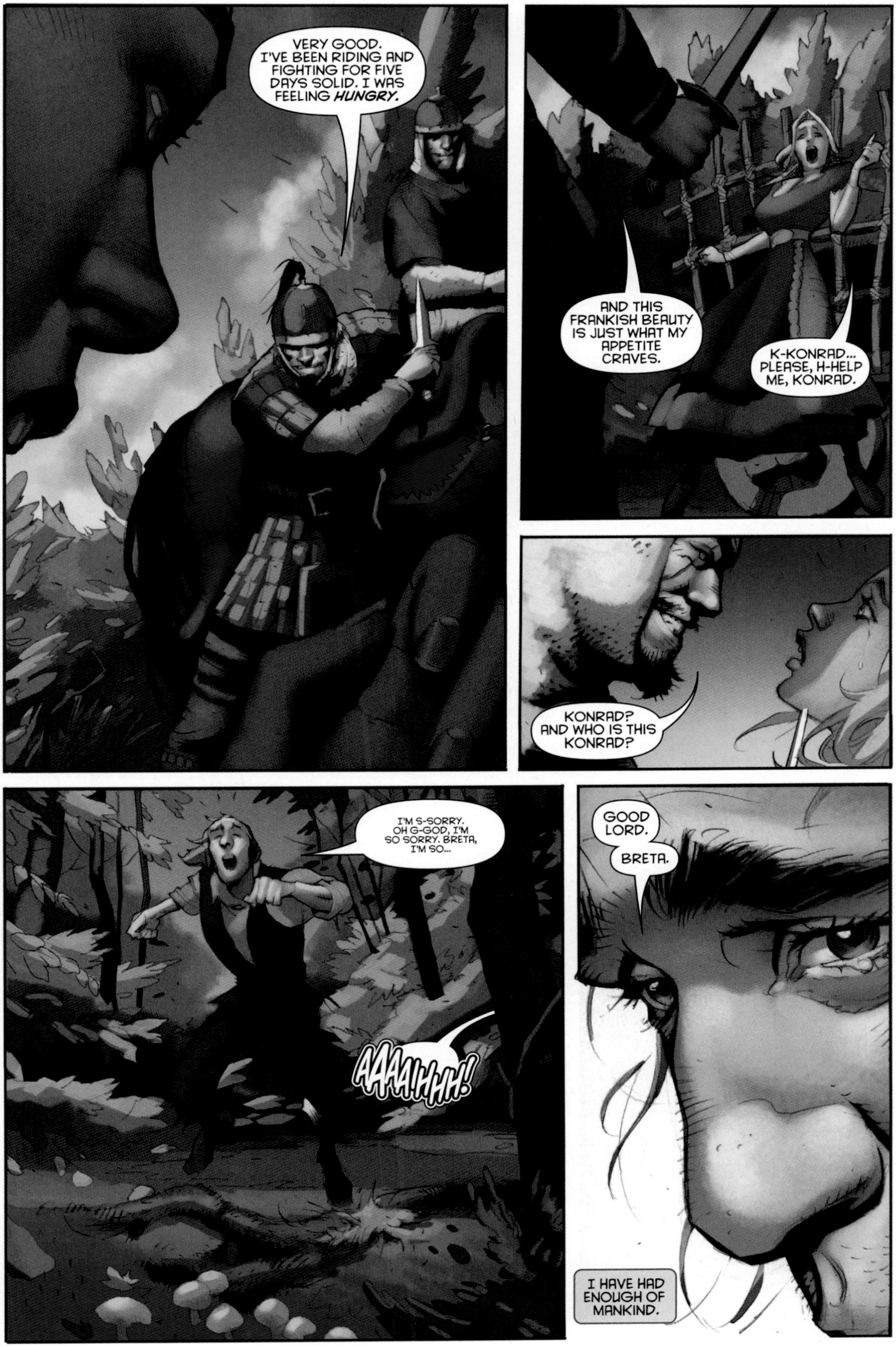
VERY GOOD. I'VE BEEN RIDING AND FIGHTING FOR FIVE DAYS SOLID. I WAS FEELING *HUNGRY.*
AND THIS FRANKISH BEAUTY IS JUST WHAT MY APPETITE CRAVES.
K-KONRAD... PLEASE, H-HELP ME, KONRAD.
KONRAD? AND WHO IS THIS KONRAD?
I'M S-SORRY. OH G-GOD, I'M SO SORRY. BRETA, I'M SO...
AAAAIHHH!
GOOD LORD.
BRETA.
I HAVE HAD ENOUGH OF MANKIND.

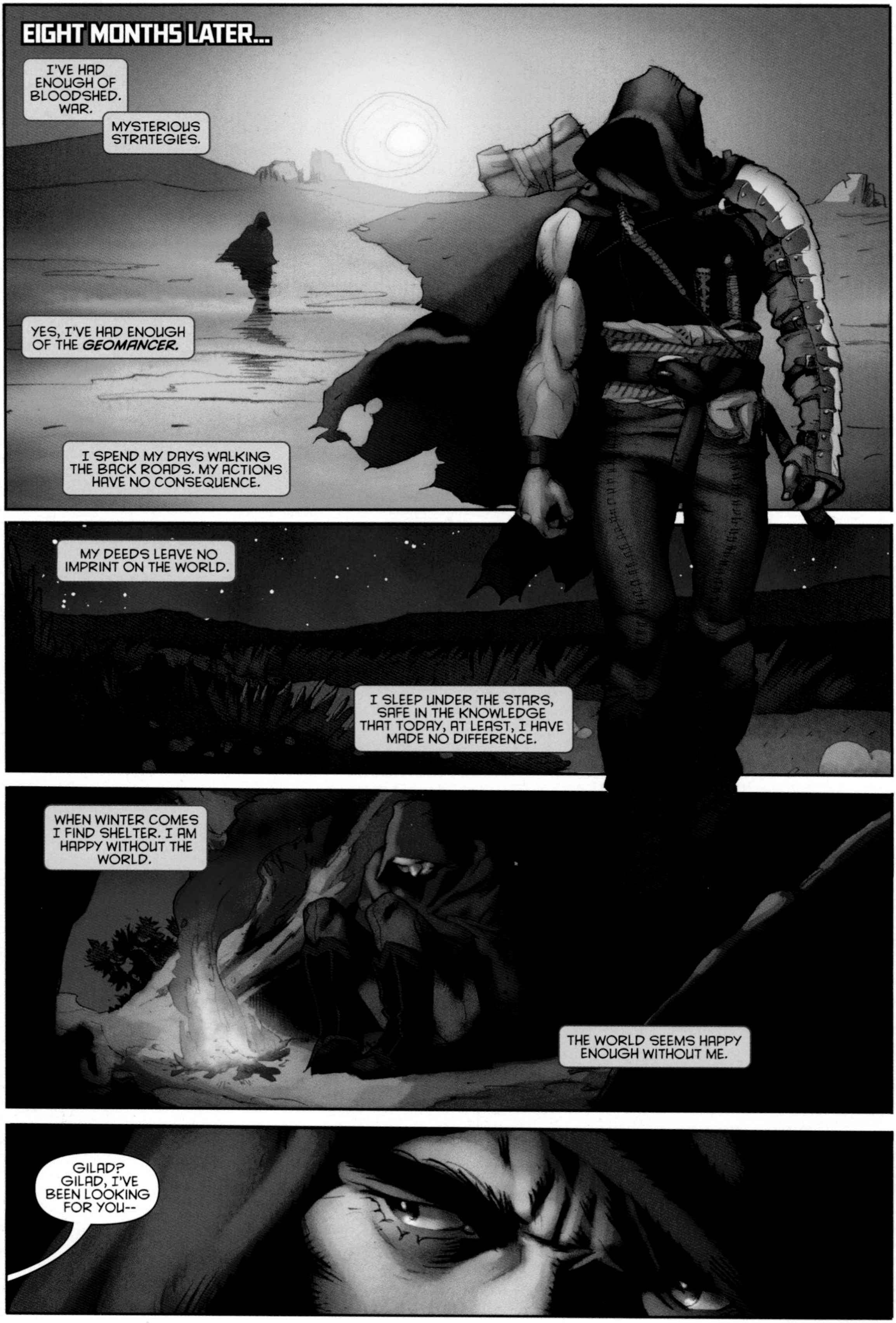
EIGHT MONTHS LATER...
I'VE HAD ENOUGH OF BLOODSHED. WAR.
MYSTERIOUS STRATEGIES.
YES, I'VE HAD ENOUGH OF THE *GEOMANCER.*
I SPEND MY DAYS WALKING THE BACK ROADS. MY ACTIONS HAVE NO CONSEQUENCE.
MY DEEDS LEAVE NO IMPRINT ON THE WORLD.
I SLEEP UNDER THE STARS, SAFE IN THE KNOWLEDGE THAT TODAY, AT LEAST, I HAVE MADE NO DIFFERENCE.
WHEN WINTER COMES I FIND SHELTER. I AM HAPPY WITHOUT THE WORLD.
THE WORLD SEEMS HAPPY ENOUGH WITHOUT ME.
GILAD? GILAD, I'VE BEEN LOOKING FOR YOU--

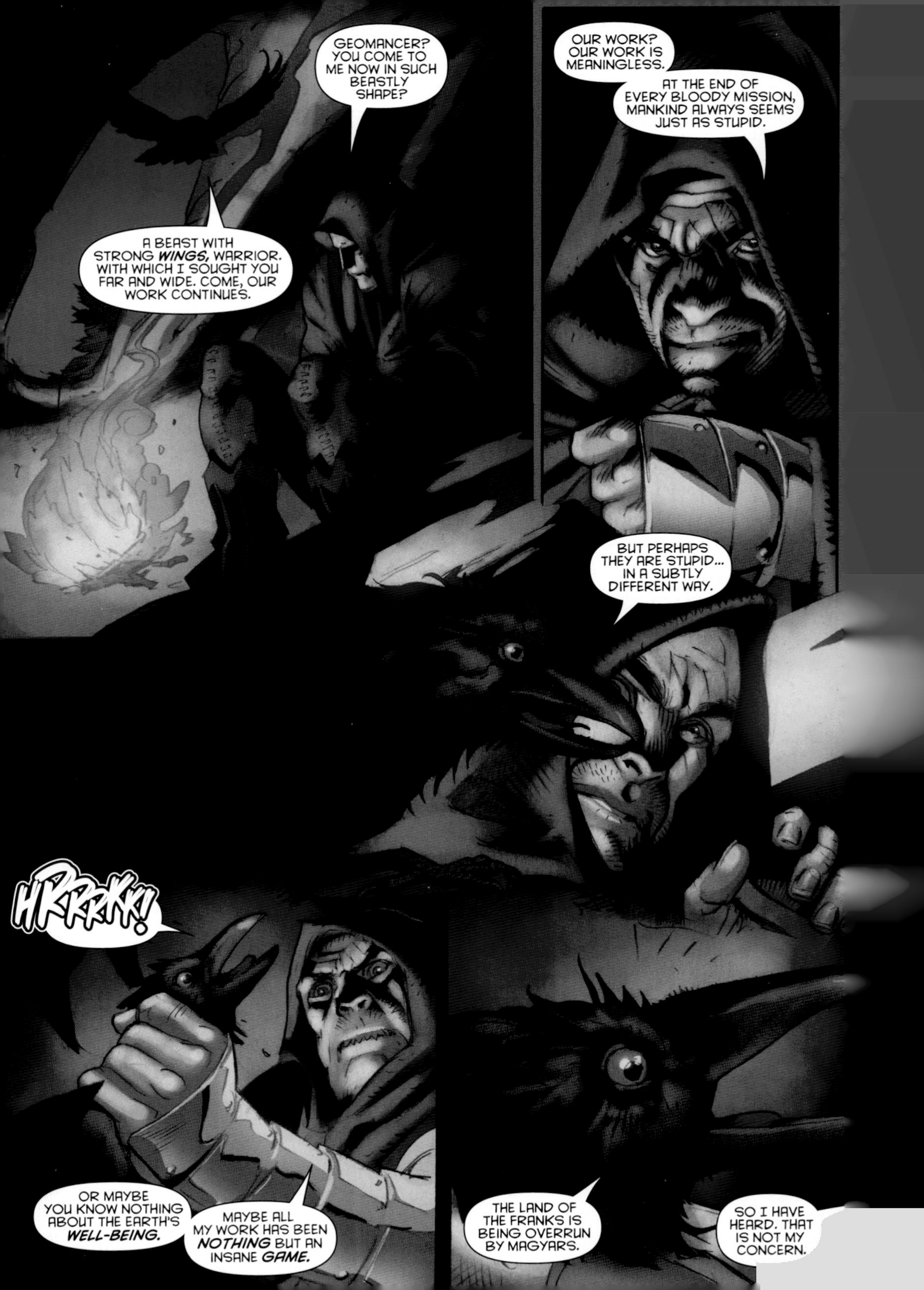
GEOMANCER? YOU COME TO ME NOW IN SUCH BEASTLY SHAPE?
A BEAST WITH STRONG *WINGS,* WARRIOR. WITH WHICH I SOUGHT YOU FAR AND WIDE. COME, OUR WORK CONTINUES.
OUR WORK? OUR WORK IS MEANINGLESS.
AT THE END OF EVERY BLOODY MISSION, MANKIND ALWAYS SEEMS JUST AS STUPID.
BUT PERHAPS THEY ARE STUPID... IN A SUBTLY DIFFERENT WAY.
HRRRKK!
OR MAYBE YOU KNOW NOTHING ABOUT THE EARTH'S *WELL-BEING.*
MAYBE ALL MY WORK HAS BEEN *NOTHING* BUT AN INSANE *GAME.*
THE LAND OF THE FRANKS IS BEING OVERRUN BY MAGYARS.
SO I HAVE HEARD. THAT IS NOT MY CONCERN.

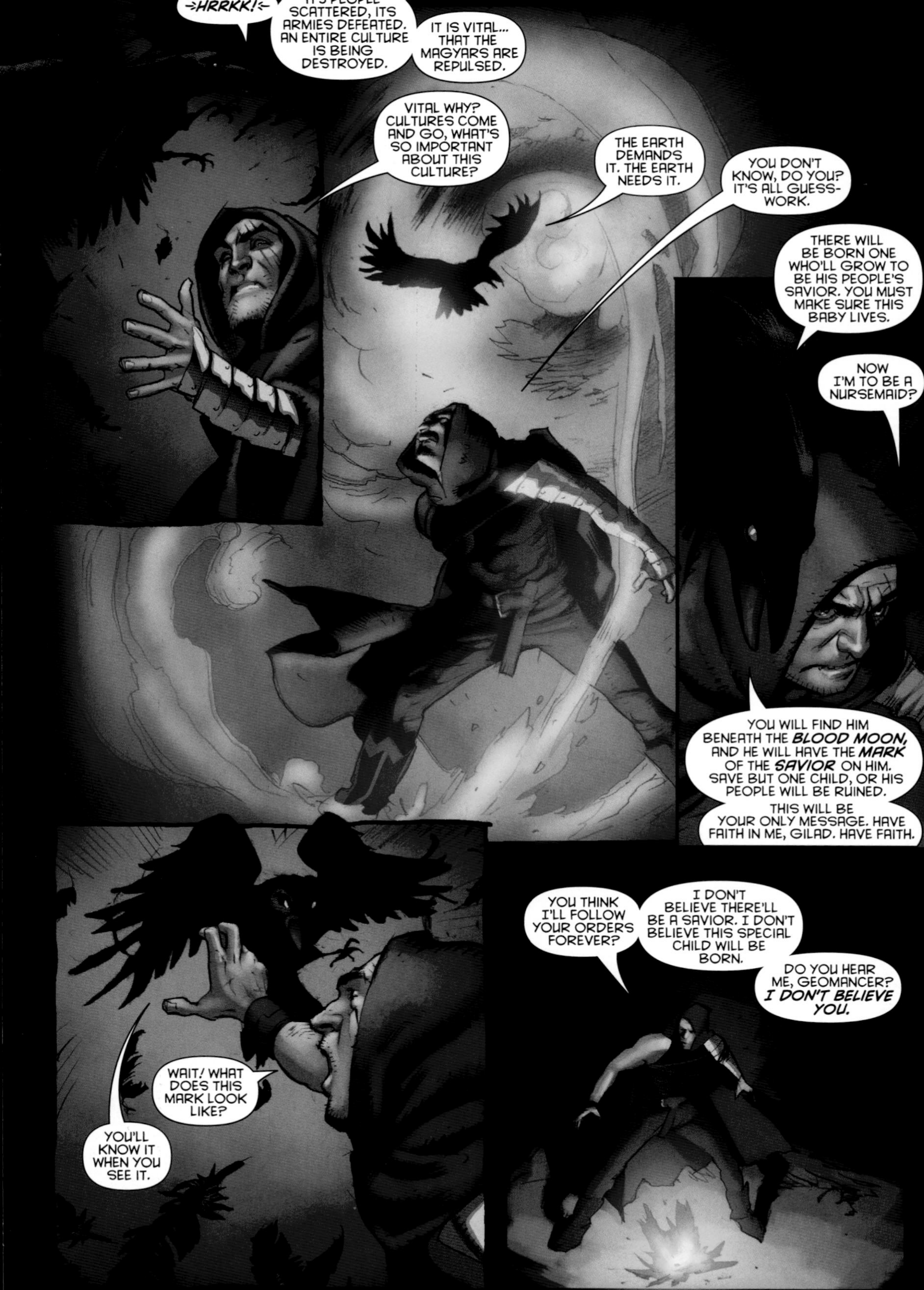

HRRKK!
SCATTERED, ITS ARMIES DEFEATED. AN ENTIRE CULTURE IS BEING DESTROYED.
IT IS VITAL... THAT THE MAGYARS ARE REPULSED.
VITAL WHY? CULTURES COME AND GO, WHAT'S SO IMPORTANT ABOUT THIS CULTURE?
THE EARTH DEMANDS IT. THE EARTH NEEDS IT.
YOU DON'T KNOW, DO YOU? IT'S ALL GUESS-WORK.
THERE WILL BE BORN ONE WHO'LL GROW TO BE HIS PEOPLE'S SAVIOR. YOU MUST MAKE SURE THIS BABY LIVES.
NOW I'M TO BE A NURSEMAID?
YOU WILL FIND HIM BENEATH THE BLOOD MOON, AND HE WILL HAVE THE MARK OF THE SAVIOR ON HIM. SAVE BUT ONE CHILD, OR HIS PEOPLE WILL BE RUINED.
THIS WILL BE YOUR ONLY MESSAGE. HAVE FAITH IN ME, GILAD. HAVE FAITH.
WAIT! WHAT DOES THIS MARK LOOK LIKE?
YOU'LL KNOW IT WHEN YOU SEE IT.
YOU THINK I'LL FOLLOW YOUR ORDERS FOREVER?
I DON'T BELIEVE THERE'LL BE A SAVIOR. I DON'T BELIEVE THIS SPECIAL CHILD WILL BE BORN.
DO YOU HEAR ME, GEOMANCER? I DON'T BELIEVE YOU.

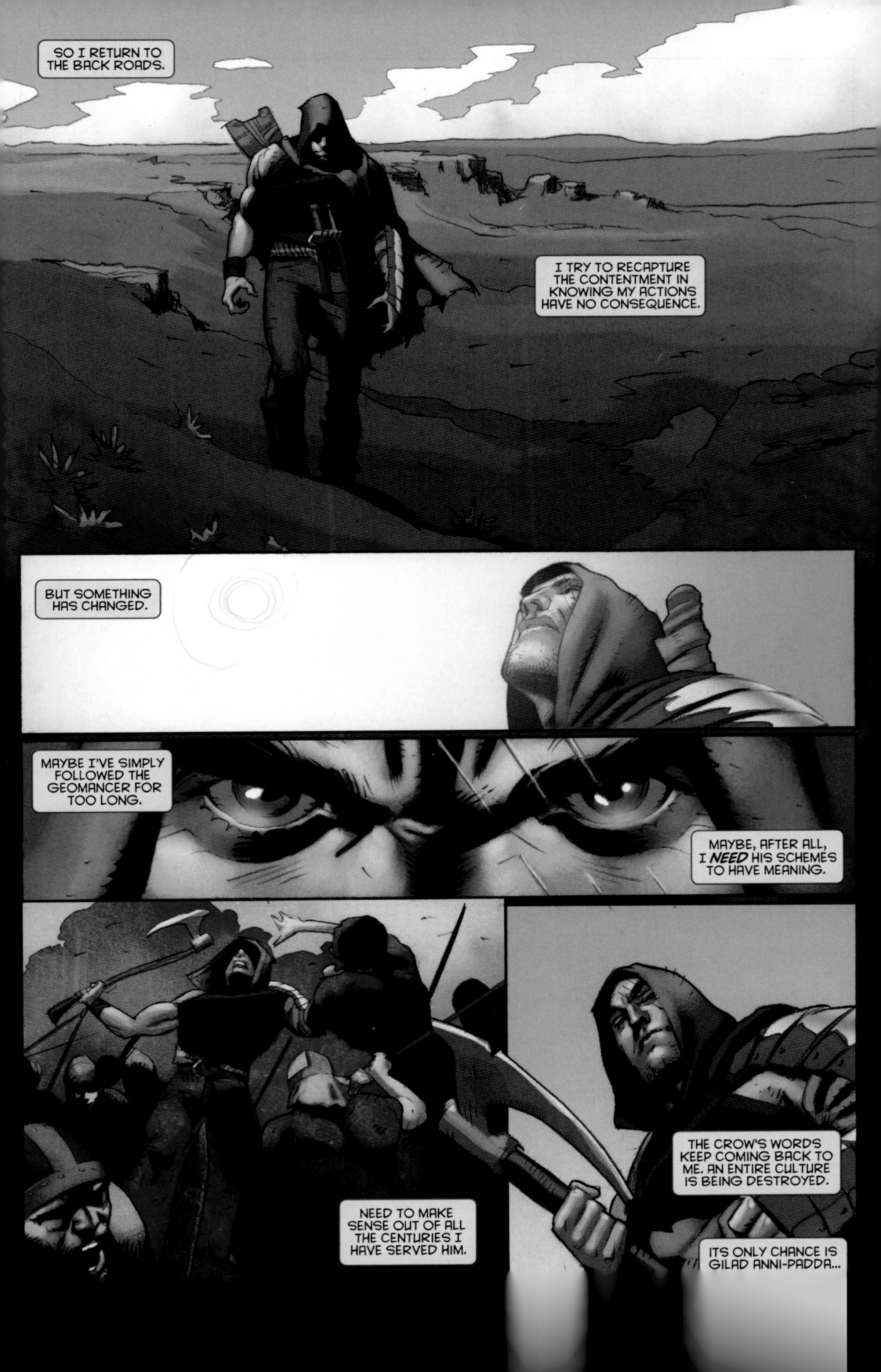
SO I RETURN TO THE BACK ROADS.
I TRY TO RECAPTURE THE CONTENTMENT IN KNOWING MY ACTIONS HAVE NO CONSEQUENCE.
BUT SOMETHING HAS CHANGED.
MAYBE I'VE SIMPLY FOLLOWED THE GEOMANCER FOR TOO LONG.
MAYBE, AFTER ALL, I *NEED* HIS SCHEMES TO HAVE MEANING.
NEED TO MAKE SENSE OUT OF ALL THE CENTURIES I HAVE SERVED HIM.
THE CROW'S WORDS KEEP COMING BACK TO ME. AN ENTIRE CULTURE IS BEING DESTROYED.
ITS ONLY CHANCE IS GILAD ANNI-PADDA...

"...ITS ONLY CHANCE IS AN UNBORN CHILD."

CAN'T YOU FORGIVE AND FORGET?

YOU THINK I CAN EVER FORGET WHAT HAPPENED?

I KNOW I COVERED MYSELF IN IGNOMINY. BUT IF I'D STAYED AND FOUGHT, WELL, THAT MAGYAR WOULD HAVE SURELY KILLED ME. AND YOU'D BE ALONE NOW.

YOU MIGHT DESPISE ME, BRETA, BUT YOU AND OUR CHILD WILL NEED LOOKING AFTER.

WE DON'T KNOW IF IT'S YOUR CHILD.

WE DON'T KNOW FOR SURE THAT IT'S *NOT*.

BRETA? WH-WHAT'S HAPPENING?

UGHH... UGH... OOOH...

I AM NEAR NINE MONTHS PREGNANT, FOOL. WH-WHAT DO YOU...*THINK* IS HAPPENING?

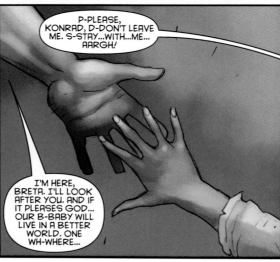

P-PLEASE, KONRAD, D-DON'T LEAVE ME. S-STAY...WITH...ME... AARGH!

I'M HERE, BRETA. I'LL LOOK AFTER YOU. AND IF IT PLEASES GOD... OUR B-BABY WILL LIVE IN A BETTER WORLD. ONE WH-WHERE...

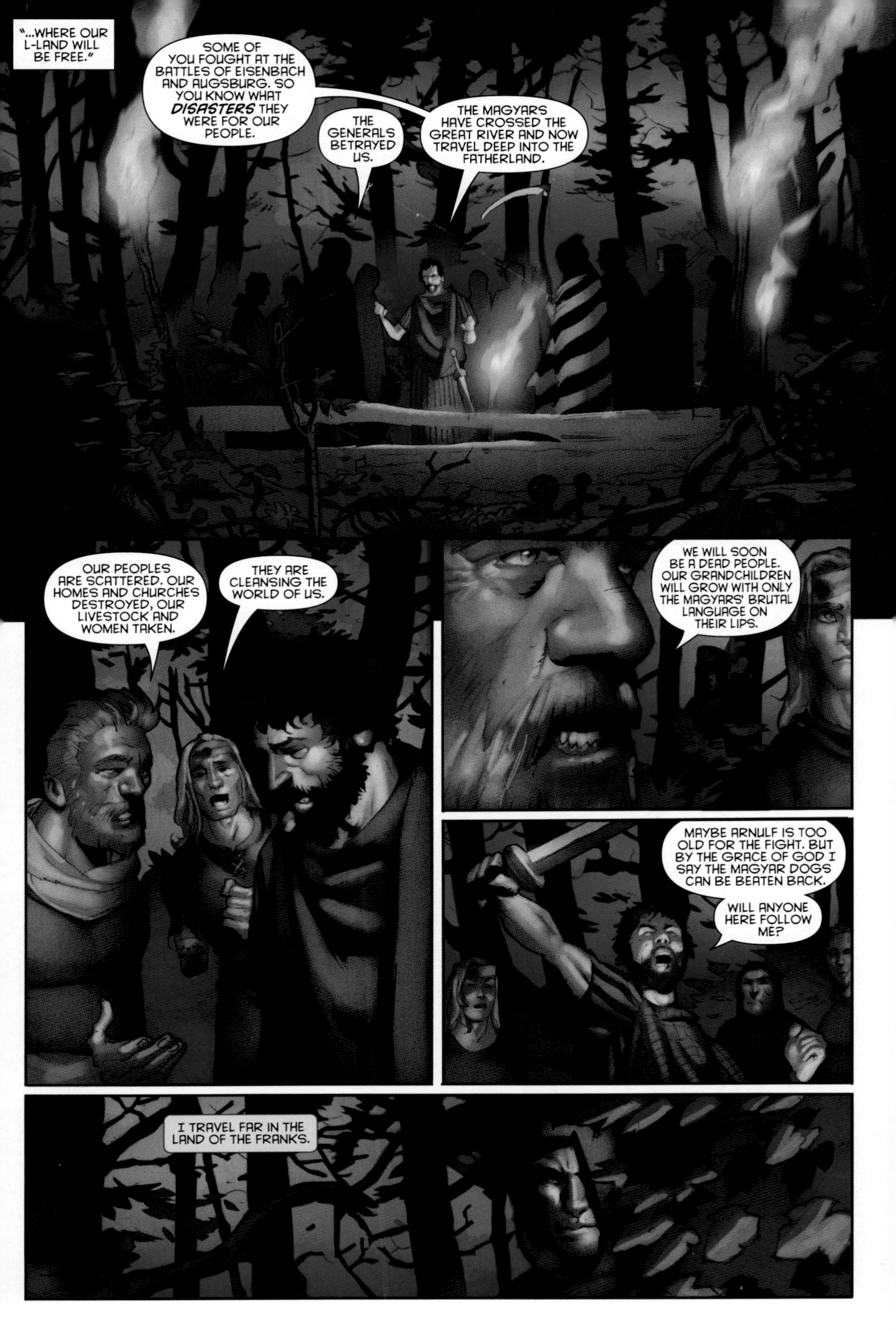
"...WHERE OUR L-LAND WILL BE FREE."
SOME OF YOU FOUGHT AT THE BATTLES OF EISENBACH AND AUGSBURG. SO YOU KNOW WHAT DISASTERS THEY WERE FOR OUR PEOPLE.
THE GENERALS BETRAYED US.
THE MAGYARS HAVE CROSSED THE GREAT RIVER AND NOW TRAVEL DEEP INTO THE FATHERLAND.
OUR PEOPLES ARE SCATTERED. OUR HOMES AND CHURCHES DESTROYED, OUR LIVESTOCK AND WOMEN TAKEN.
THEY ARE CLEANSING THE WORLD OF US.
WE WILL SOON BE A DEAD PEOPLE. OUR GRANDCHILDREN WILL GROW WITH ONLY THE MAGYARS' BRUTAL LANGUAGE ON THEIR LIPS.
MAYBE ARNULF IS TOO OLD FOR THE FIGHT. BUT BY THE GRACE OF GOD I SAY THE MAGYAR DOGS CAN BE BEATEN BACK.
WILL ANYONE HERE FOLLOW ME?
I TRAVEL FAR IN THE LAND OF THE FRANKS.

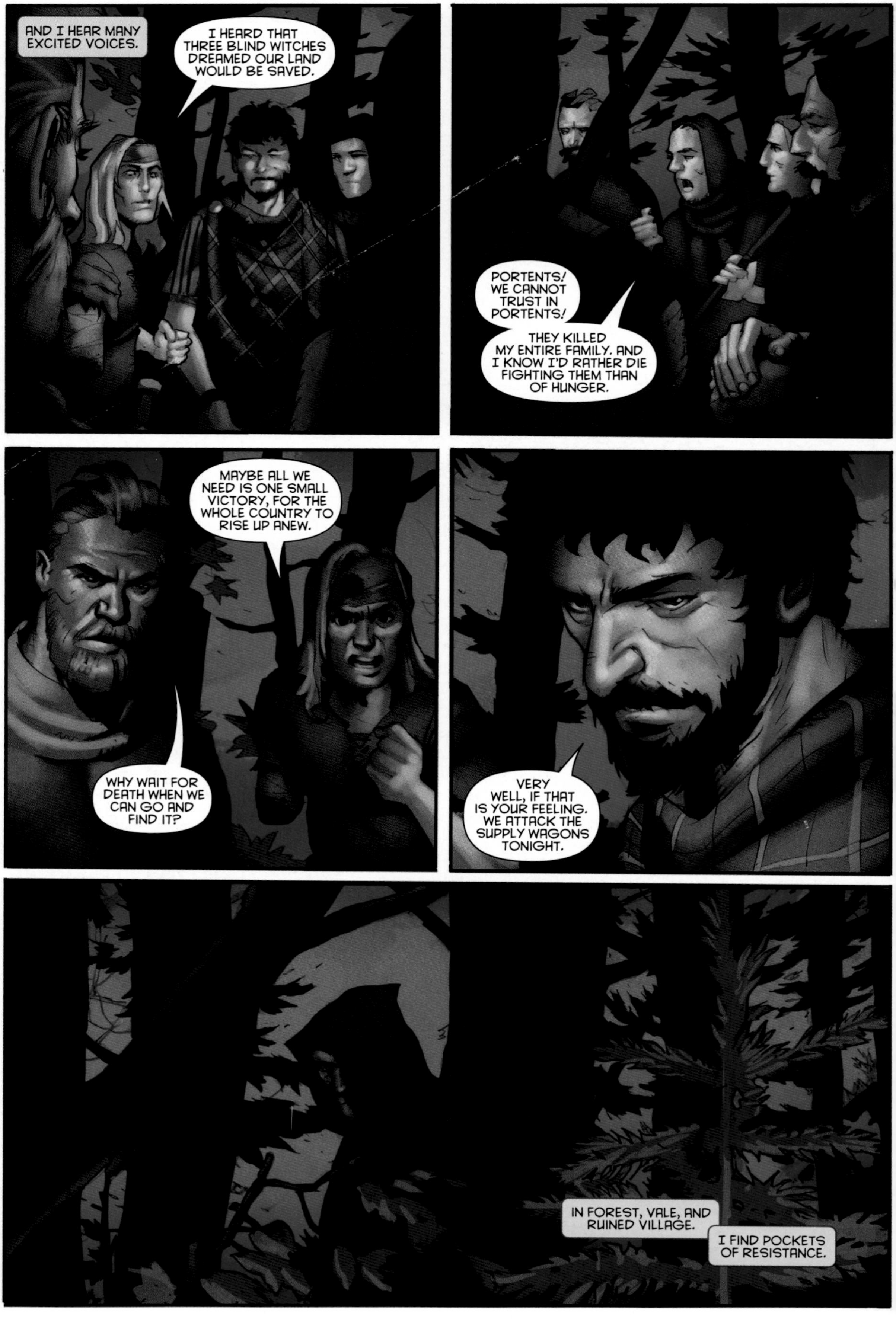
AND I HEAR MANY EXCITED VOICES.
I HEARD THAT THREE BLIND WITCHES DREAMED OUR LAND WOULD BE SAVED.
PORTENTS! WE CANNOT TRUST IN PORTENTS!
THEY KILLED MY ENTIRE FAMILY. AND I KNOW I'D RATHER DIE FIGHTING THEM THAN OF HUNGER.
MAYBE ALL WE NEED IS ONE SMALL VICTORY, FOR THE WHOLE COUNTRY TO RISE UP ANEW.
WHY WAIT FOR DEATH WHEN WE CAN GO AND FIND IT?
VERY WELL, IF THAT IS YOUR FEELING. WE ATTACK THE SUPPLY WAGONS TONIGHT.
IN FOREST, VALE, AND RUINED VILLAGE.
I FIND POCKETS OF RESISTANCE.

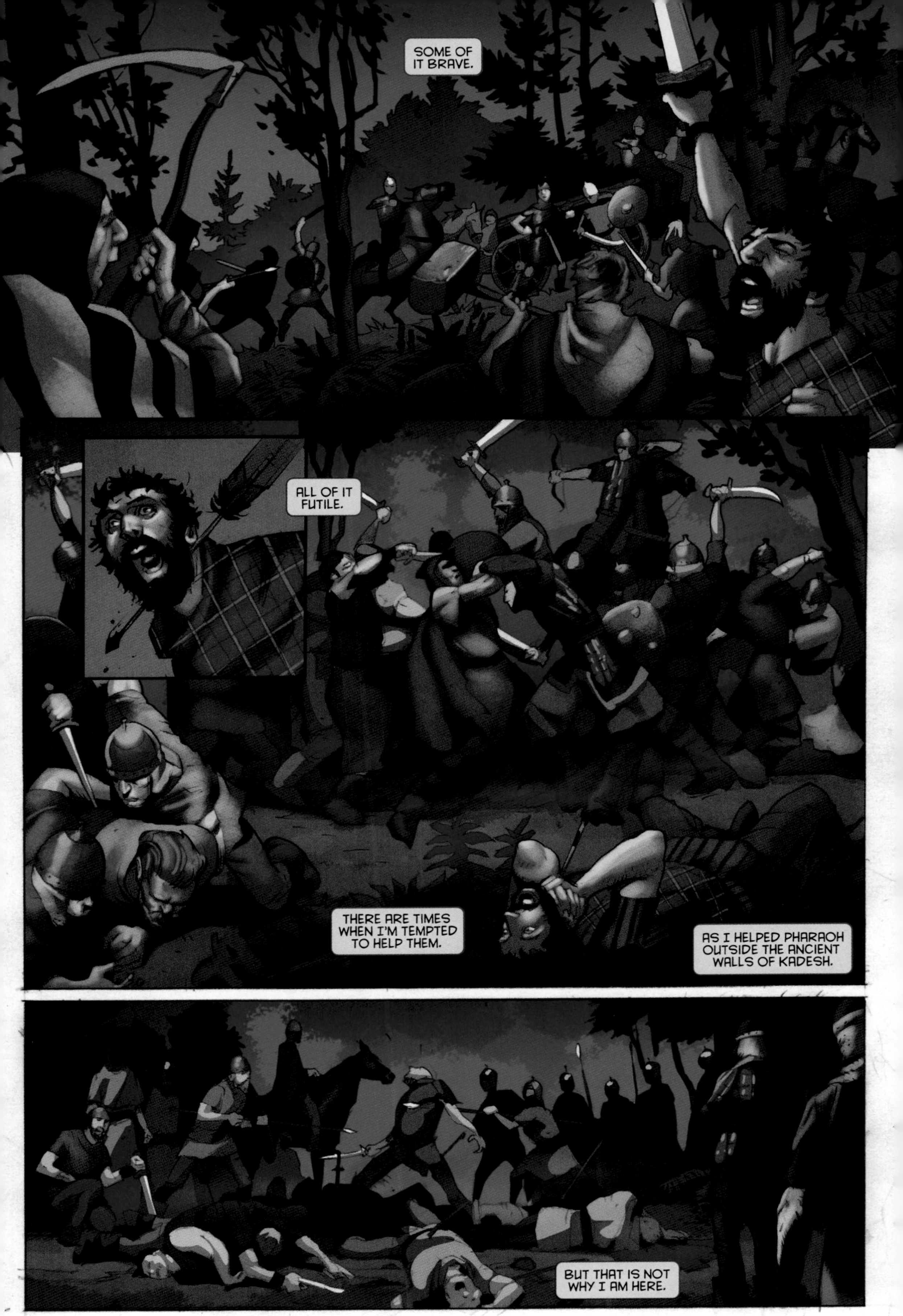
SOME OF IT BRAVE.
ALL OF IT FUTILE.
THERE ARE TIMES WHEN I'M TEMPTED TO HELP THEM.
AS I HELPED PHARAOH OUTSIDE THE ANCIENT WALLS OF KADESH.
BUT THAT IS NOT WHY I AM HERE.

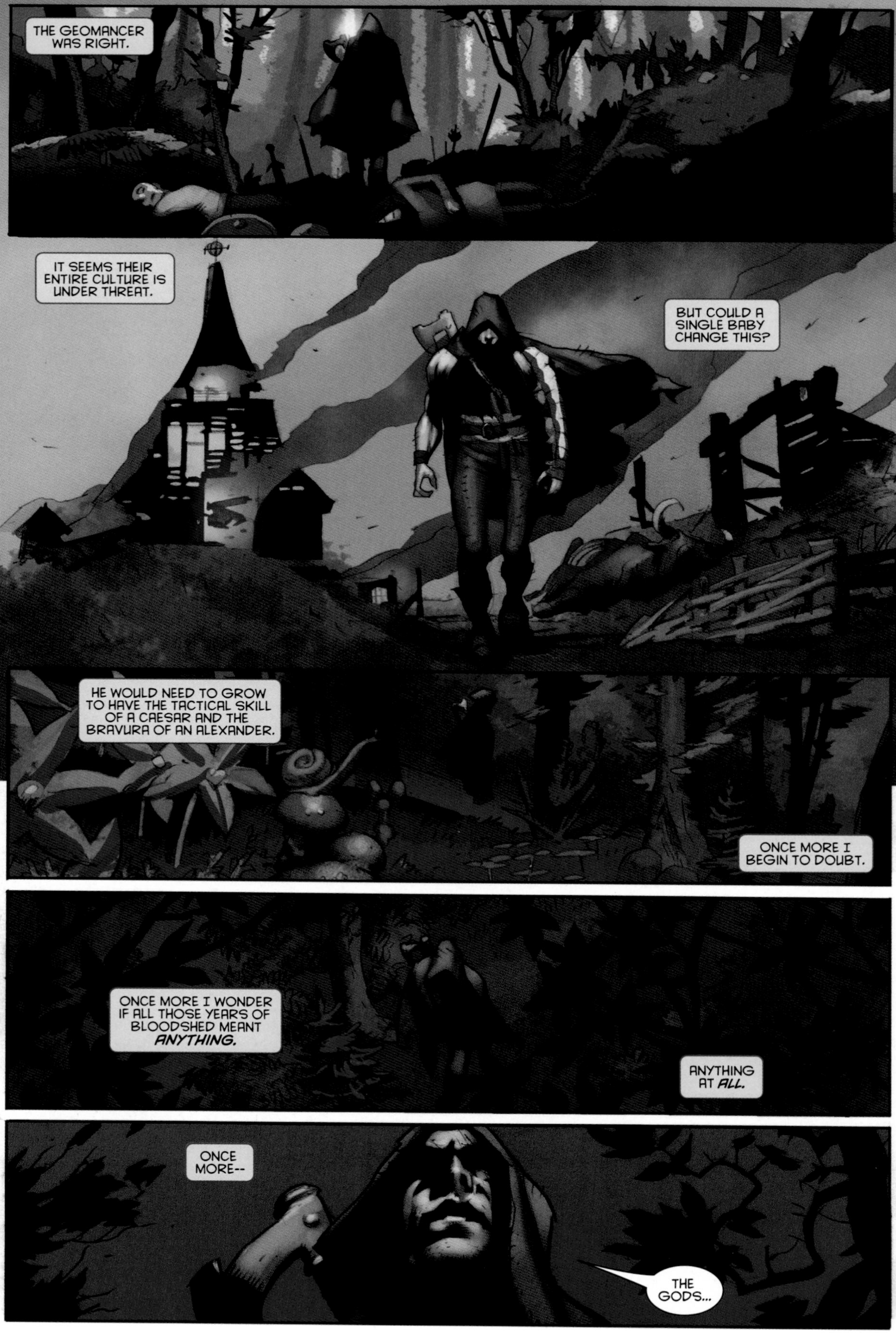
THE GEOMANCER WAS RIGHT.
IT SEEMS THEIR ENTIRE CULTURE IS UNDER THREAT.
BUT COULD A SINGLE BABY CHANGE THIS?
HE WOULD NEED TO GROW TO HAVE THE TACTICAL SKILL OF A CAESAR AND THE BRAVURA OF AN ALEXANDER.
ONCE MORE I BEGIN TO DOUBT.
ONCE MORE I WONDER IF ALL THOSE YEARS OF BLOODSHED MEANT ANYTHING.
ANYTHING AT ALL.
ONCE MORE--
THE GODS...

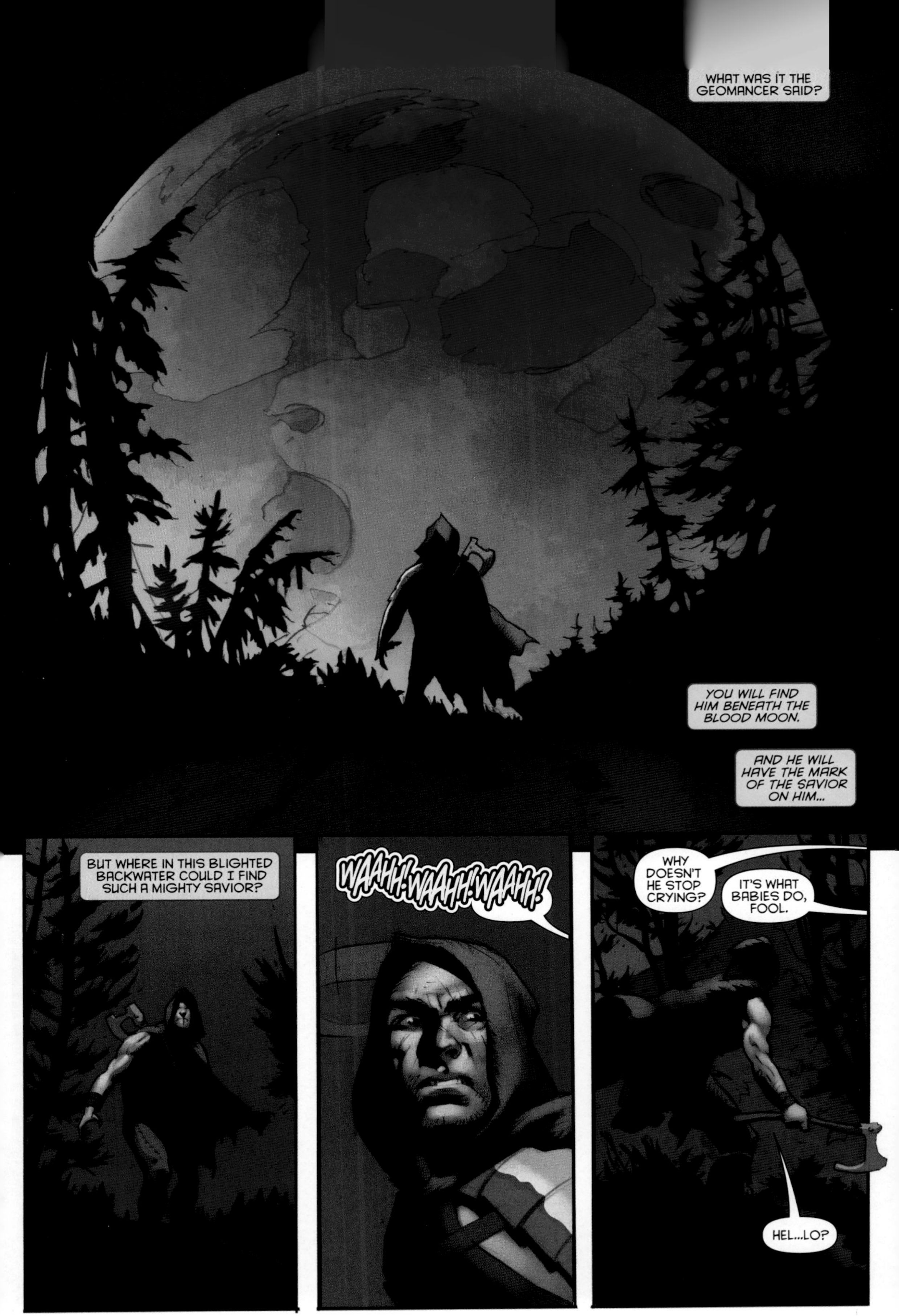
WHAT WAS IT THE GEOMANCER SAID?
YOU WILL FIND HIM BENEATH THE BLOOD MOON.
AND HE WILL HAVE THE MARK OF THE SAVIOR ON HIM...
BUT WHERE IN THIS BLIGHTED BACKWATER COULD I FIND SUCH A MIGHTY SAVIOR?
WAAHH! WAAHH! WAAHH!
WHY DOESN'T HE STOP CRYING?
IT'S WHAT BABIES DO, FOOL.
HEL...LO?

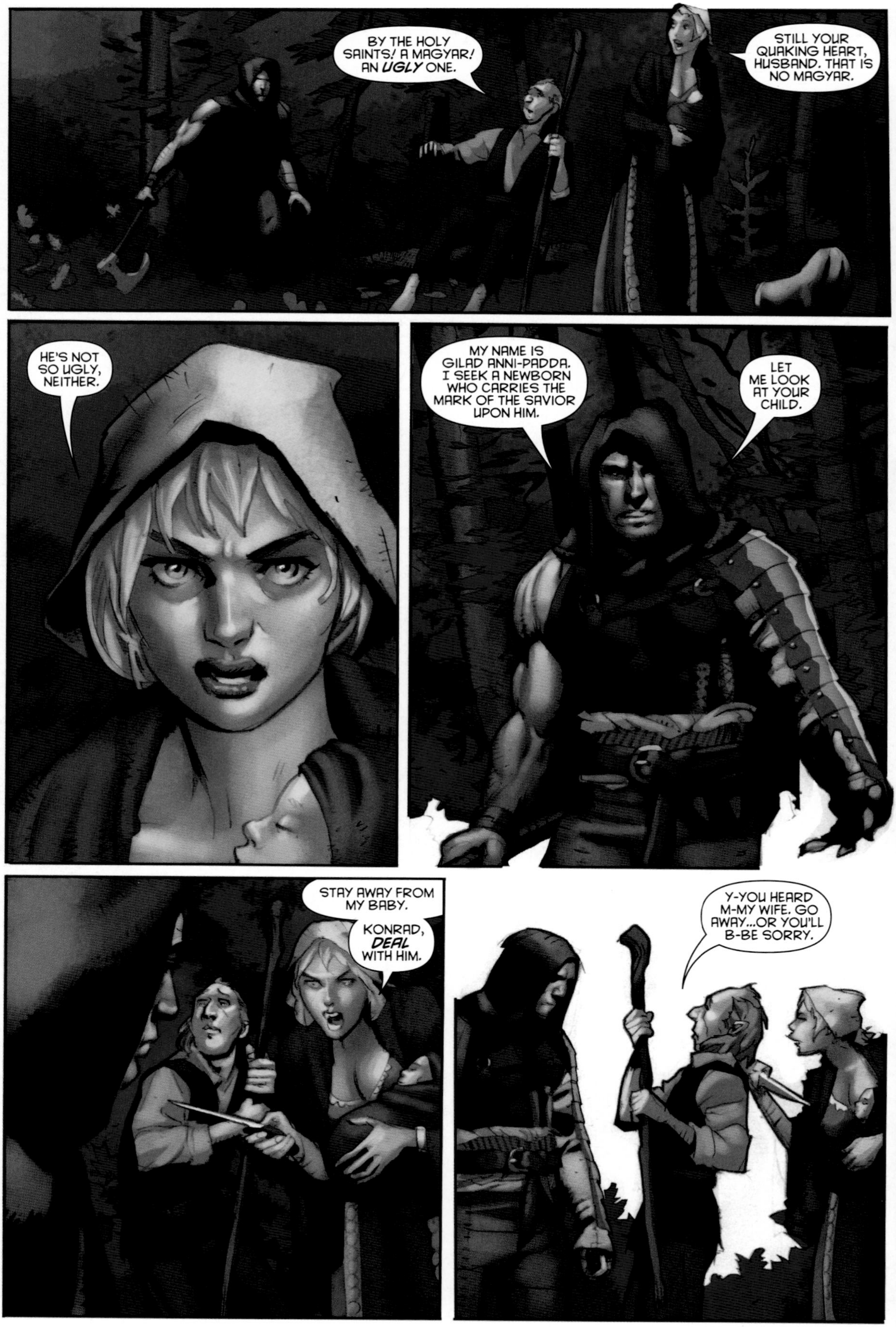
BY THE HOLY SAINTS! A MAGYAR! AN UGLY ONE.
STILL YOUR QUAKING HEART, HUSBAND. THAT IS NO MAGYAR.
HE'S NOT SO UGLY, NEITHER.
MY NAME IS GILAD ANNI-PADDA. I SEEK A NEWBORN WHO CARRIES THE MARK OF THE SAVIOR UPON HIM.
LET ME LOOK AT YOUR CHILD.
STAY AWAY FROM MY BABY.
KONRAD, DEAL WITH HIM.
Y-YOU HEARD M-MY WIFE. GO AWAY...OR YOU'LL B-BE SORRY.

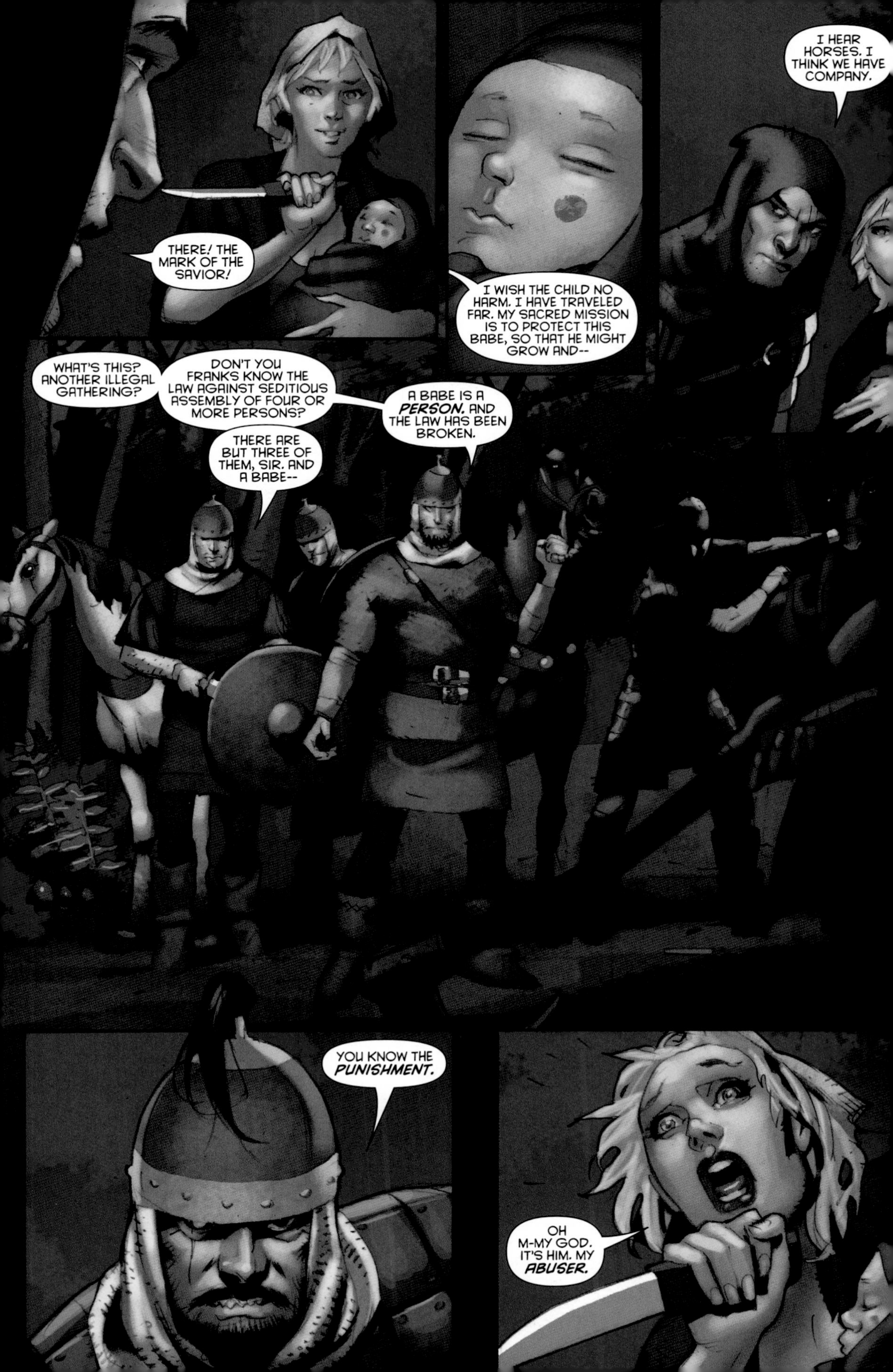
THERE! THE MARK OF THE SAVIOR!
I WISH THE CHILD NO HARM. I HAVE TRAVELED FAR. MY SACRED MISSION IS TO PROTECT THIS BABE, SO THAT HE MIGHT GROW AND--
I HEAR HORSES. I THINK WE HAVE COMPANY.
WHAT'S THIS? ANOTHER ILLEGAL GATHERING?
DON'T YOU FRANKS KNOW THE LAW AGAINST SEDITIOUS ASSEMBLY OF FOUR OR MORE PERSONS?
THERE ARE BUT THREE OF THEM, SIR. AND A BABE--
A BABE IS A PERSON. AND THE LAW HAS BEEN BROKEN.
YOU KNOW THE PUNISHMENT.
OH M-MY GOD. IT'S HIM. MY ABUSER.

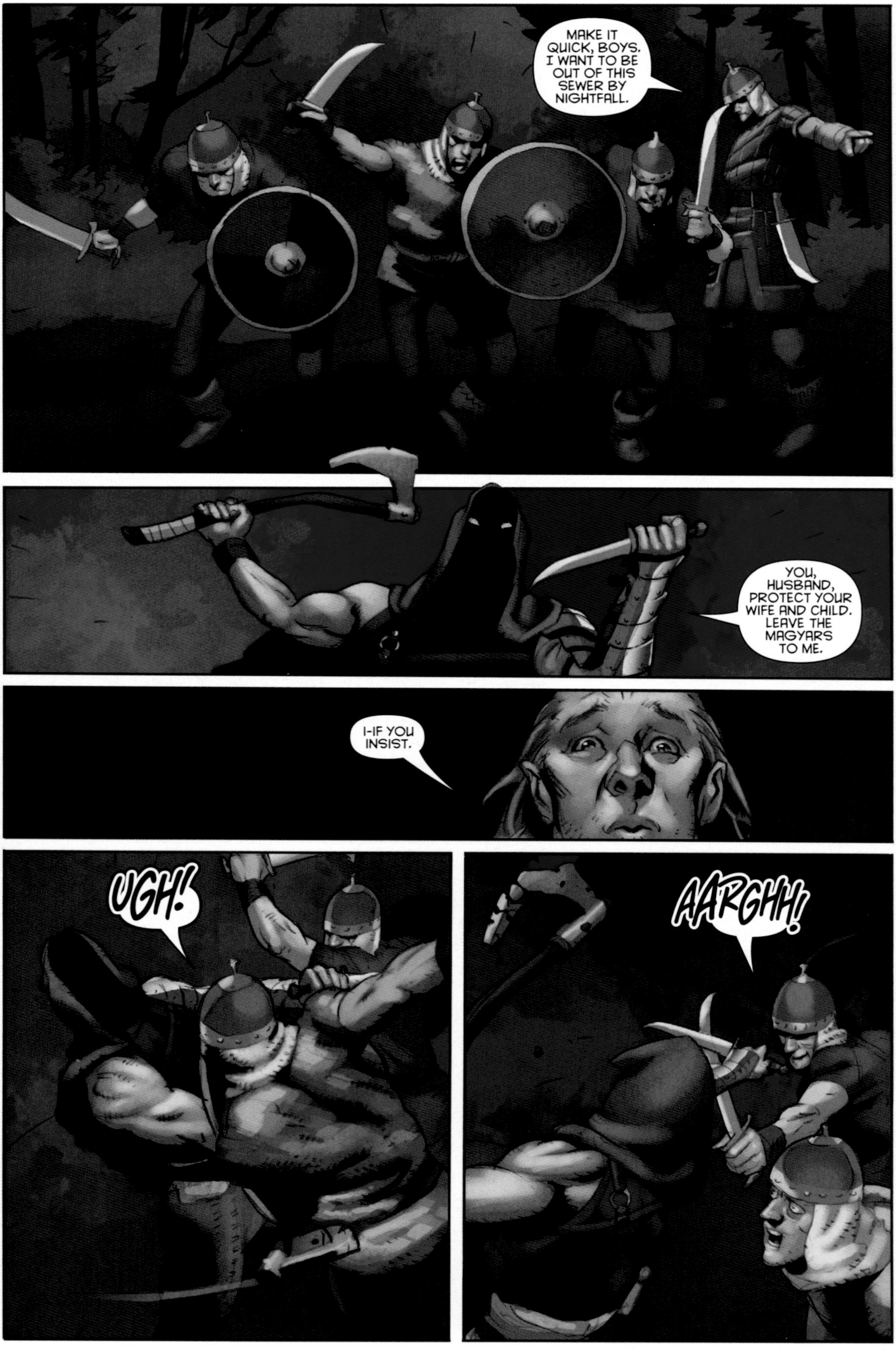
MAKE IT QUICK, BOYS. I WANT TO BE OUT OF THIS SEWER BY NIGHTFALL.
YOU, HUSBAND, PROTECT YOUR WIFE AND CHILD. LEAVE THE MAGYARS TO ME.
I-IF YOU INSIST.
UGH!
AARGHH!

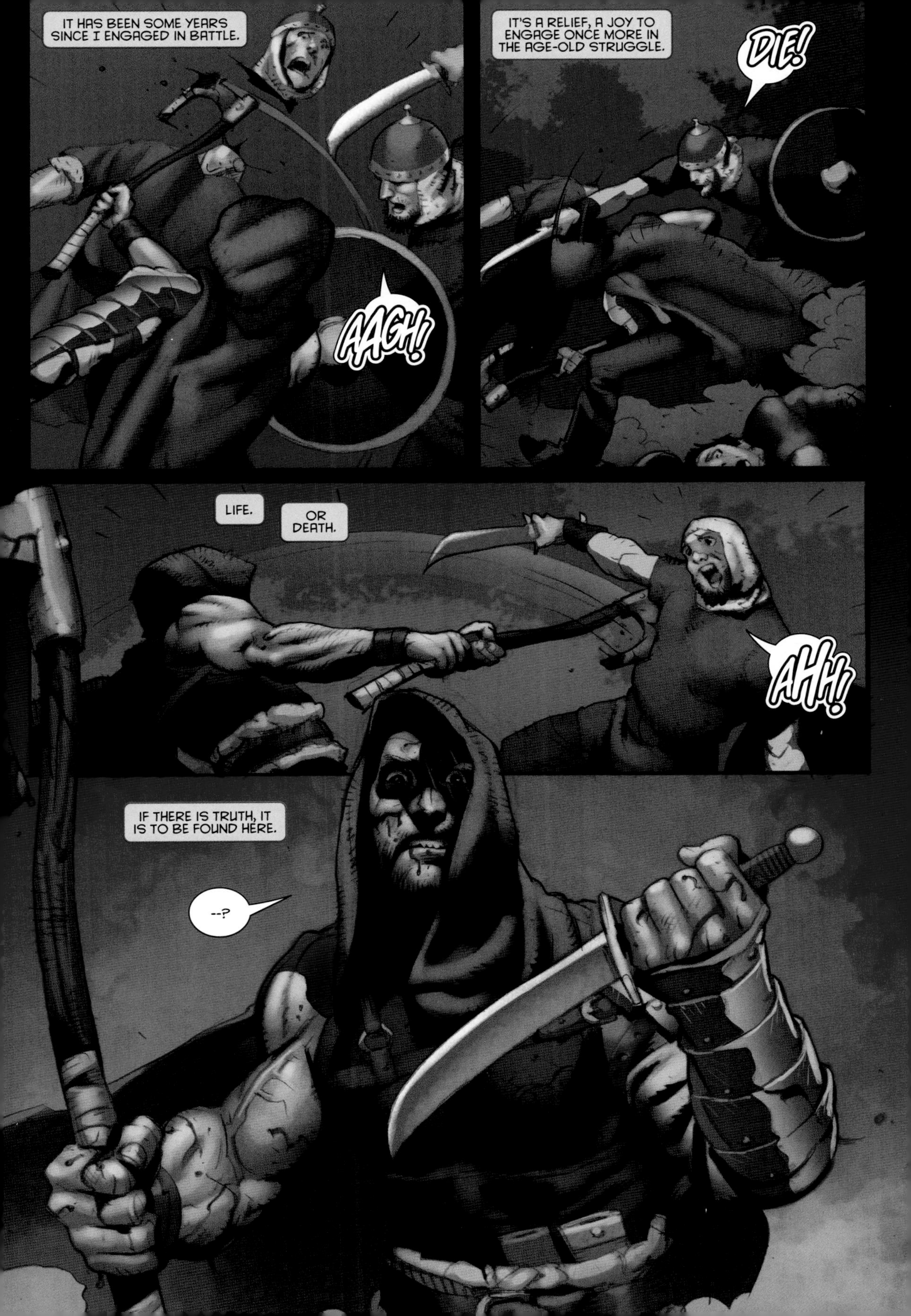
IT HAS BEEN SOME YEARS SINCE I ENGAGED IN BATTLE.
AAGH!
IT'S A RELIEF, A JOY TO ENGAGE ONCE MORE IN THE AGE-OLD STRUGGLE.
DIE!
LIFE.
OR DEATH.
AHH!
IF THERE IS TRUTH, IT IS TO BE FOUND HERE.
--?

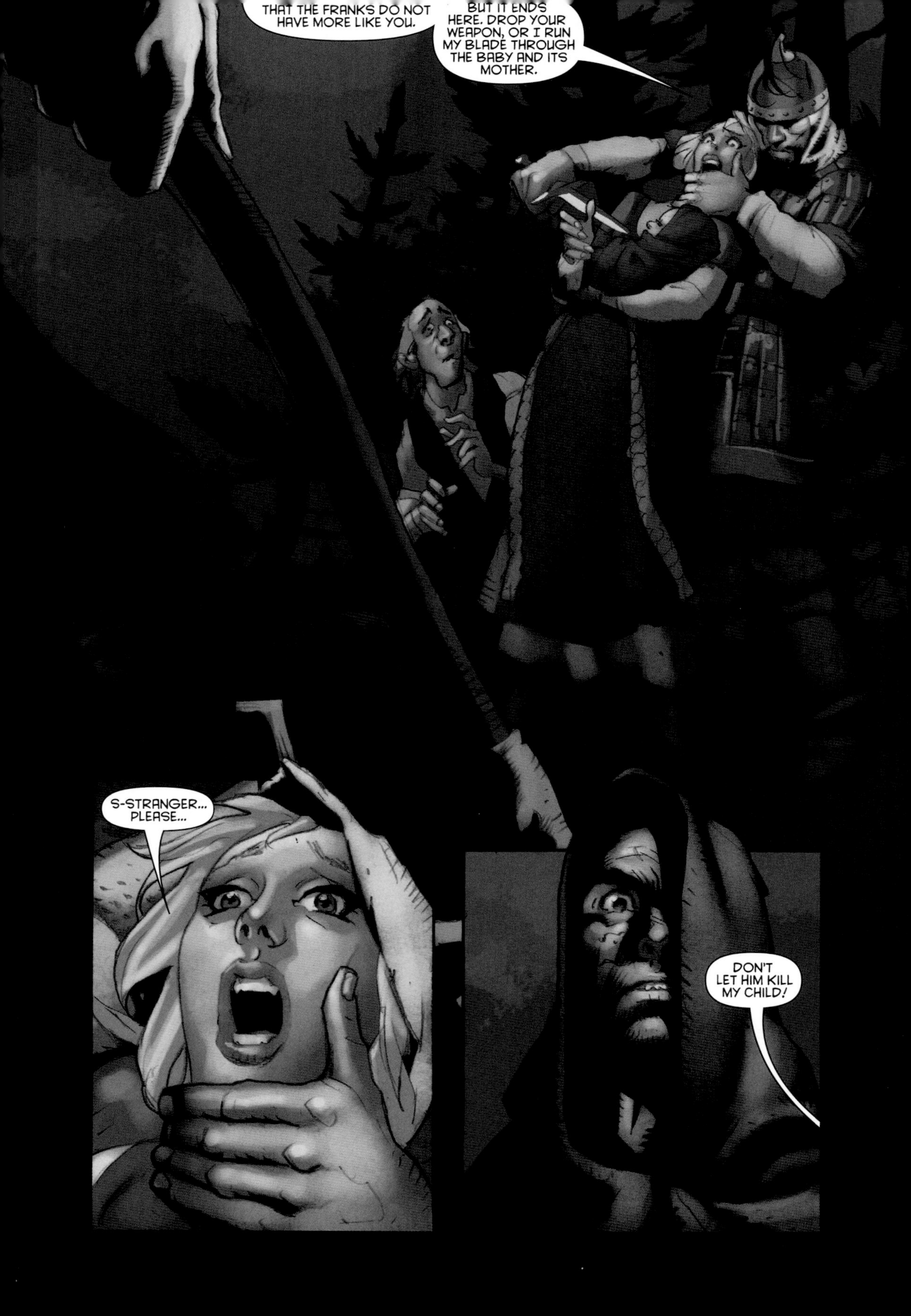
THAT THE FRANKS DO NOT HAVE MORE LIKE YOU.
BUT IT ENDS HERE. DROP YOUR WEAPON, OR I RUN MY BLADE THROUGH THE BABY AND ITS MOTHER.
S-STRANGER... PLEASE...
DON'T LET HIM KILL MY CHILD!

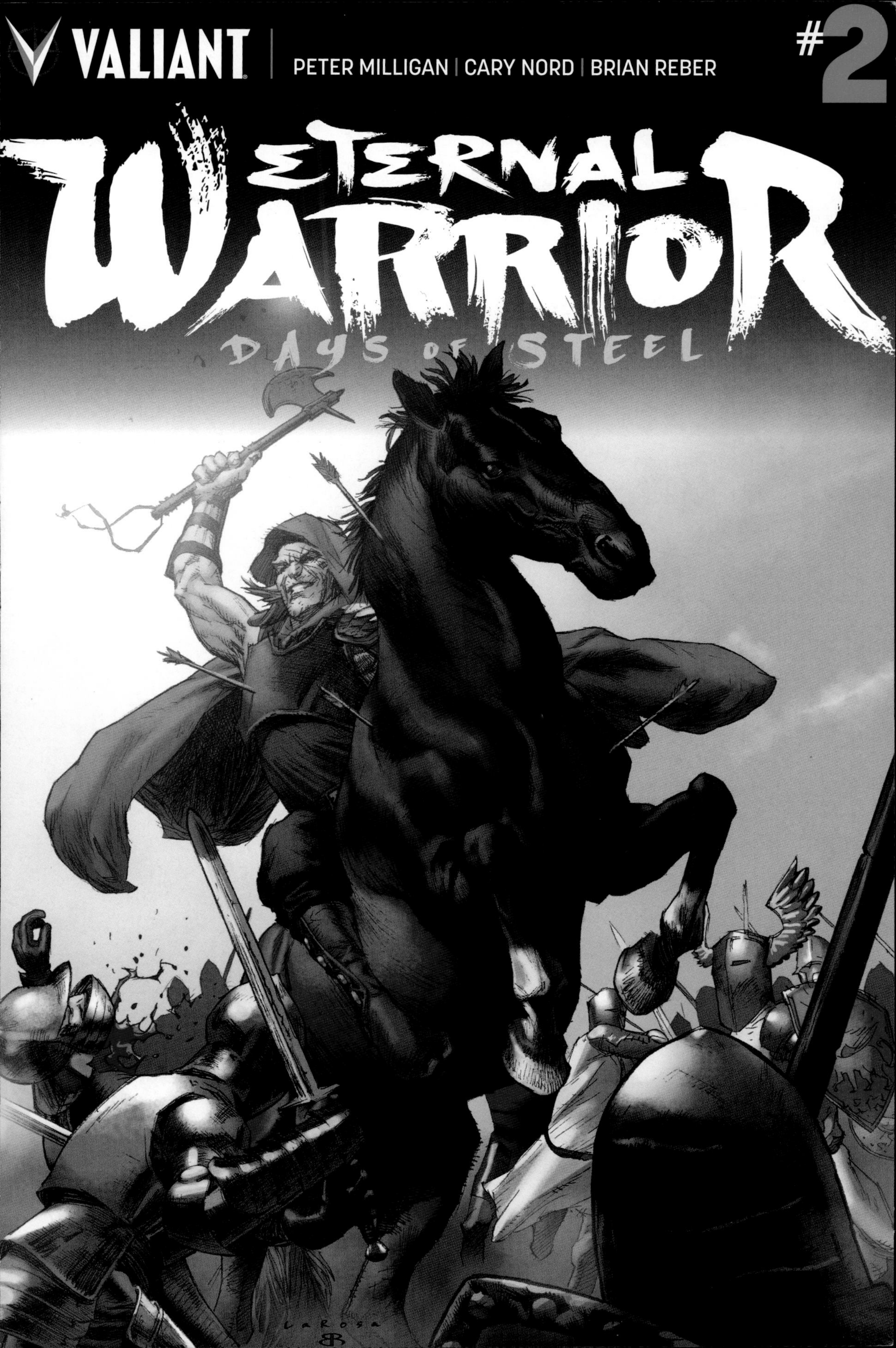
VALIANT
PETER MILLIGAN | CARY NORD | BRIAN REBER
#2
ETERNAL WARRIOR
DAYS OF STEEL
LAROSA

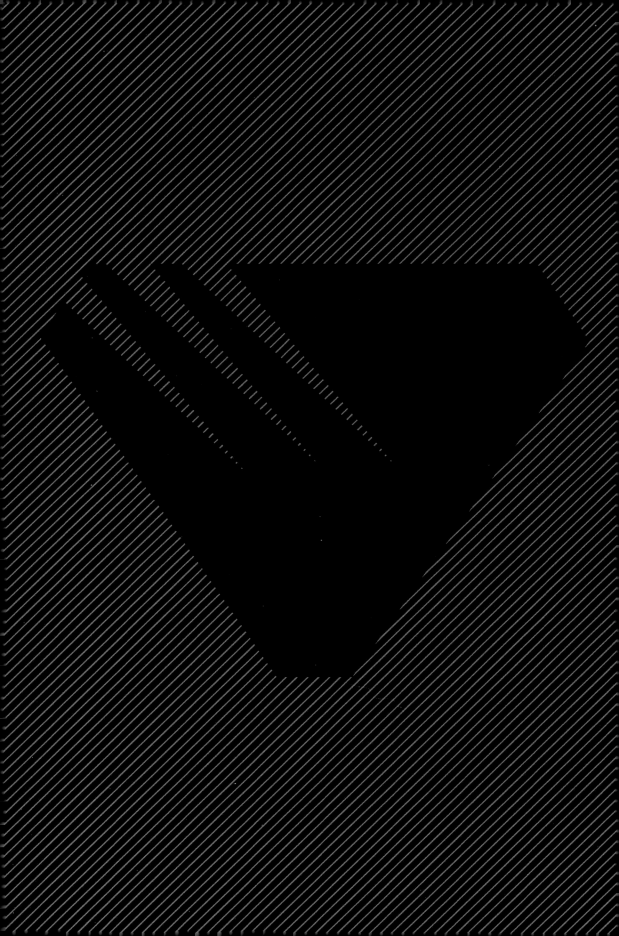

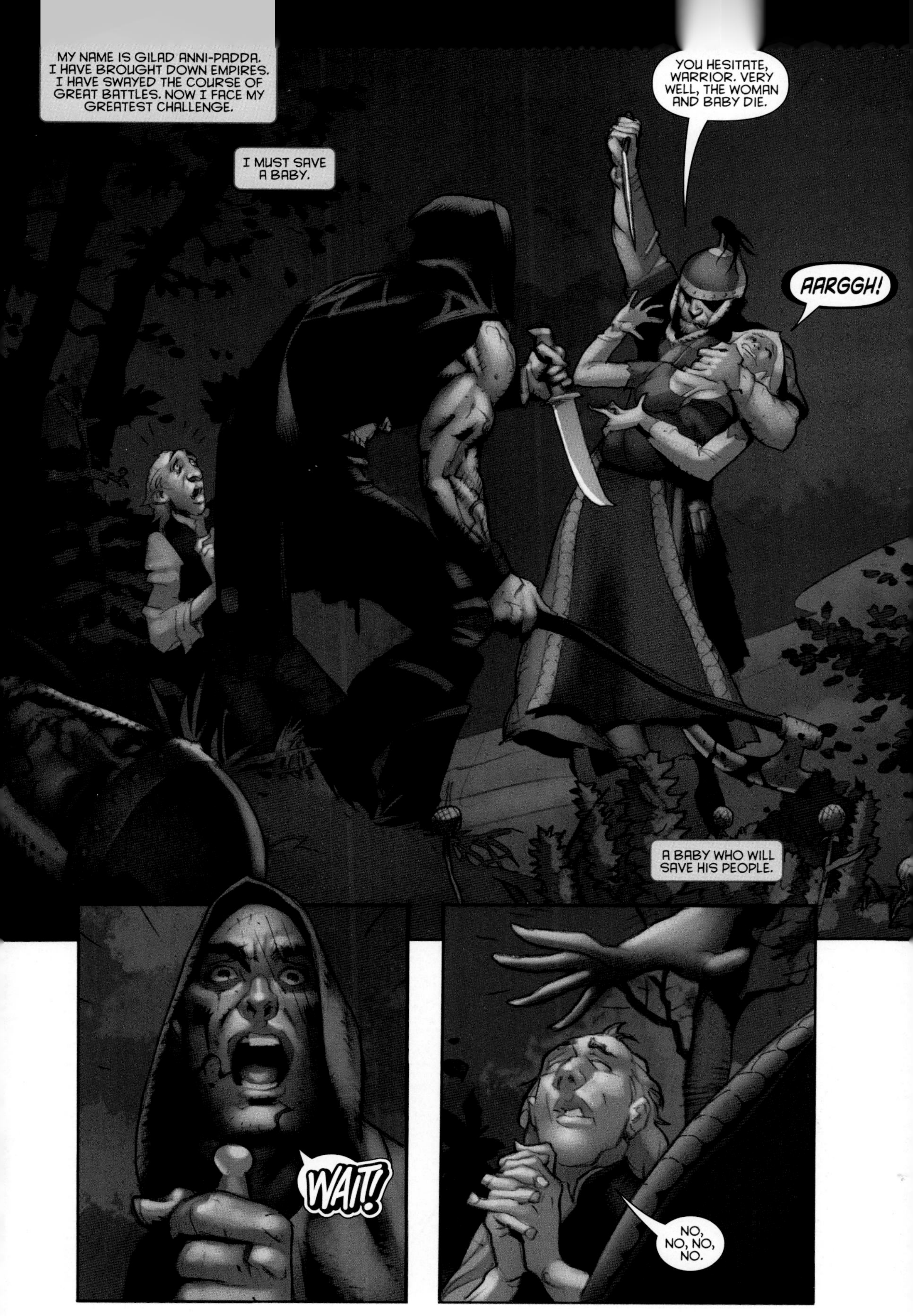
MY NAME IS GILAD ANNI-PADDA. I HAVE BROUGHT DOWN EMPIRES. I HAVE SWAYED THE COURSE OF GREAT BATTLES. NOW I FACE MY GREATEST CHALLENGE.
I MUST SAVE A BABY.
YOU HESITATE, WARRIOR. VERY WELL, THE WOMAN AND BABY DIE.
AARGGH!
A BABY WHO WILL SAVE HIS PEOPLE.
WAIT!
NO, NO, NO, NO.

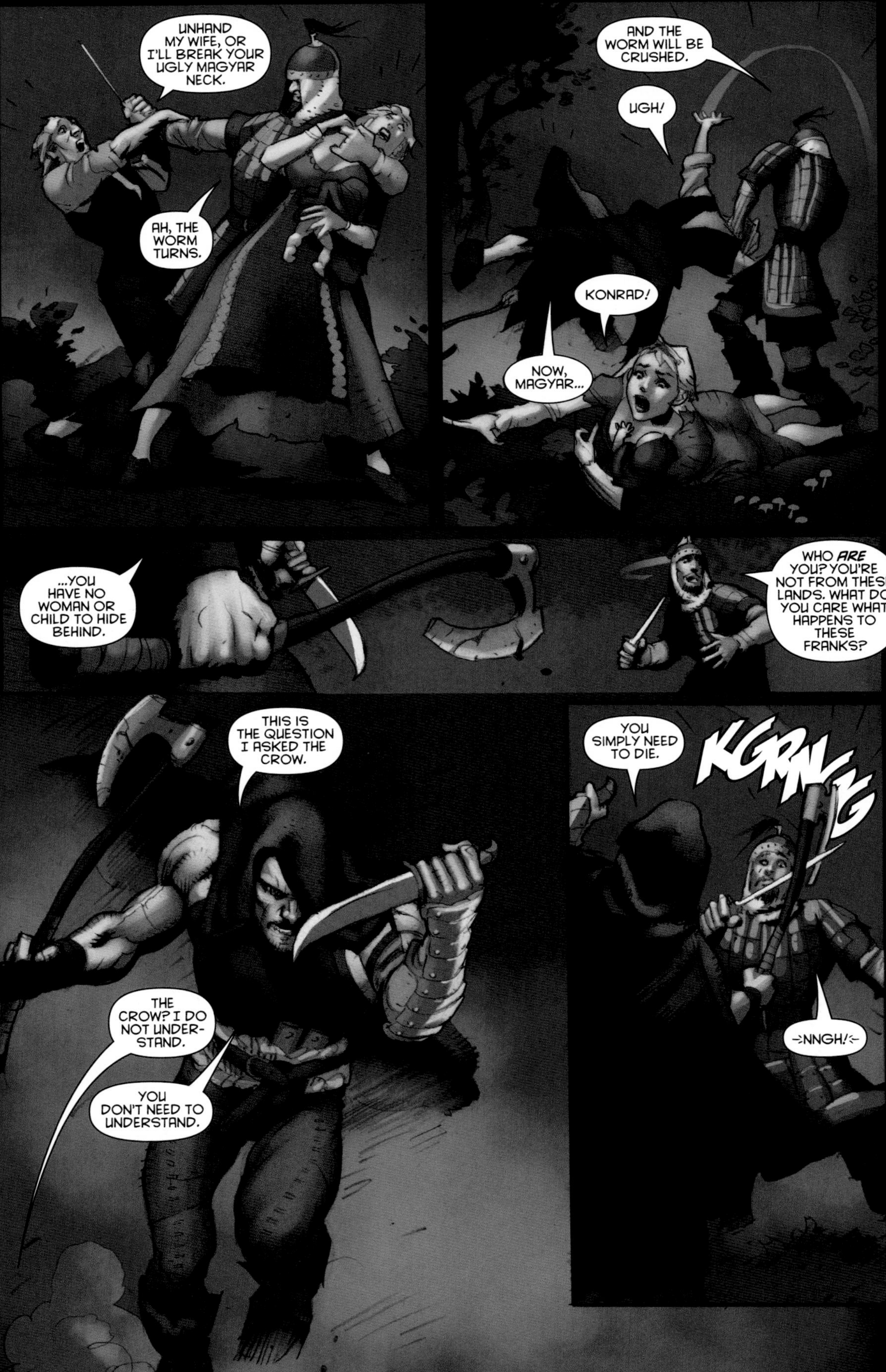
UNHAND MY WIFE, OR I'LL BREAK YOUR UGLY MAGYAR NECK.
AH, THE WORM TURNS.
AND THE WORM WILL BE CRUSHED.
UGH!
KONRAD!
NOW, MAGYAR...
...YOU HAVE NO WOMAN OR CHILD TO HIDE BEHIND.
WHO ARE YOU? YOU'RE NOT FROM THESE LANDS. WHAT DO YOU CARE WHAT HAPPENS TO THESE FRANKS?
THIS IS THE QUESTION I ASKED THE CROW.
THE CROW? I DO NOT UNDER-STAND.
YOU DON'T NEED TO UNDERSTAND.
YOU SIMPLY NEED TO DIE.
KGRNNNG
-NNGH!-

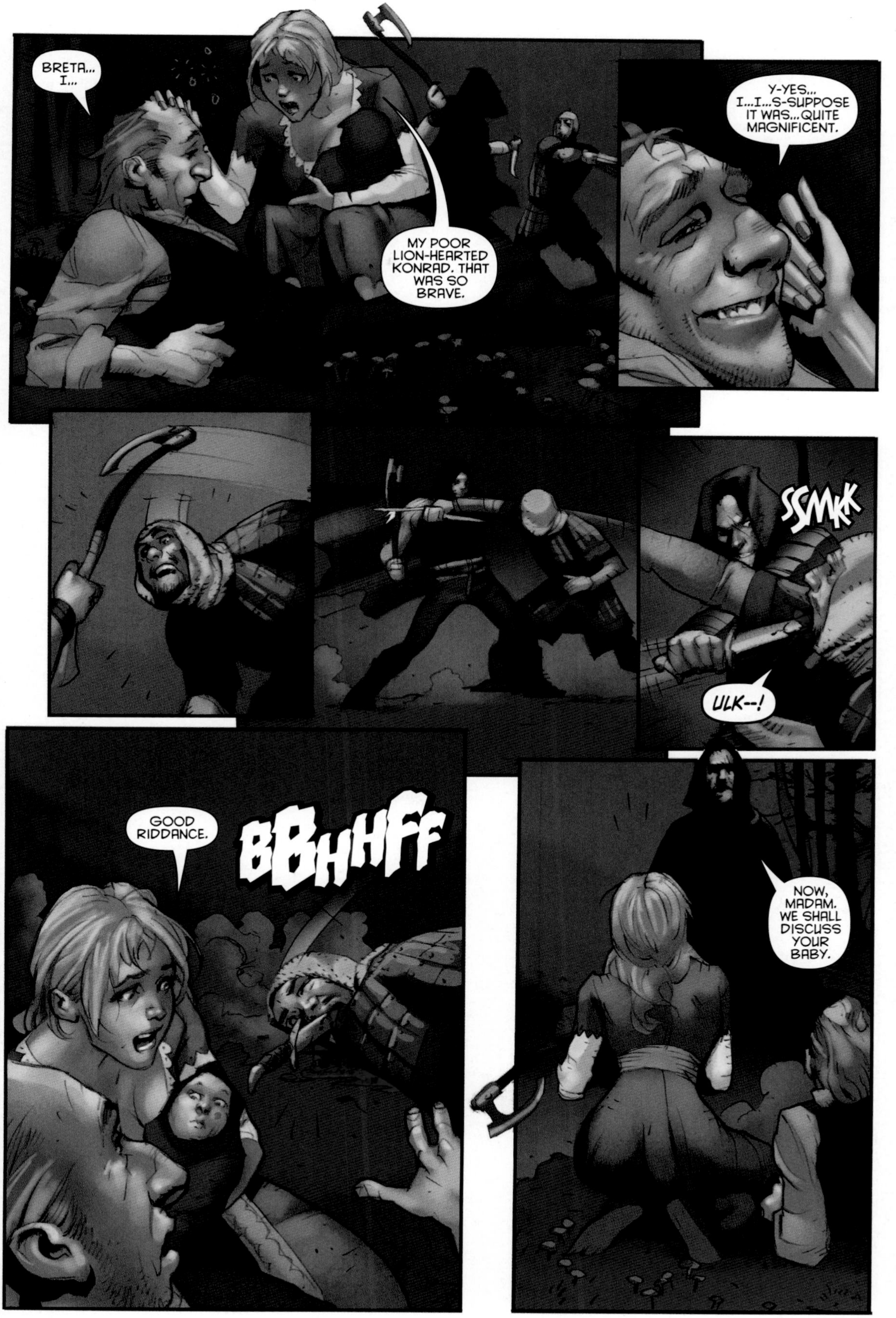
BRETA... I...
MY POOR LION-HEARTED KONRAD. THAT WAS SO BRAVE.
Y-YES... I...I...S-SUPPOSE IT WAS...QUITE MAGNIFICENT.
SSMKK
ULK--!
GOOD RIDDANCE.
BBHHFF
NOW, MADAM. WE SHALL DISCUSS YOUR BABY.

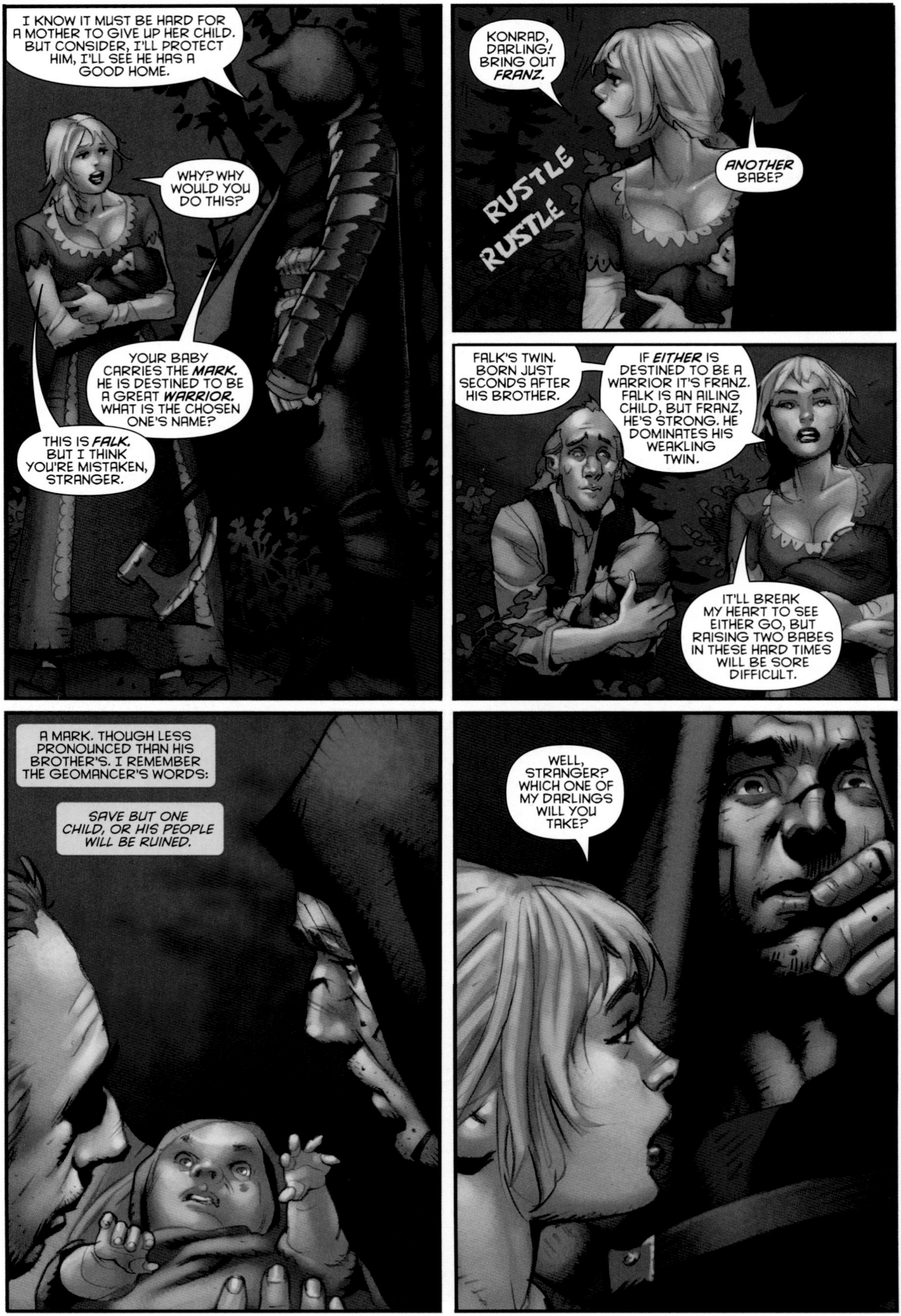
I KNOW IT MUST BE HARD FOR A MOTHER TO GIVE UP HER CHILD. BUT CONSIDER, I'LL PROTECT HIM, I'LL SEE HE HAS A GOOD HOME.
WHY? WHY WOULD YOU DO THIS?
YOUR BABY CARRIES THE *MARK.* HE IS DESTINED TO BE A GREAT *WARRIOR.* WHAT IS THE CHOSEN ONE'S NAME?
THIS IS *FALK.* BUT I THINK YOU'RE MISTAKEN, STRANGER.
KONRAD, DARLING! BRING OUT *FRANZ.*
RUSTLE
RUSTLE
ANOTHER BABE?
FALK'S TWIN. BORN JUST SECONDS AFTER HIS BROTHER.
IF *EITHER* IS DESTINED TO BE A WARRIOR IT'S FRANZ. FALK IS AN AILING CHILD, BUT FRANZ, HE'S STRONG. HE DOMINATES HIS WEAKLING TWIN.
IT'LL BREAK MY HEART TO SEE EITHER GO, BUT RAISING TWO BABES IN THESE HARD TIMES WILL BE SORE DIFFICULT.
A MARK. THOUGH LESS PRONOUNCED THAN HIS BROTHER'S. I REMEMBER THE GEOMANCER'S WORDS:
SAVE BUT ONE CHILD, OR HIS PEOPLE WILL BE RUINED.
WELL, STRANGER? WHICH ONE OF MY DARLINGS WILL YOU TAKE?

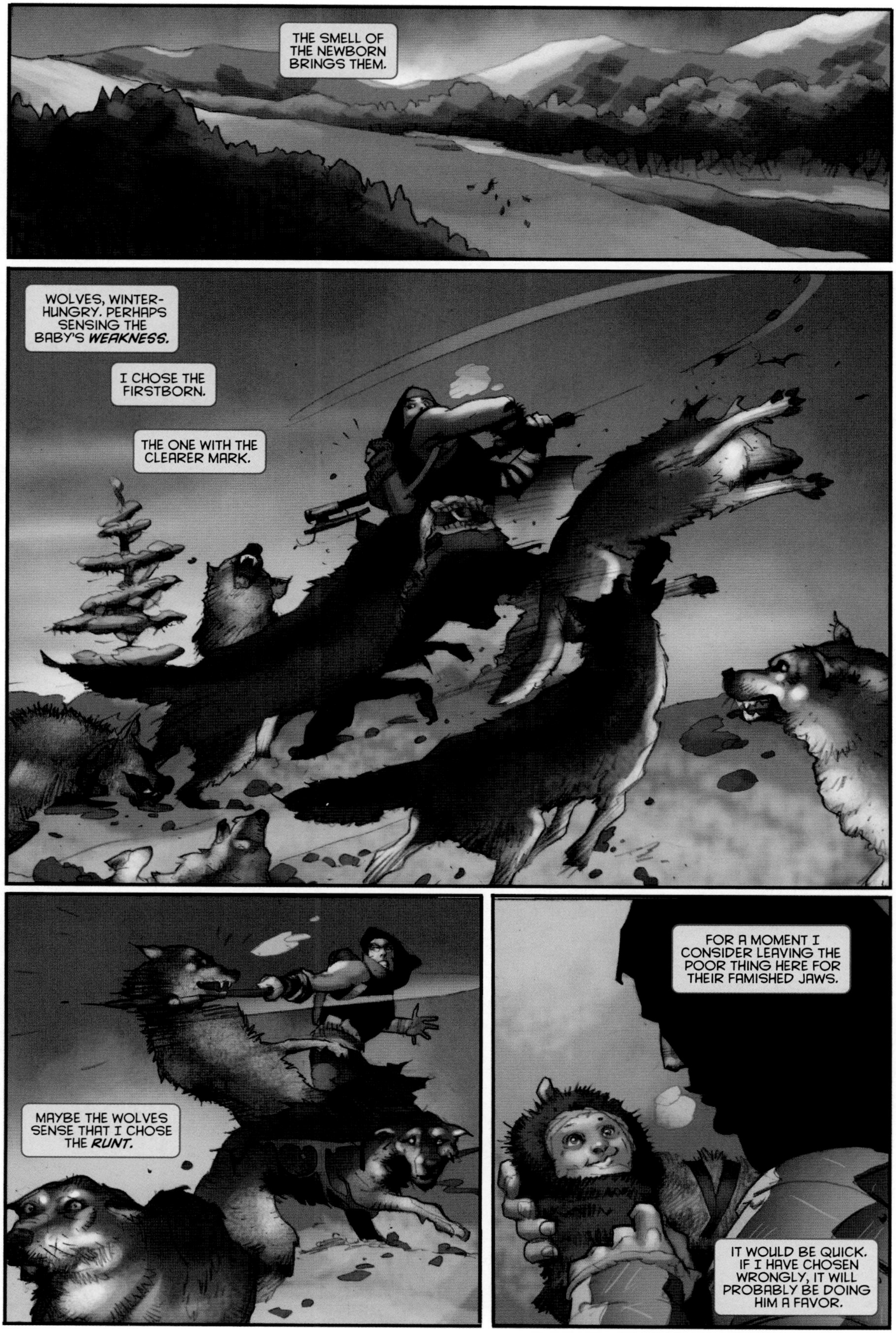

THE SMELL OF THE NEWBORN BRINGS THEM.
WOLVES, WINTER-HUNGRY. PERHAPS SENSING THE BABY'S *WEAKNESS.*
I CHOSE THE FIRSTBORN.
THE ONE WITH THE CLEARER MARK.
MAYBE THE WOLVES SENSE THAT I CHOSE THE *RUNT.*
FOR A MOMENT I CONSIDER LEAVING THE POOR THING HERE FOR THEIR FAMISHED JAWS.
IT WOULD BE QUICK. IF I HAVE CHOSEN WRONGLY, IT WILL PROBABLY BE DOING HIM A FAVOR.

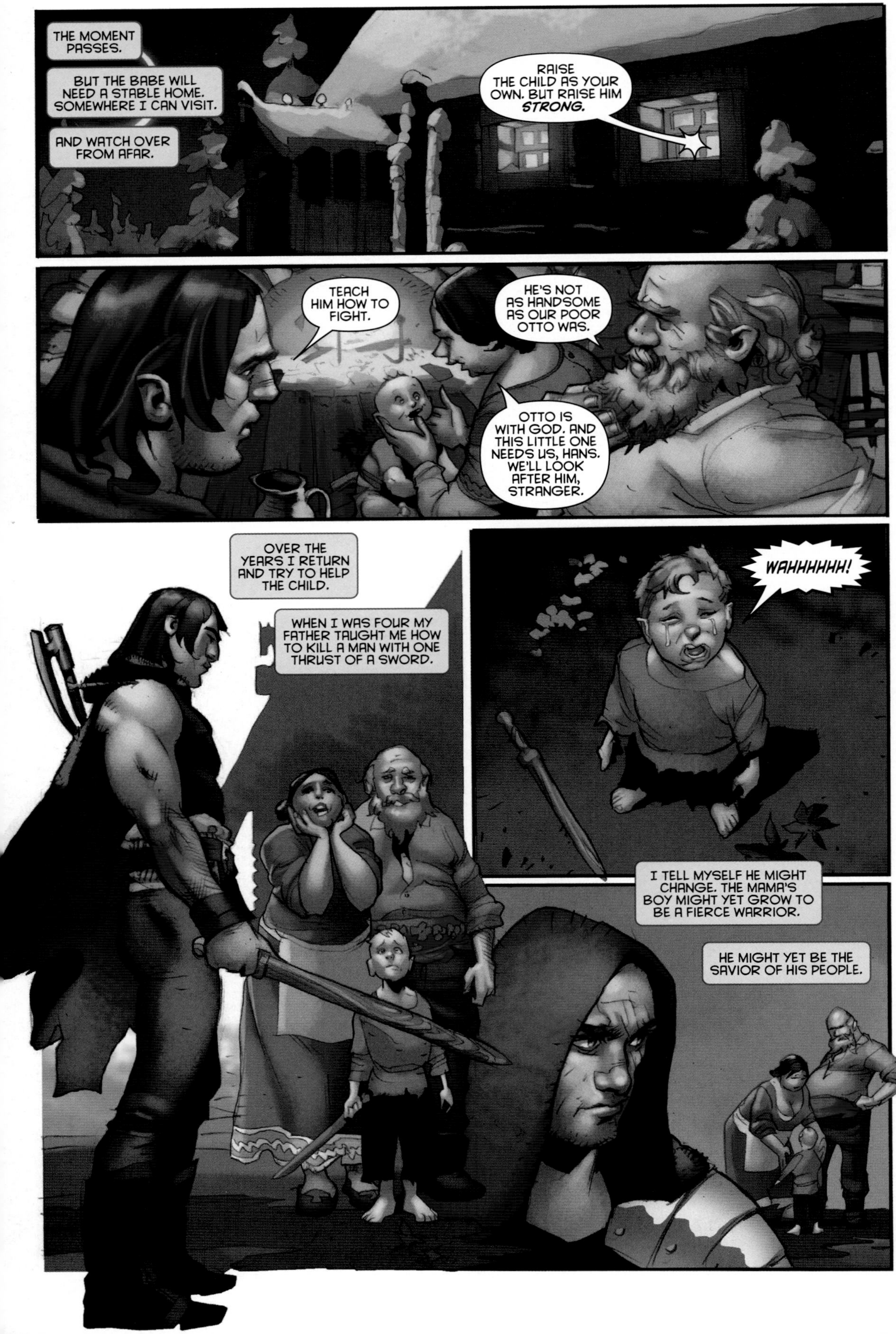
THE MOMENT PASSES.
BUT THE BABE WILL NEED A STABLE HOME. SOMEWHERE I CAN VISIT.
AND WATCH OVER FROM AFAR.
RAISE THE CHILD AS YOUR OWN. BUT RAISE HIM STRONG.
TEACH HIM HOW TO FIGHT.
HE'S NOT AS HANDSOME AS OUR POOR OTTO WAS.
OTTO IS WITH GOD. AND THIS LITTLE ONE NEEDS US, HANS. WE'LL LOOK AFTER HIM, STRANGER.
OVER THE YEARS I RETURN AND TRY TO HELP THE CHILD.
WHEN I WAS FOUR MY FATHER TAUGHT ME HOW TO KILL A MAN WITH ONE THRUST OF A SWORD.
WAHHHHHH!
I TELL MYSELF HE MIGHT CHANGE. THE MAMA'S BOY MIGHT YET GROW TO BE A FIERCE WARRIOR.
HE MIGHT YET BE THE SAVIOR OF HIS PEOPLE.

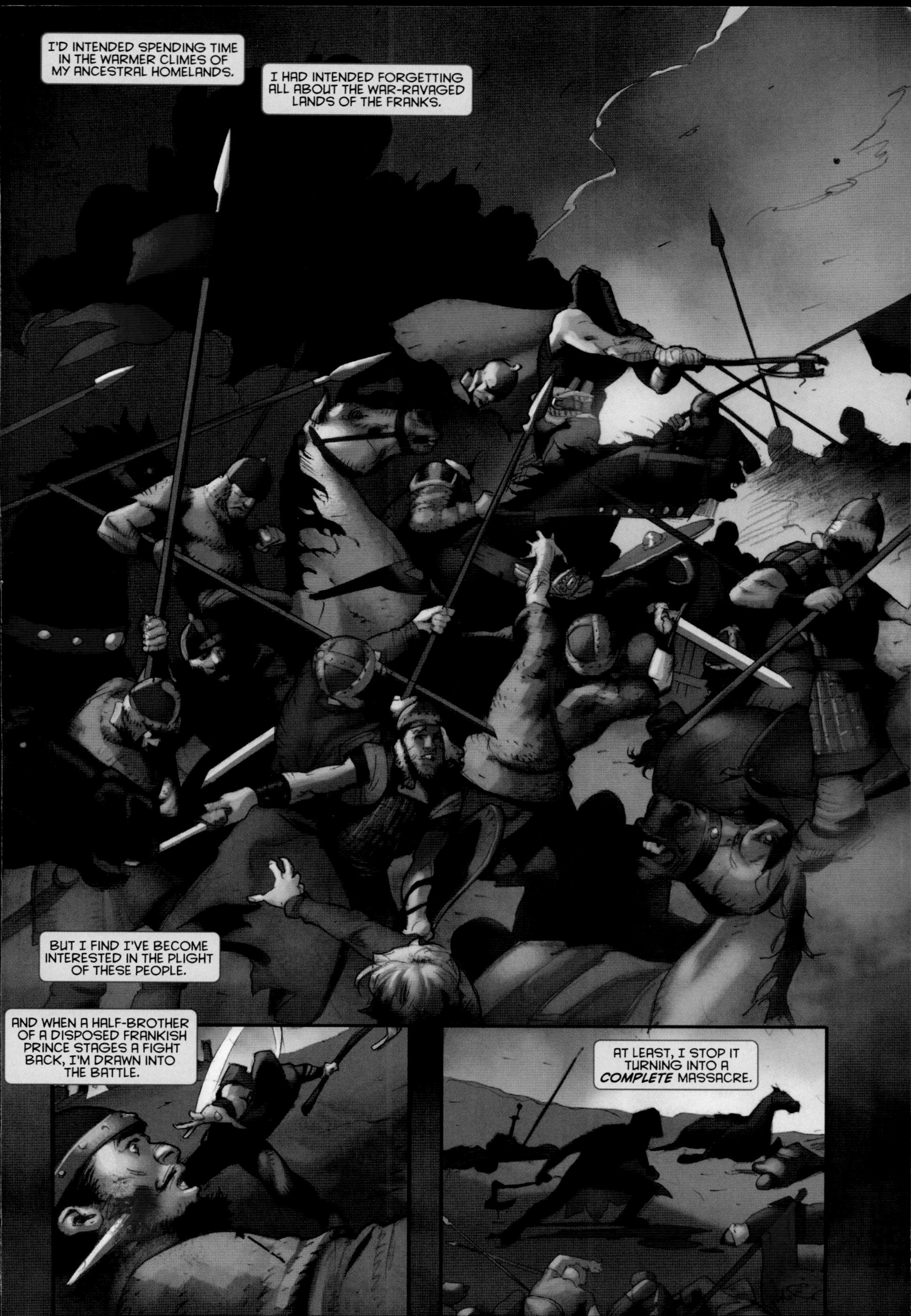
I'D INTENDED SPENDING TIME IN THE WARMER CLIMES OF MY ANCESTRAL HOMELANDS.
I HAD INTENDED FORGETTING ALL ABOUT THE WAR-RAVAGED LANDS OF THE FRANKS.
BUT I FIND I'VE BECOME INTERESTED IN THE PLIGHT OF THESE PEOPLE.
AND WHEN A HALF-BROTHER OF A DISPOSED FRANKISH PRINCE STAGES A FIGHT BACK, I'M DRAWN INTO THE BATTLE.
AT LEAST, I STOP IT TURNING INTO A *COMPLETE* MASSACRE.

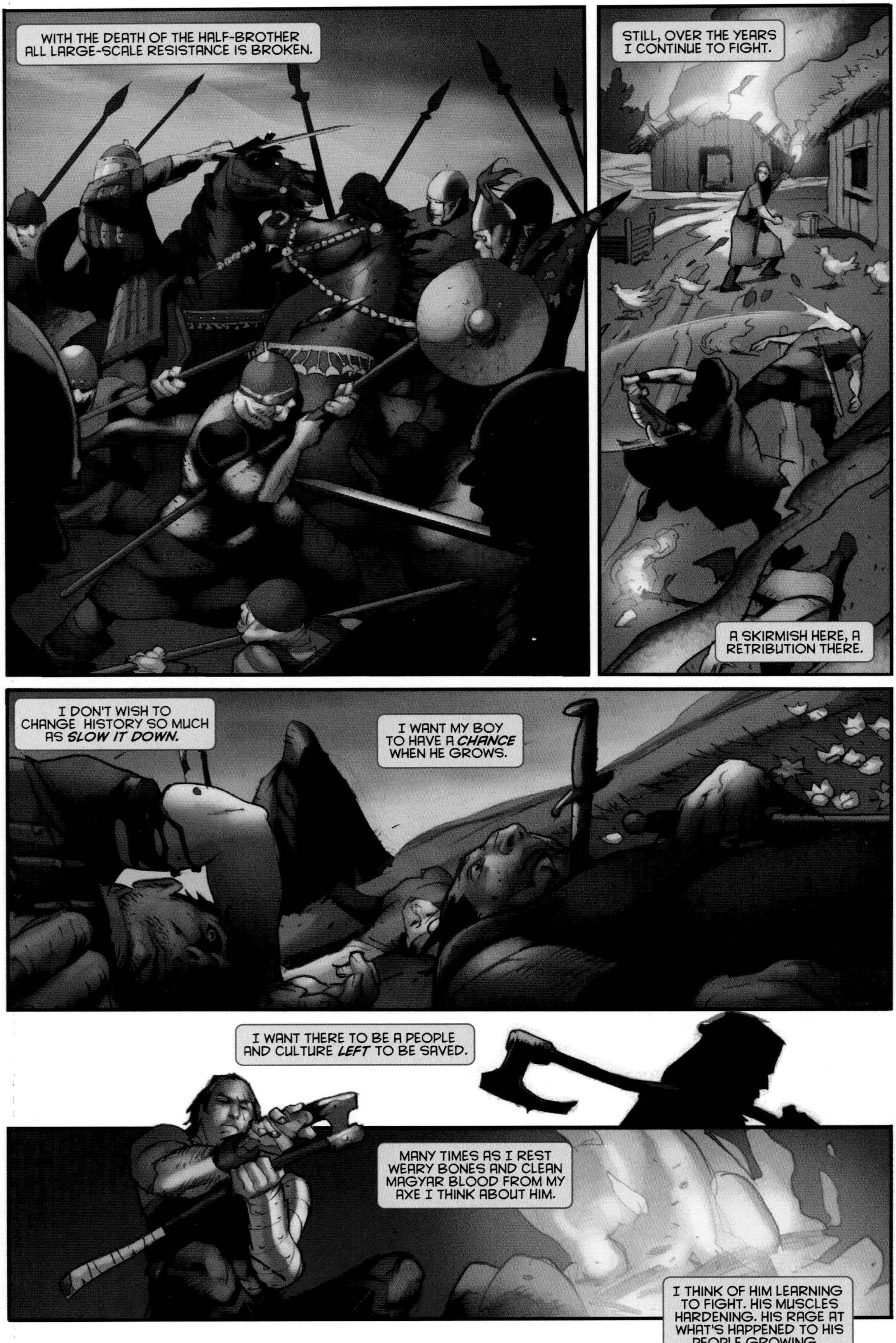
WITH THE DEATH OF THE HALF-BROTHER ALL LARGE-SCALE RESISTANCE IS BROKEN.
STILL, OVER THE YEARS I CONTINUE TO FIGHT.
A SKIRMISH HERE, A RETRIBUTION THERE.
I DON'T WISH TO CHANGE HISTORY SO MUCH AS *SLOW IT DOWN.*
I WANT MY BOY TO HAVE A *CHANCE* WHEN HE GROWS.
I WANT THERE TO BE A PEOPLE AND CULTURE *LEFT* TO BE SAVED.
MANY TIMES AS I REST WEARY BONES AND CLEAN MAGYAR BLOOD FROM MY AXE I THINK ABOUT HIM.
I THINK OF HIM LEARNING TO FIGHT. HIS MUSCLES HARDENING. HIS RAGE AT WHAT'S HAPPENED TO HIS PEOPLE GROWING...

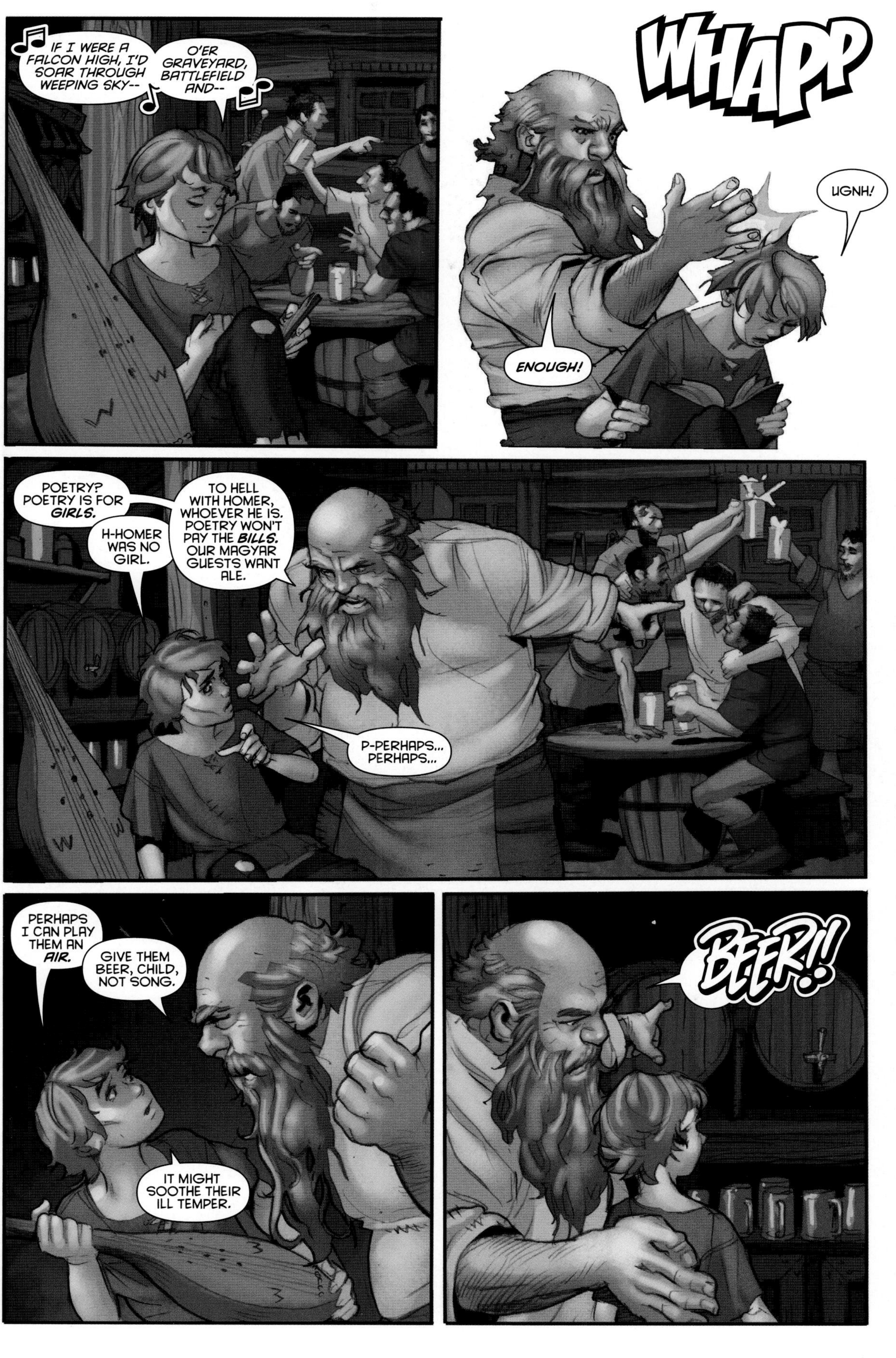
IF I WERE A FALCON HIGH, I'D SOAR THROUGH WEEPING SKY--
O'ER GRAVEYARD, BATTLEFIELD AND--
WHAPP
UGNH!
ENOUGH!
POETRY? POETRY IS FOR GIRLS.
H-HOMER WAS NO GIRL.
TO HELL WITH HOMER, WHOEVER HE IS. POETRY WON'T PAY THE BILLS. OUR MAGYAR GUESTS WANT ALE.
P-PERHAPS... PERHAPS...
PERHAPS I CAN PLAY THEM AN AIR.
GIVE THEM BEER, CHILD, NOT SONG.
IT MIGHT SOOTHE THEIR ILL TEMPER.
BEER!!

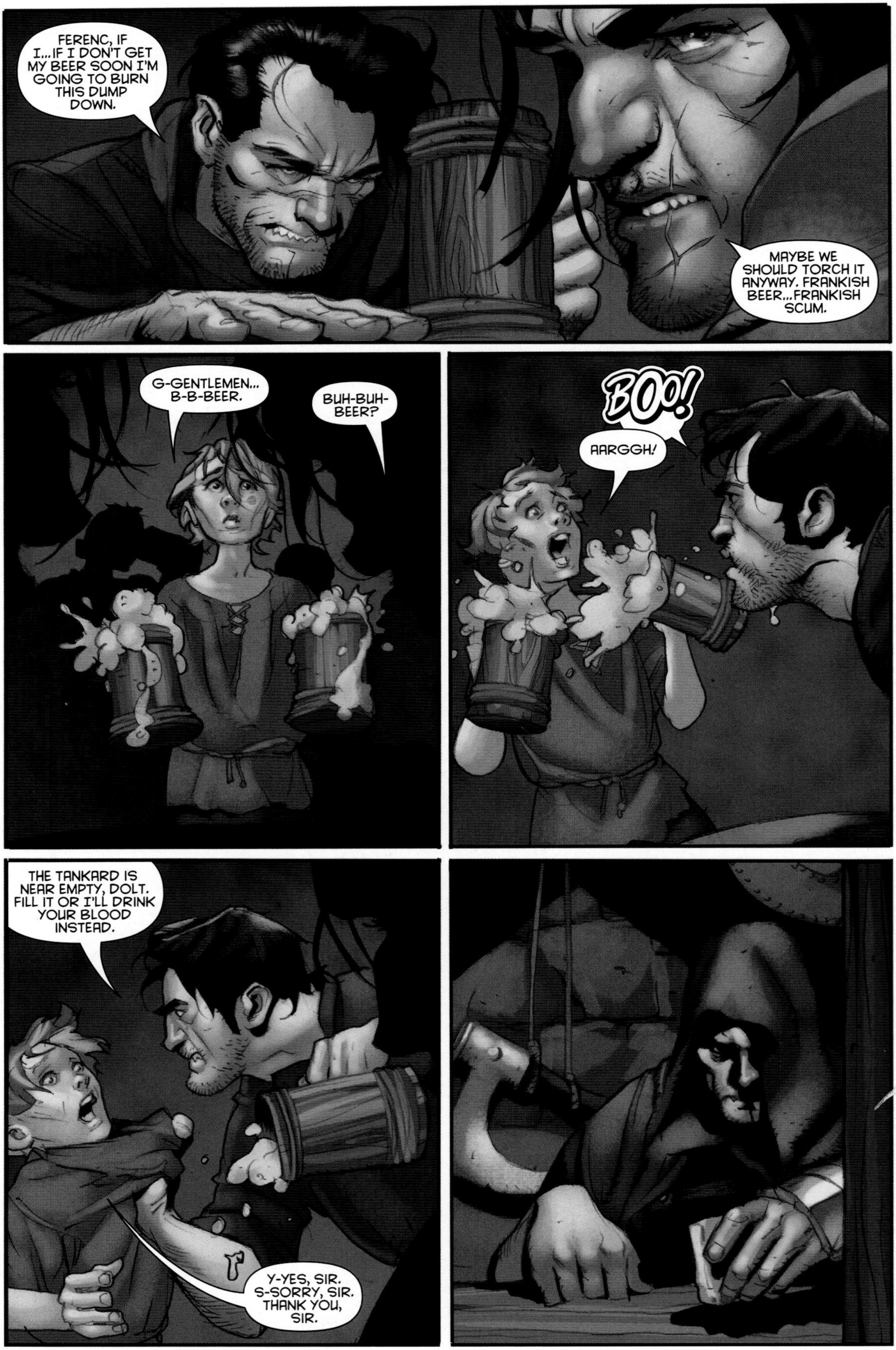
FERENC, IF I...IF I DON'T GET MY BEER SOON I'M GOING TO BURN THIS DUMP DOWN.
MAYBE WE SHOULD TORCH IT ANYWAY. FRANKISH BEER...FRANKISH SCUM.
G-GENTLEMEN... B-B-BEER.
BUH-BUH-BEER?
BOO!
AARGGH!
THE TANKARD IS NEAR EMPTY, DOLT. FILL IT OR I'LL DRINK YOUR BLOOD INSTEAD.
Y-YES, SIR. S-SORRY, SIR. THANK YOU, SIR.

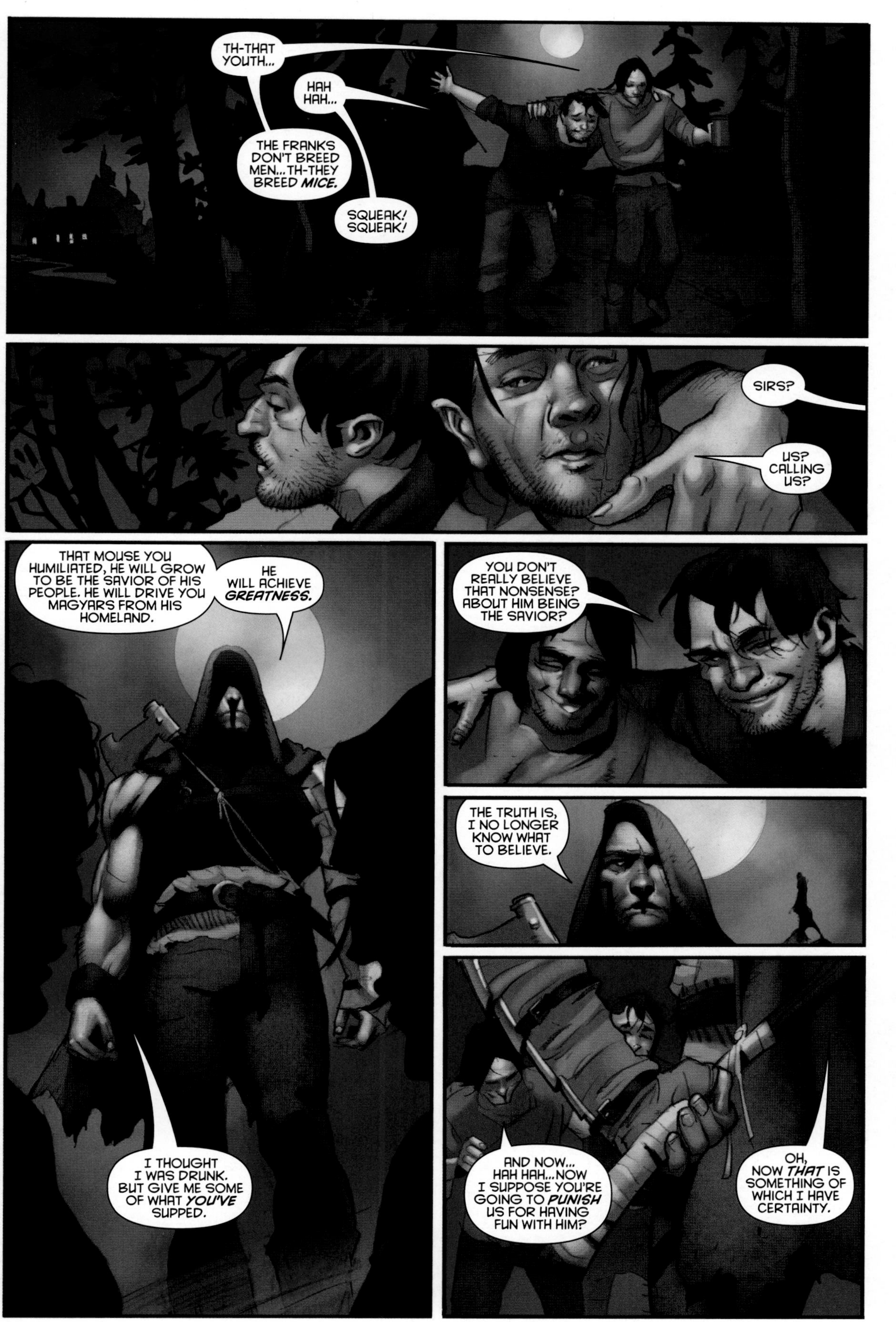
TH-THAT YOUTH...
HAH HAH...
THE FRANKS DON'T BREED MEN...TH-THEY BREED *MICE.*
SQUEAK! SQUEAK!
SIRS?
US? CALLING US?
THAT MOUSE YOU HUMILIATED, HE WILL GROW TO BE THE SAVIOR OF HIS PEOPLE. HE WILL DRIVE YOU MAGYARS FROM HIS HOMELAND.
HE WILL ACHIEVE *GREATNESS.*
I THOUGHT I WAS DRUNK. BUT GIVE ME SOME OF WHAT *YOU'VE* SUPPED.
YOU DON'T REALLY BELIEVE THAT NONSENSE? ABOUT HIM BEING THE SAVIOR?
THE TRUTH IS, I NO LONGER KNOW WHAT TO BELIEVE.
AND NOW... HAH HAH...NOW I SUPPOSE YOU'RE GOING TO *PUNISH* US FOR HAVING FUN WITH HIM?
OH, NOW *THAT* IS SOMETHING OF WHICH I HAVE CERTAINTY.

"GEOMANCER! HEAR ME, GEOMANCER!"
COME ON, CROW. SHOW YOUR UGLY FACE.
I WANT TO KNOW. I WANT TO KNOW FOR CERTAIN.
I CHOSE THE CHILD WITH THE CLEAREST MARK. I CHOSE THE FIRSTBORN...
BUT... DID I CHOOSE CORRECTLY?
THE BOY SEEMS A WEAKLING. A COWARD. BUT...BUT MAYBE HE WILL CHANGE. MAYBE HE HIDES HIS POTENTIAL.
AND WHAT OF THE OTHER BABY...?

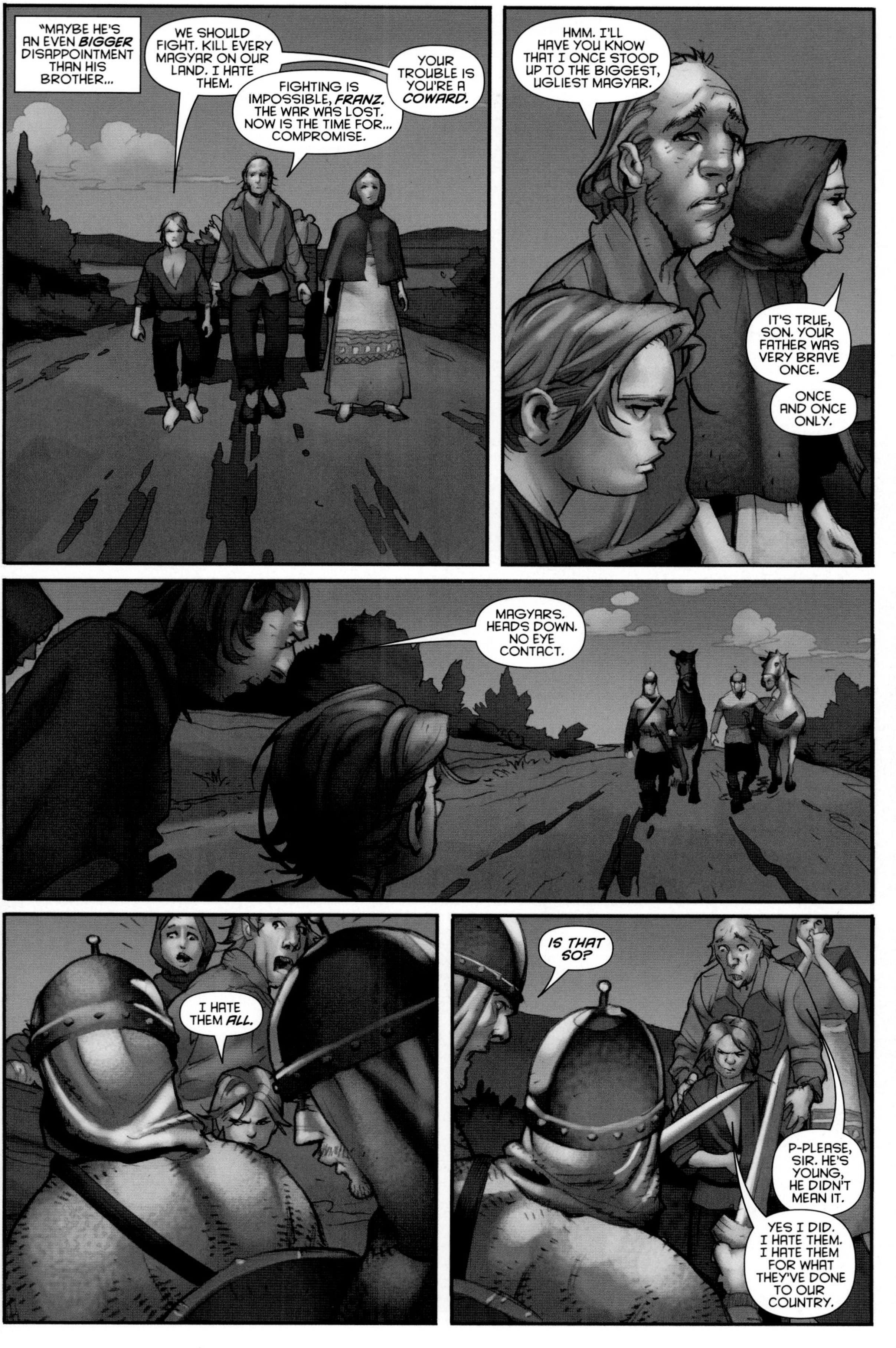
"MAYBE HE'S AN EVEN BIGGER DISAPPOINTMENT THAN HIS BROTHER...
WE SHOULD FIGHT. KILL EVERY MAGYAR ON OUR LAND. I HATE THEM.
FIGHTING IS IMPOSSIBLE, FRANZ. THE WAR WAS LOST. NOW IS THE TIME FOR... COMPROMISE.
YOUR TROUBLE IS YOU'RE A COWARD.
HMM. I'LL HAVE YOU KNOW THAT I ONCE STOOD UP TO THE BIGGEST, UGLIEST MAGYAR.
IT'S TRUE, SON. YOUR FATHER WAS VERY BRAVE ONCE.
ONCE AND ONCE ONLY.
MAGYARS. HEADS DOWN. NO EYE CONTACT.
I HATE THEM ALL.
IS THAT SO?
P-PLEASE, SIR. HE'S YOUNG, HE DIDN'T MEAN IT.
YES I DID. I HATE THEM. I HATE THEM FOR WHAT THEY'VE DONE TO OUR COUNTRY.

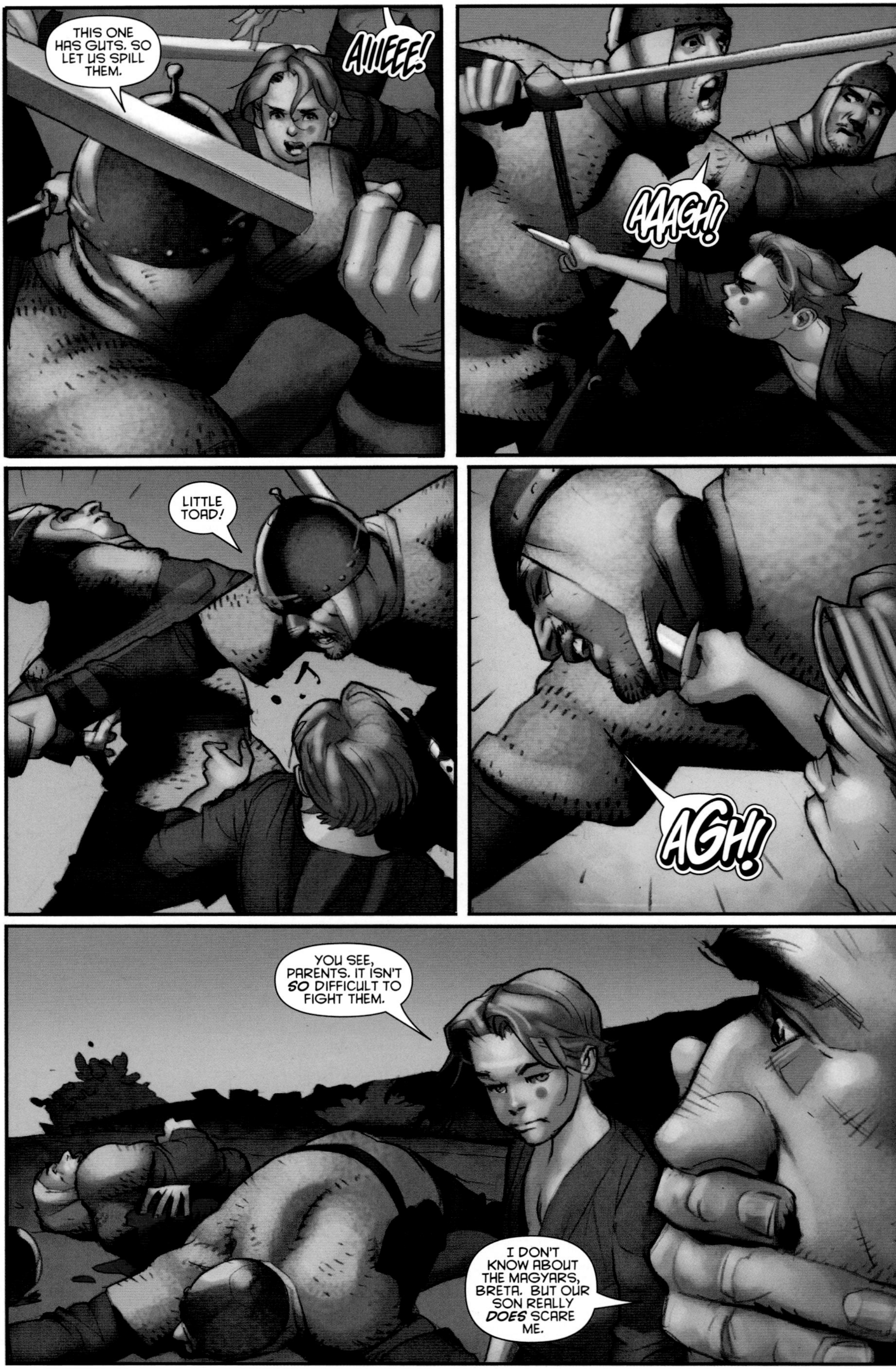
THIS ONE HAS GUTS. SO LET US SPILL THEM.
AIIIEEE!
AAAGH!
LITTLE TOAD!
AGH!
YOU SEE, PARENTS. IT ISN'T *SO* DIFFICULT TO FIGHT THEM.
I DON'T KNOW ABOUT THE MAGYARS, BRETA. BUT OUR SON REALLY *DOES* SCARE ME.

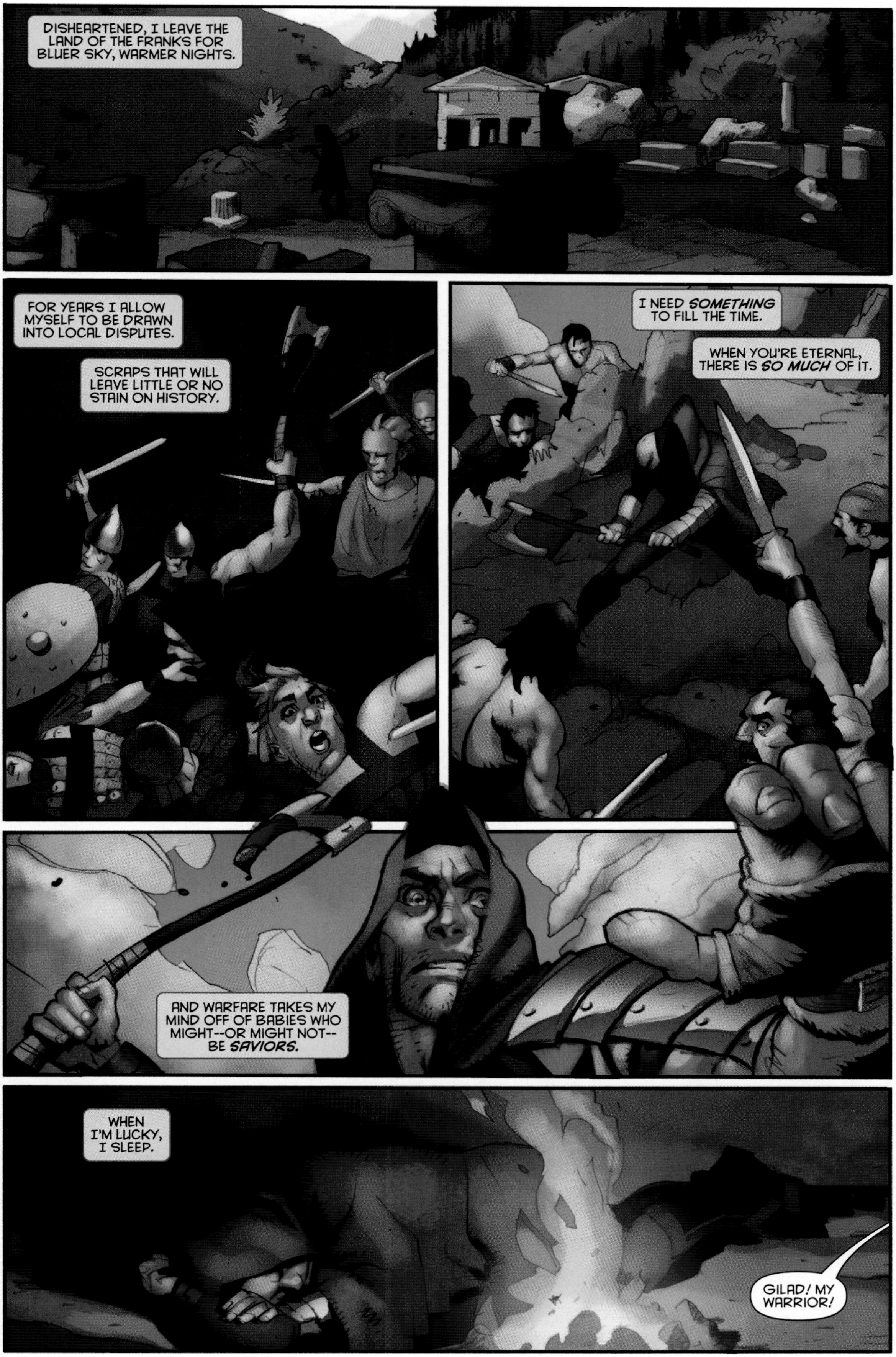
DISHEARTENED, I LEAVE THE LAND OF THE FRANKS FOR BLUER SKY, WARMER NIGHTS.
FOR YEARS I ALLOW MYSELF TO BE DRAWN INTO LOCAL DISPUTES.
SCRAPS THAT WILL LEAVE LITTLE OR NO STAIN ON HISTORY.
I NEED SOMETHING TO FILL THE TIME.
WHEN YOU'RE ETERNAL, THERE IS SO MUCH OF IT.
AND WARFARE TAKES MY MIND OFF OF BABIES WHO MIGHT--OR MIGHT NOT--BE SAVIORS.
WHEN I'M LUCKY, I SLEEP.
GILAD! MY WARRIOR!

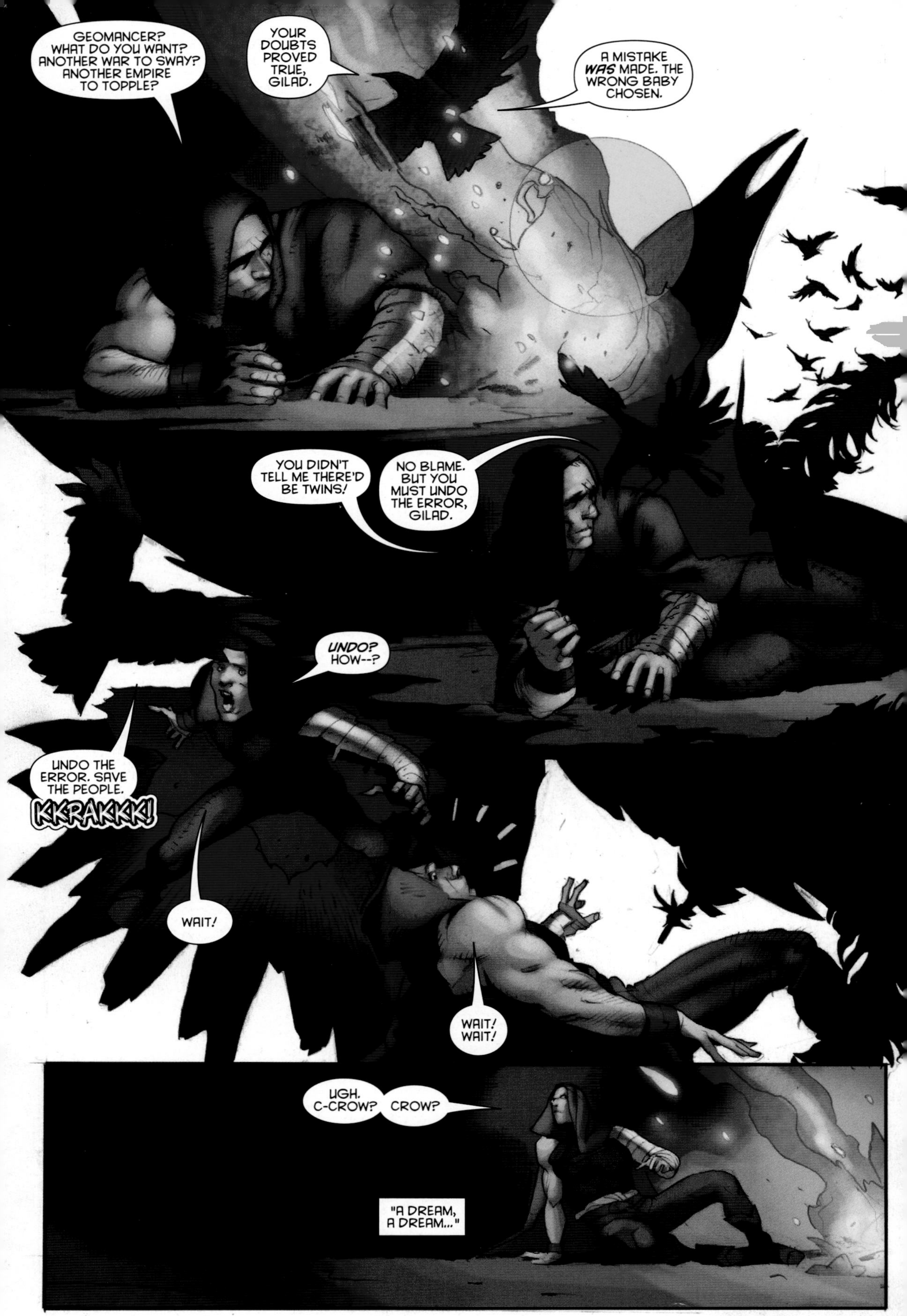
GEOMANCER? WHAT DO YOU WANT? ANOTHER WAR TO SWAY? ANOTHER EMPIRE TO TOPPLE?
YOUR DOUBTS PROVED TRUE, GILAD.
A MISTAKE *WAS* MADE. THE WRONG BABY CHOSEN.
YOU DIDN'T TELL ME THERE'D BE TWINS!
NO BLAME. BUT YOU MUST UNDO THE ERROR, GILAD.
UNDO? HOW--?
UNDO THE ERROR. SAVE THE PEOPLE.
KKRAKKK!
WAIT!
WAIT! WAIT!
UGH. C-CROW?
CROW?
"A DREAM, A DREAM..."

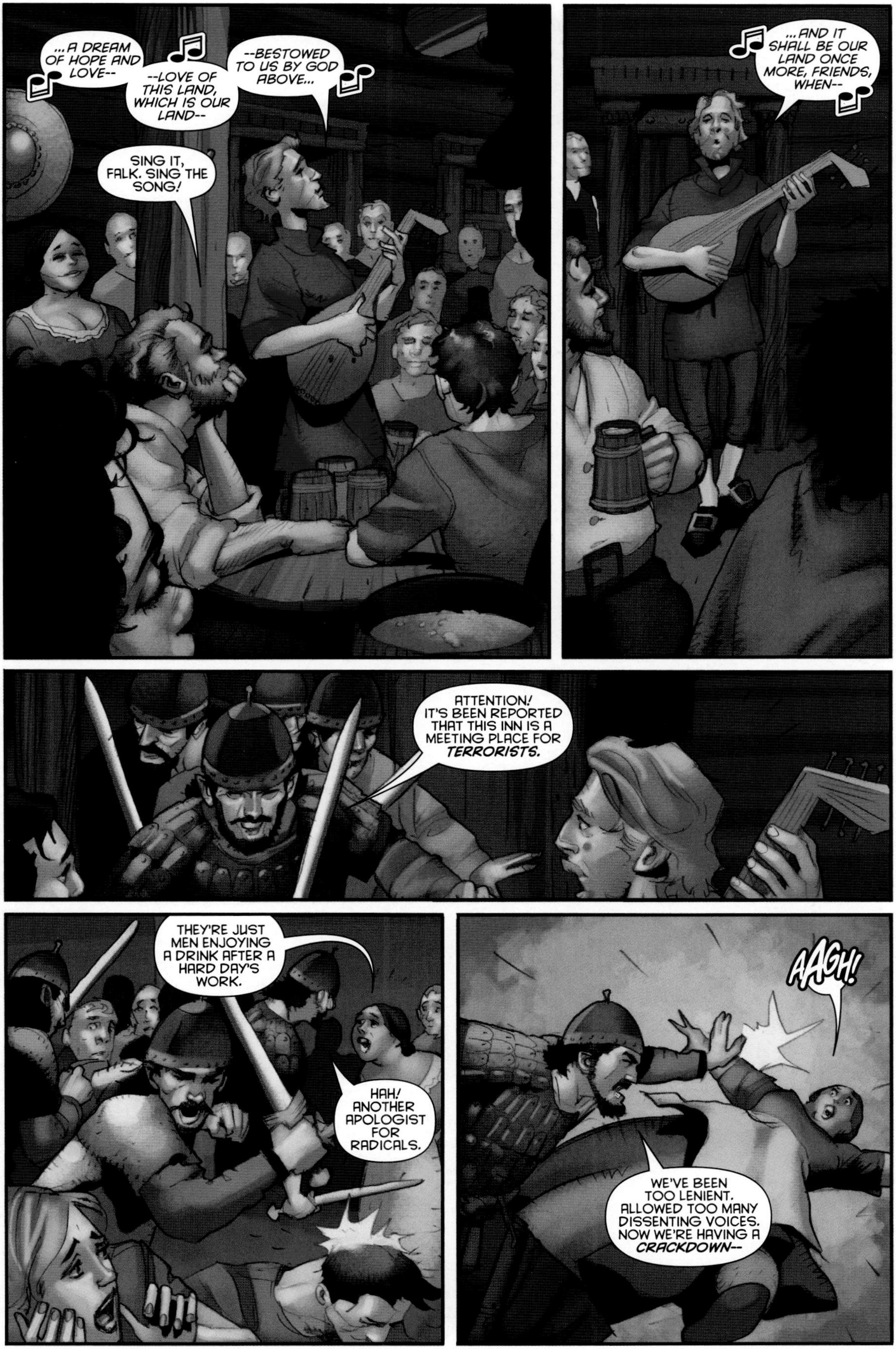
...A DREAM OF HOPE AND LOVE--
--LOVE OF THIS LAND, WHICH IS OUR LAND--
--BESTOWED TO US BY GOD ABOVE...
SING IT, FALK. SING THE SONG!
...AND IT SHALL BE OUR LAND ONCE MORE, FRIENDS, WHEN--
ATTENTION! IT'S BEEN REPORTED THAT THIS INN IS A MEETING PLACE FOR *TERRORISTS.*
THEY'RE JUST MEN ENJOYING A DRINK AFTER A HARD DAY'S WORK.
HAH! ANOTHER APOLOGIST FOR RADICALS.
AAGH!
WE'VE BEEN TOO LENIENT. ALLOWED TOO MANY DISSENTING VOICES. NOW WE'RE HAVING A *CRACKDOWN*--

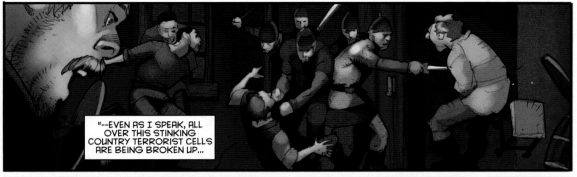

"--EVEN AS I SPEAK, ALL OVER THIS STINKING COUNTRY TERRORIST CELLS ARE BEING BROKEN UP...

"...DANGEROUS EXTREMISTS ARE BEING HUNTED DOWN..."

FRANZ! LOOK OUT!

"...AND ELIMINATED."

AAAGGH!

AAAGGH!

M-MY HEART!

HAH! THIS ONE GROANS WITHOUT BEING TOUCHED!

DID I SAY YOU COULD LEAVE?

AARGH!

NOW, GROANER. I'LL GIVE YOU SOMETHING TO GROAN ABOUT.

PLEASE, HE MEANS YOU NO HARM. HE'S BUT A MINSTREL.

I... I...

A MINSTREL? THEN I WILL LET HIM LIVE. SO HE CAN SING A SONG OF HOW WE MAGYARS DEAL WITH OUR ENEMIES.

--!

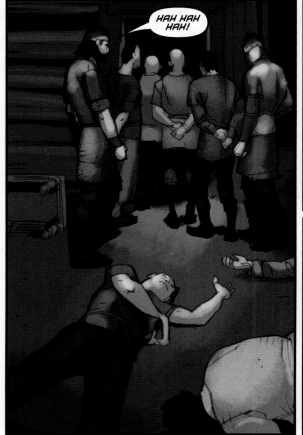

HAH HAH HAH!

I HAVE DECIDED. I MUST GO, MOTHER. I MUST GO TRAVEL THE ROAD.

MY SON, WHY?

THAT MAGYAR WAS RIGHT. I MUST SING A SONG OF HOW THEY TREAT US. I MUST SING A SONG FOR OUR PEOPLE...

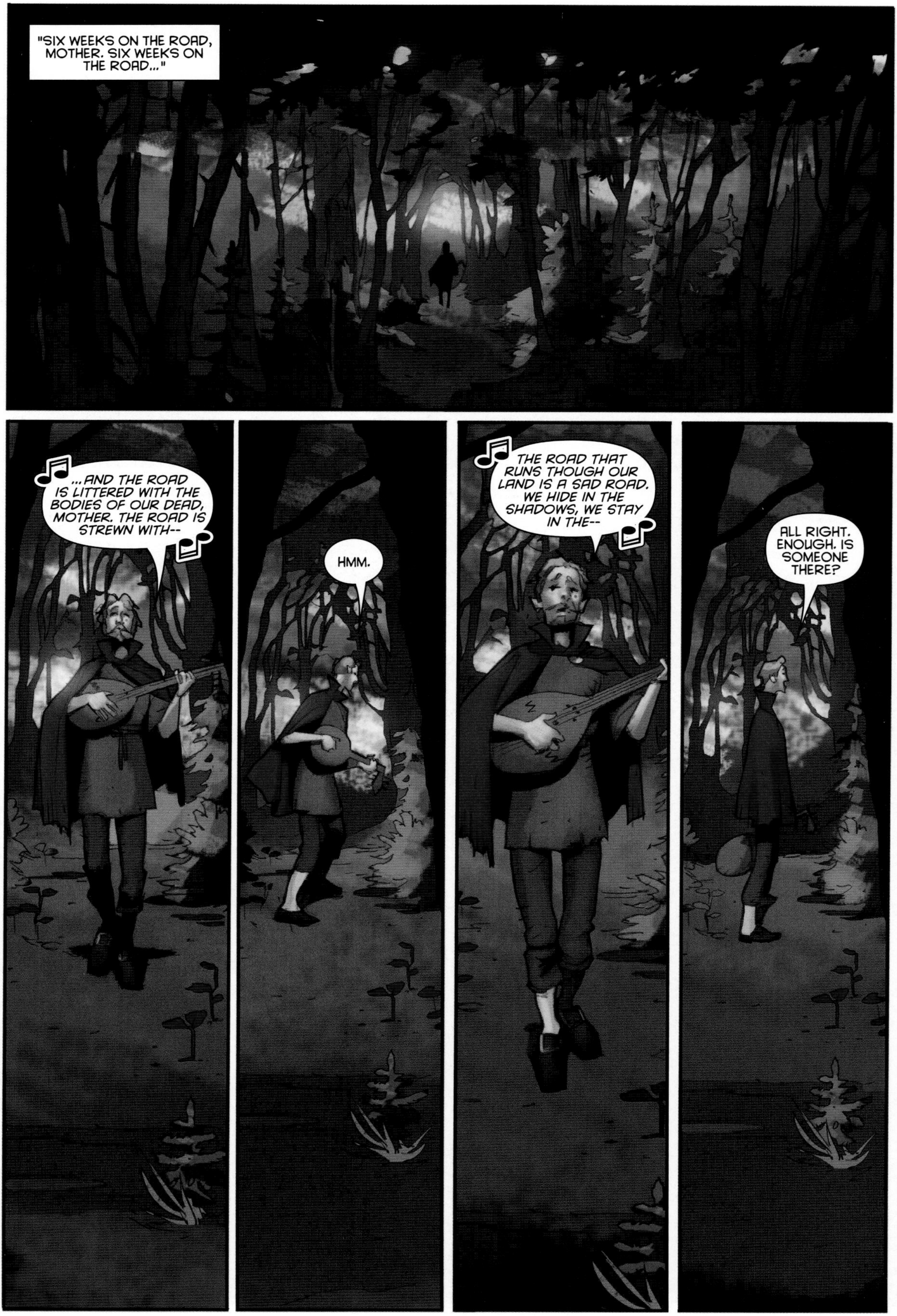
"SIX WEEKS ON THE ROAD, MOTHER. SIX WEEKS ON THE ROAD..."
...AND THE ROAD IS LITTERED WITH THE BODIES OF OUR DEAD, MOTHER. THE ROAD IS STREWN WITH--
HMM.
THE ROAD THAT RUNS THOUGH OUR LAND IS A SAD ROAD. WE HIDE IN THE SHADOWS, WE STAY IN THE--
ALL RIGHT. ENOUGH. IS SOMEONE THERE?

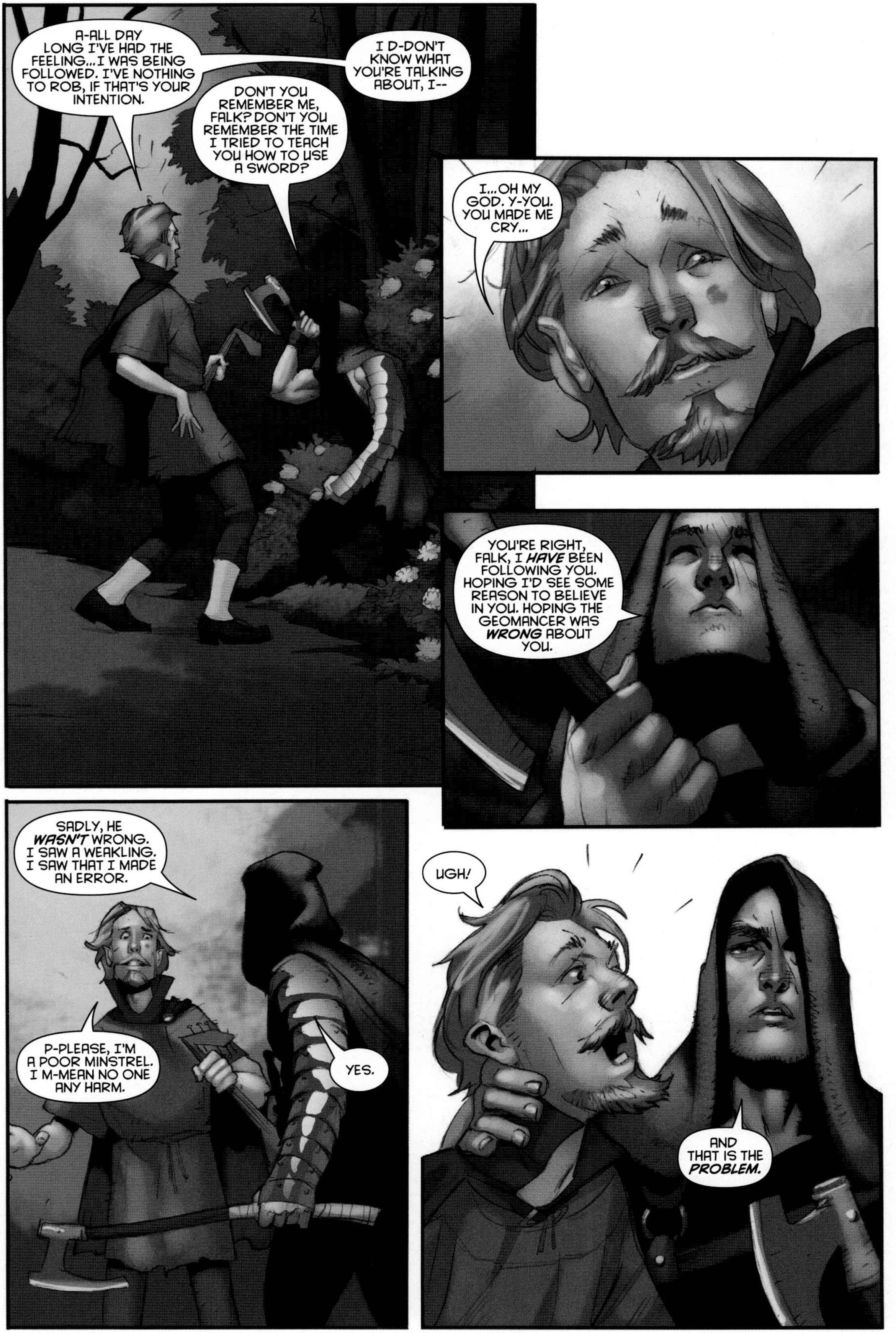
A-ALL DAY LONG I'VE HAD THE FEELING...I WAS BEING FOLLOWED. I'VE NOTHING TO ROB, IF THAT'S YOUR INTENTION.
DON'T YOU REMEMBER ME, FALK? DON'T YOU REMEMBER THE TIME I TRIED TO TEACH YOU HOW TO USE A SWORD?
I D-DON'T KNOW WHAT YOU'RE TALKING ABOUT, I--
I...OH MY GOD. Y-YOU. YOU MADE ME CRY...
YOU'RE RIGHT, FALK, I *HAVE* BEEN FOLLOWING YOU. HOPING I'D SEE SOME REASON TO BELIEVE IN YOU. HOPING THE GEOMANCER WAS *WRONG* ABOUT YOU.
SADLY, HE *WASN'T* WRONG. I SAW A WEAKLING. I SAW THAT I MADE AN ERROR.
P-PLEASE, I'M A POOR MINSTREL. I M-MEAN NO ONE ANY HARM.
YES.
UGH!
AND THAT IS THE *PROBLEM.*

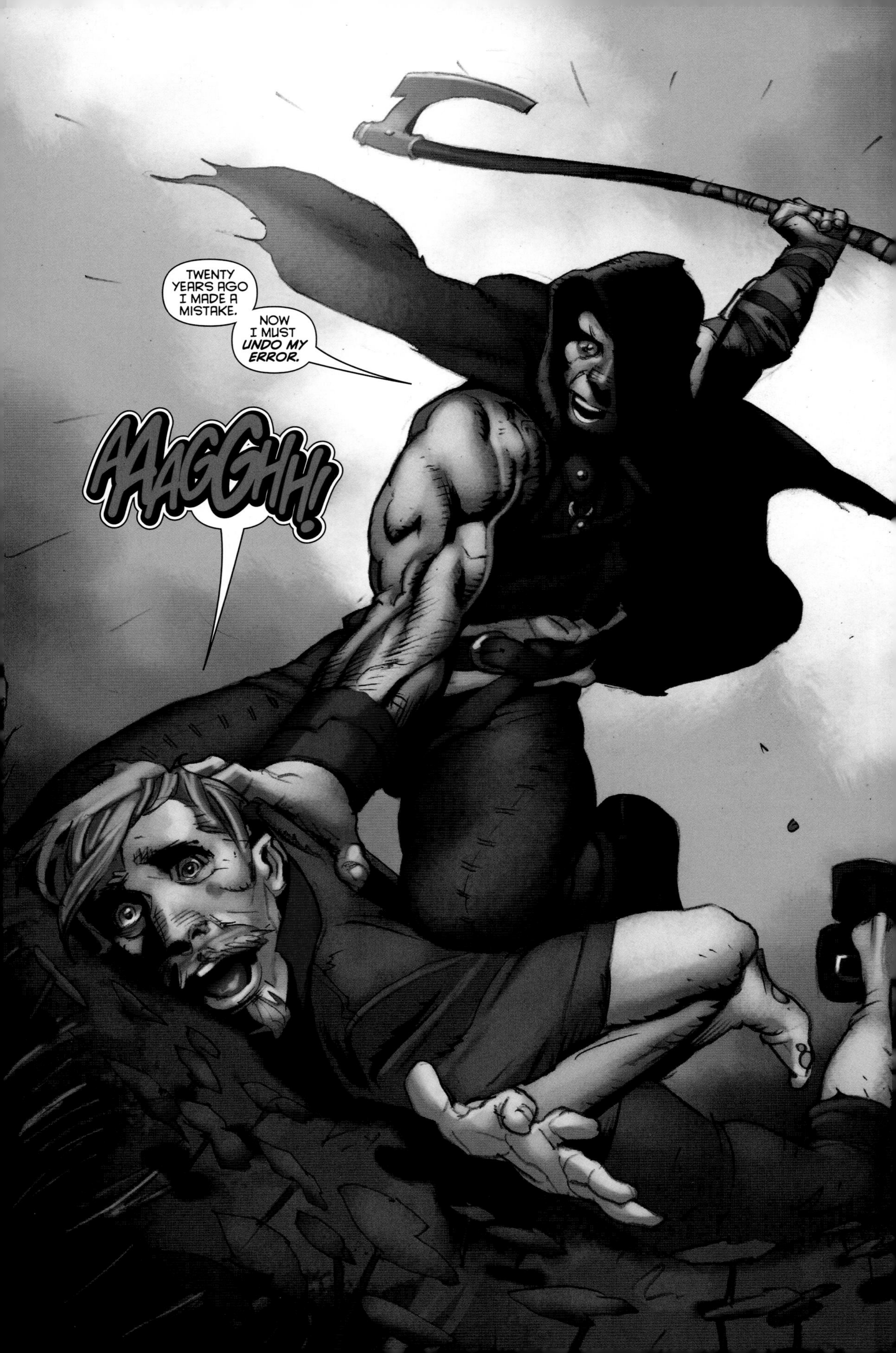
TWENTY YEARS AGO I MADE A MISTAKE.
NOW I MUST *UNDO MY ERROR.*
AAAGGHH!

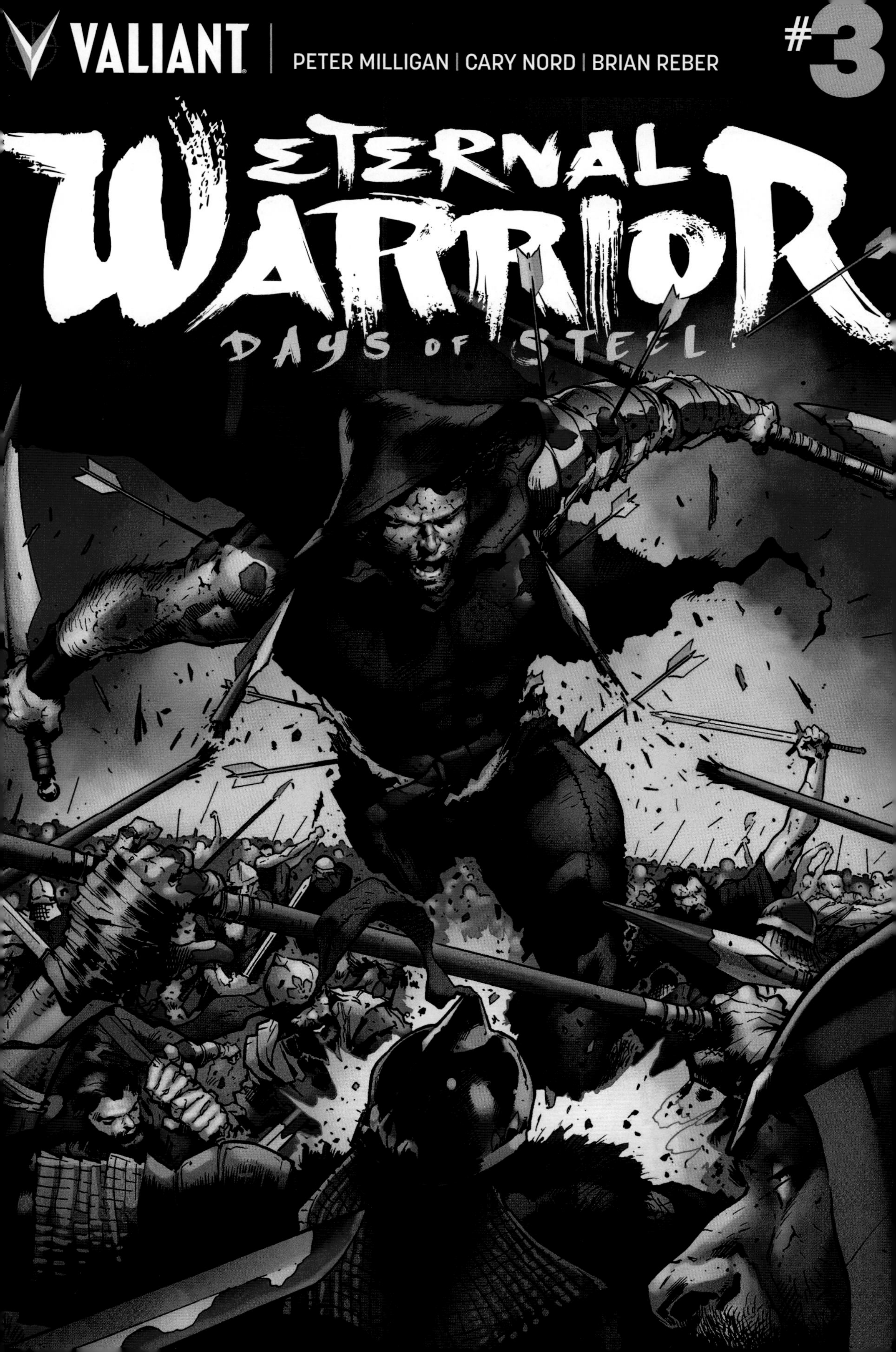
VALIANT
PETER MILLIGAN | CARY NORD | BRIAN REBER
#3
ETERNAL WARRIOR
DAYS OF STEEL

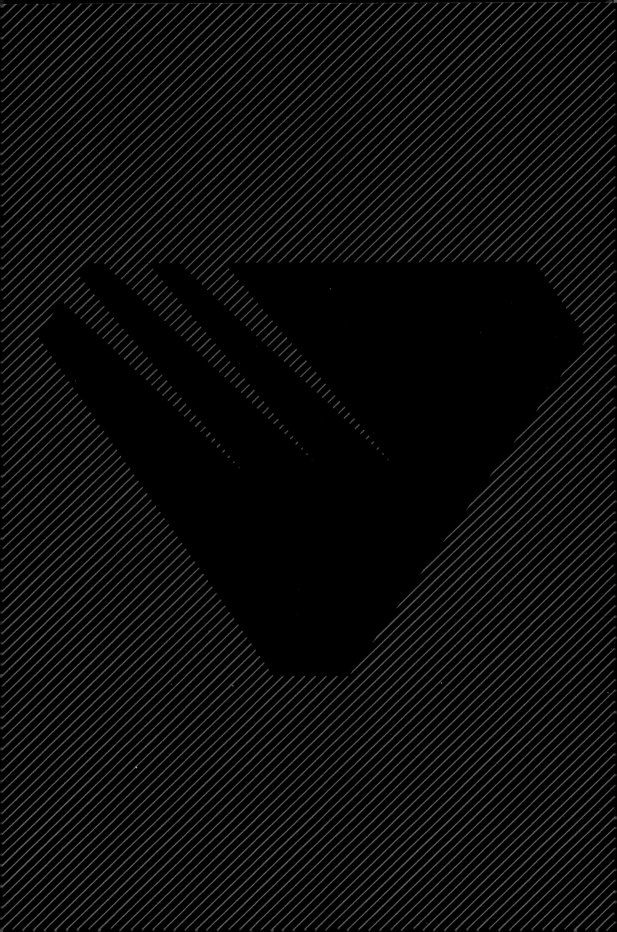

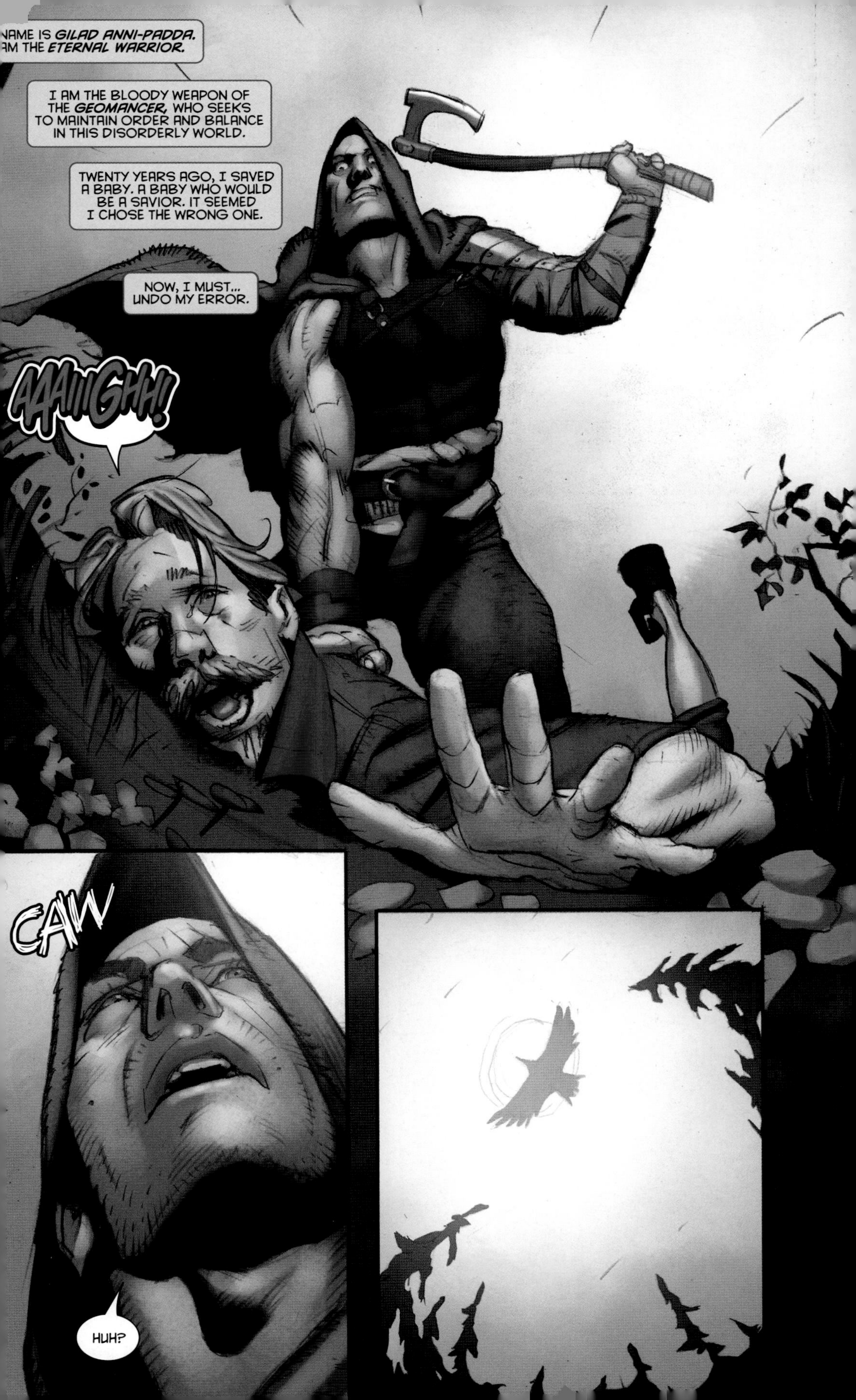
NAME IS GILAD ANNI-PADDA. AM THE ETERNAL WARRIOR.
I AM THE BLOODY WEAPON OF THE GEOMANCER, WHO SEEKS TO MAINTAIN ORDER AND BALANCE IN THIS DISORDERLY WORLD.
TWENTY YEARS AGO, I SAVED A BABY. A BABY WHO WOULD BE A SAVIOR. IT SEEMED I CHOSE THE WRONG ONE.
NOW, I MUST... UNDO MY ERROR.
AAAIIIGHH!
CAW
HUH?

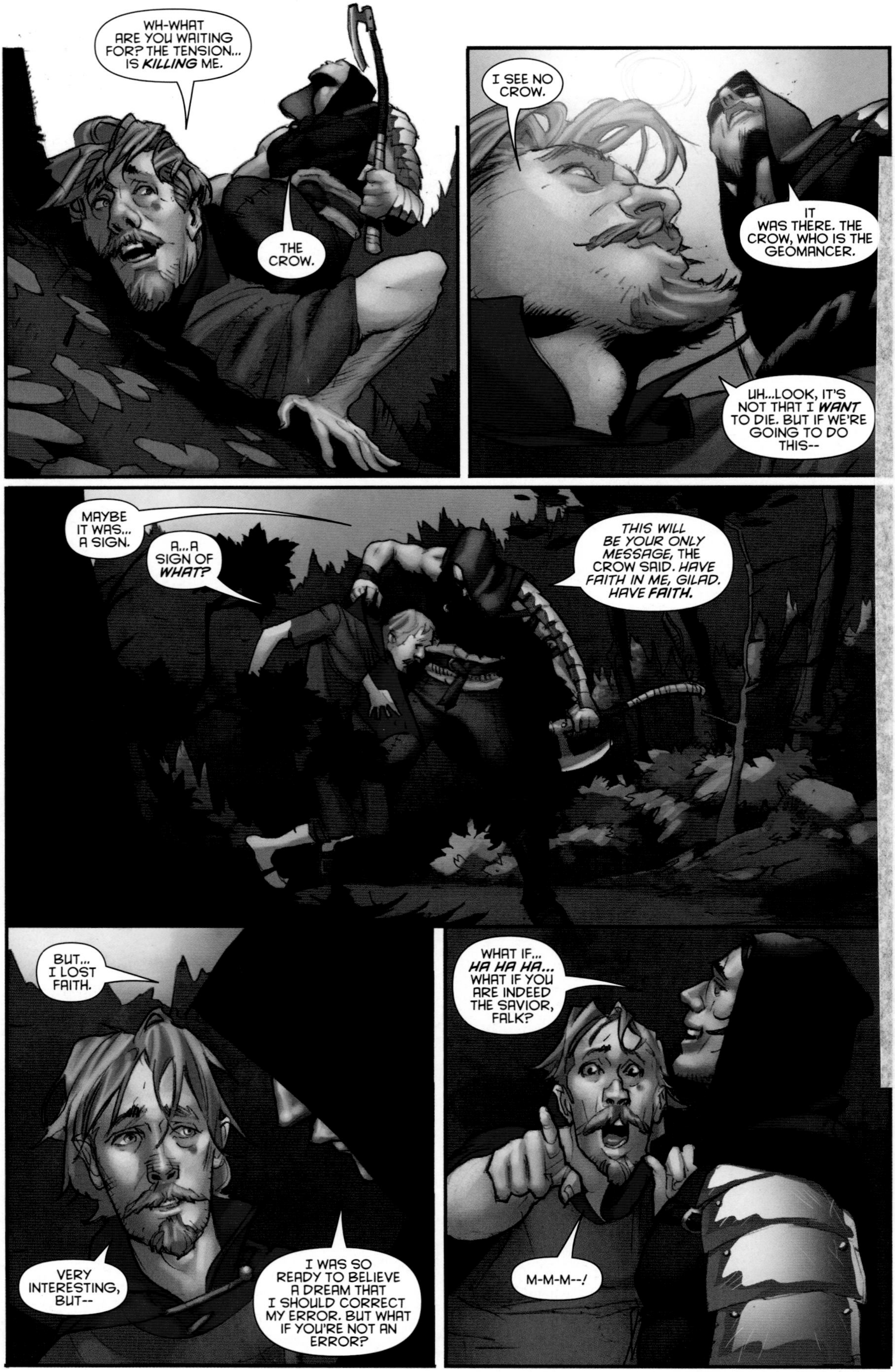
WH-WHAT ARE YOU WAITING FOR? THE TENSION... IS *KILLING* ME.
THE CROW.
I SEE NO CROW.
IT WAS THERE. THE CROW, WHO IS THE GEOMANCER.
UH...LOOK, IT'S NOT THAT I *WANT* TO DIE. BUT IF WE'RE GOING TO DO THIS--
MAYBE IT WAS... A SIGN.
A...A SIGN OF *WHAT?*
THIS WILL BE YOUR ONLY MESSAGE, THE CROW SAID. *HAVE FAITH IN ME, GILAD. HAVE* ***FAITH.***
BUT... I LOST FAITH.
VERY INTERESTING, BUT--
I WAS SO READY TO BELIEVE A DREAM THAT I SHOULD CORRECT MY ERROR. BUT WHAT IF YOU'RE NOT AN ERROR?
WHAT IF... ***HA HA HA...*** WHAT IF YOU ARE INDEED THE SAVIOR, FALK?
M-M-M--!

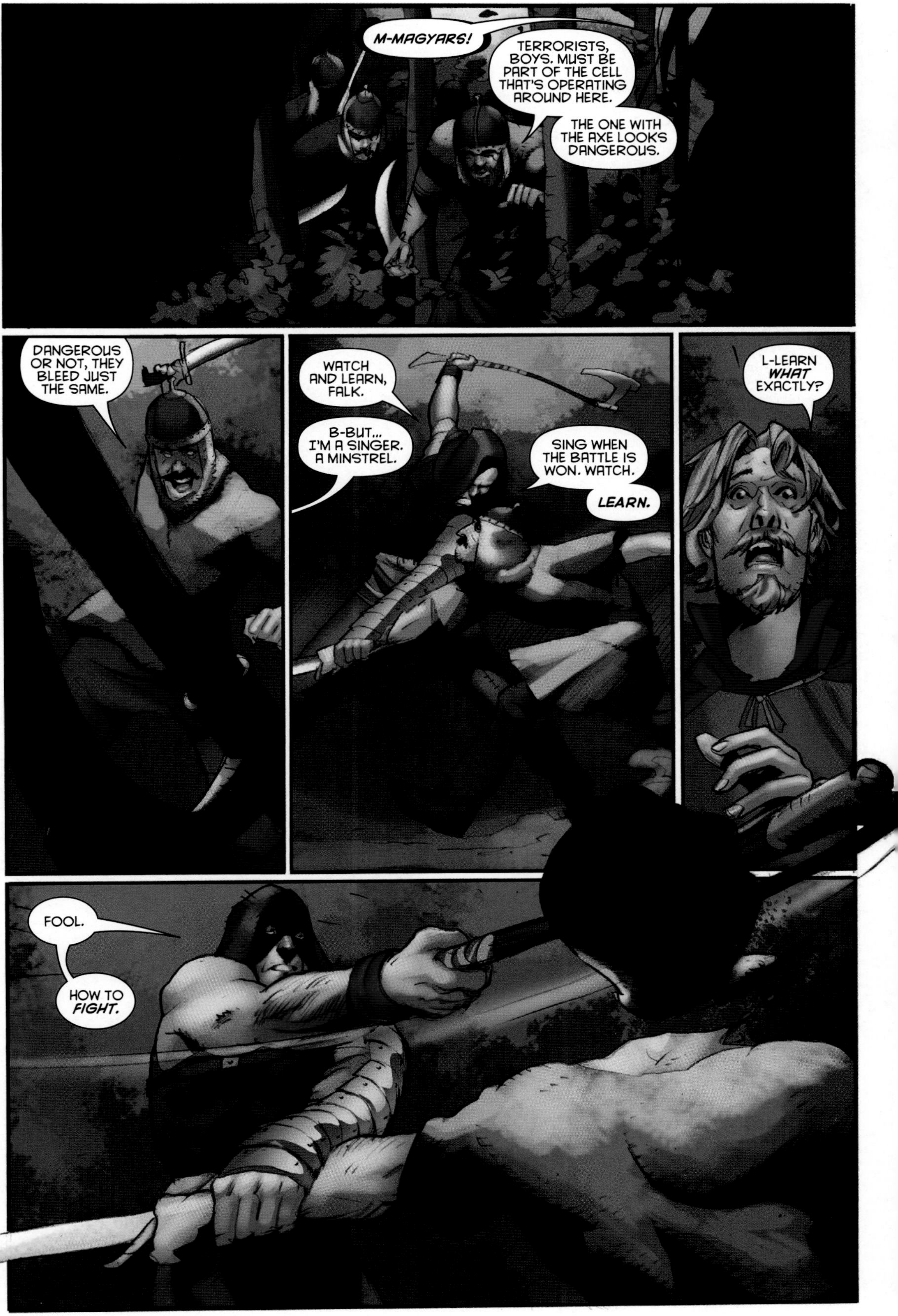
M-MAGYARS!
TERRORISTS, BOYS. MUST BE PART OF THE CELL THAT'S OPERATING AROUND HERE.
THE ONE WITH THE AXE LOOKS DANGEROUS.
DANGEROUS OR NOT, THEY BLEED JUST THE SAME.
WATCH AND LEARN, FALK.
B-BUT... I'M A SINGER. A MINSTREL.
SING WHEN THE BATTLE IS WON. WATCH.
LEARN.
L-LEARN WHAT EXACTLY?
FOOL.
HOW TO FIGHT.

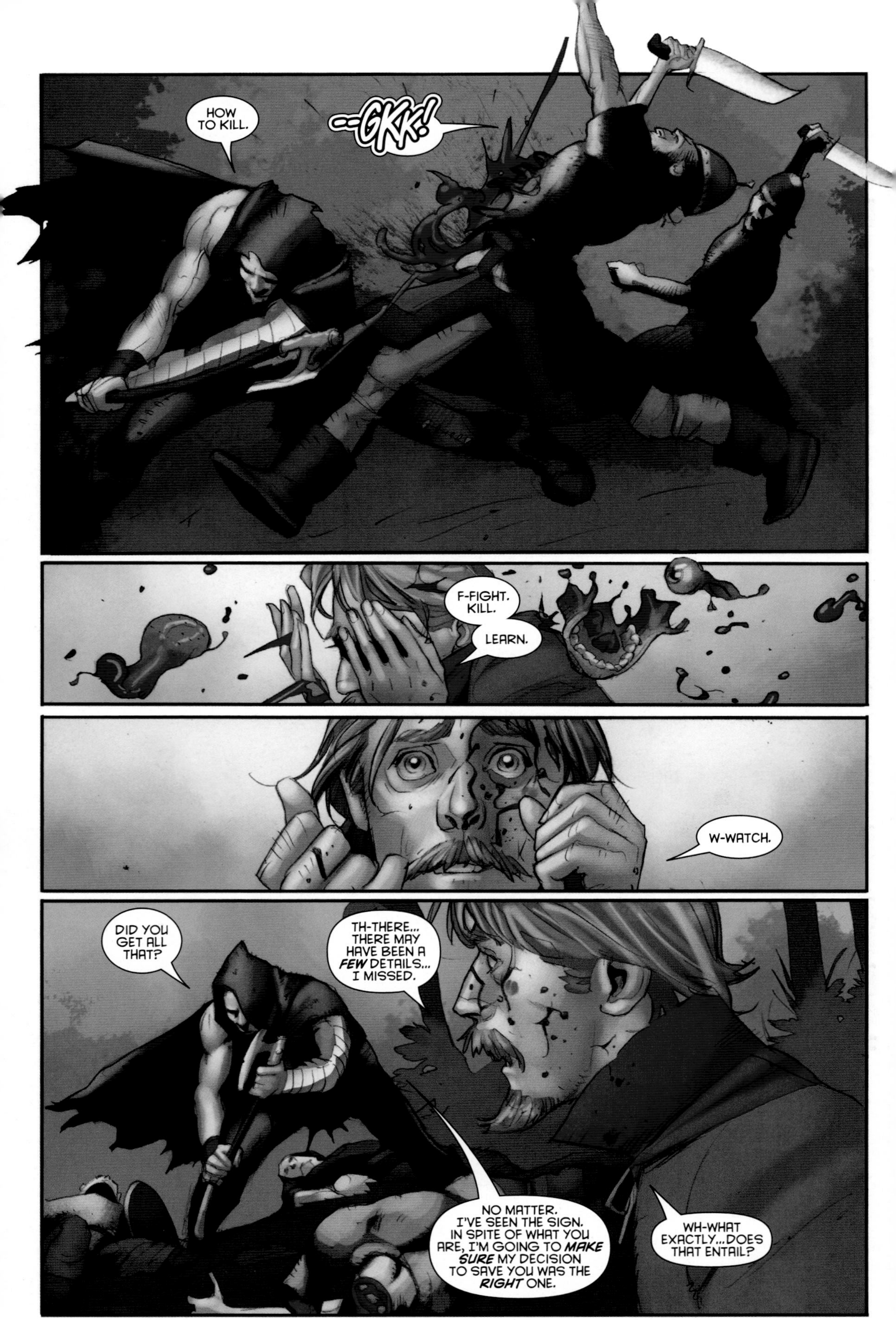
HOW TO KILL.
--GKK!
F-FIGHT. KILL.
LEARN.
W-WATCH.
DID YOU GET ALL THAT?
TH-THERE... THERE MAY HAVE BEEN A *FEW* DETAILS... I MISSED.
NO MATTER. I'VE SEEN THE SIGN. IN SPITE OF WHAT YOU ARE, I'M GOING TO *MAKE SURE* MY DECISION TO SAVE YOU WAS THE *RIGHT* ONE.
WH-WHAT EXACTLY...DOES THAT ENTAIL?

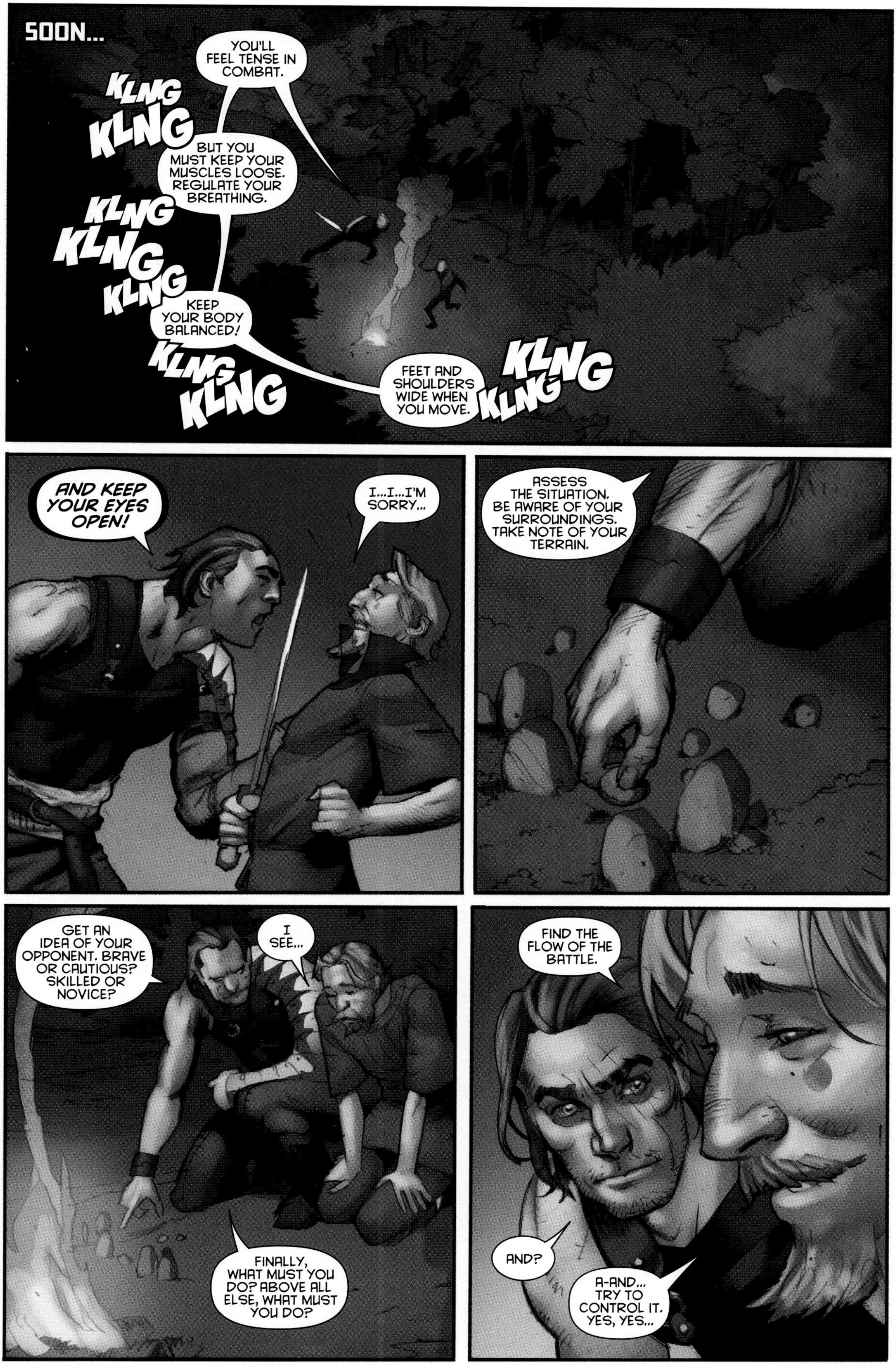
SOON...
YOU'LL FEEL TENSE IN COMBAT.
KLNG KLNG
BUT YOU MUST KEEP YOUR MUSCLES LOOSE. REGULATE YOUR BREATHING.
KLNG KLNG KLNG
KEEP YOUR BODY BALANCED!
KLNG KLNG
FEET AND SHOULDERS WIDE WHEN YOU MOVE.
KLNG KLNG
AND KEEP YOUR EYES OPEN!
I...I...I'M SORRY...
ASSESS THE SITUATION. BE AWARE OF YOUR SURROUNDINGS. TAKE NOTE OF YOUR TERRAIN.
GET AN IDEA OF YOUR OPPONENT. BRAVE OR CAUTIOUS? SKILLED OR NOVICE?
I SEE...
FINALLY, WHAT MUST YOU DO? ABOVE ALL ELSE, WHAT MUST YOU DO?
FIND THE FLOW OF THE BATTLE.
AND?
A-AND... TRY TO CONTROL IT. YES, YES...

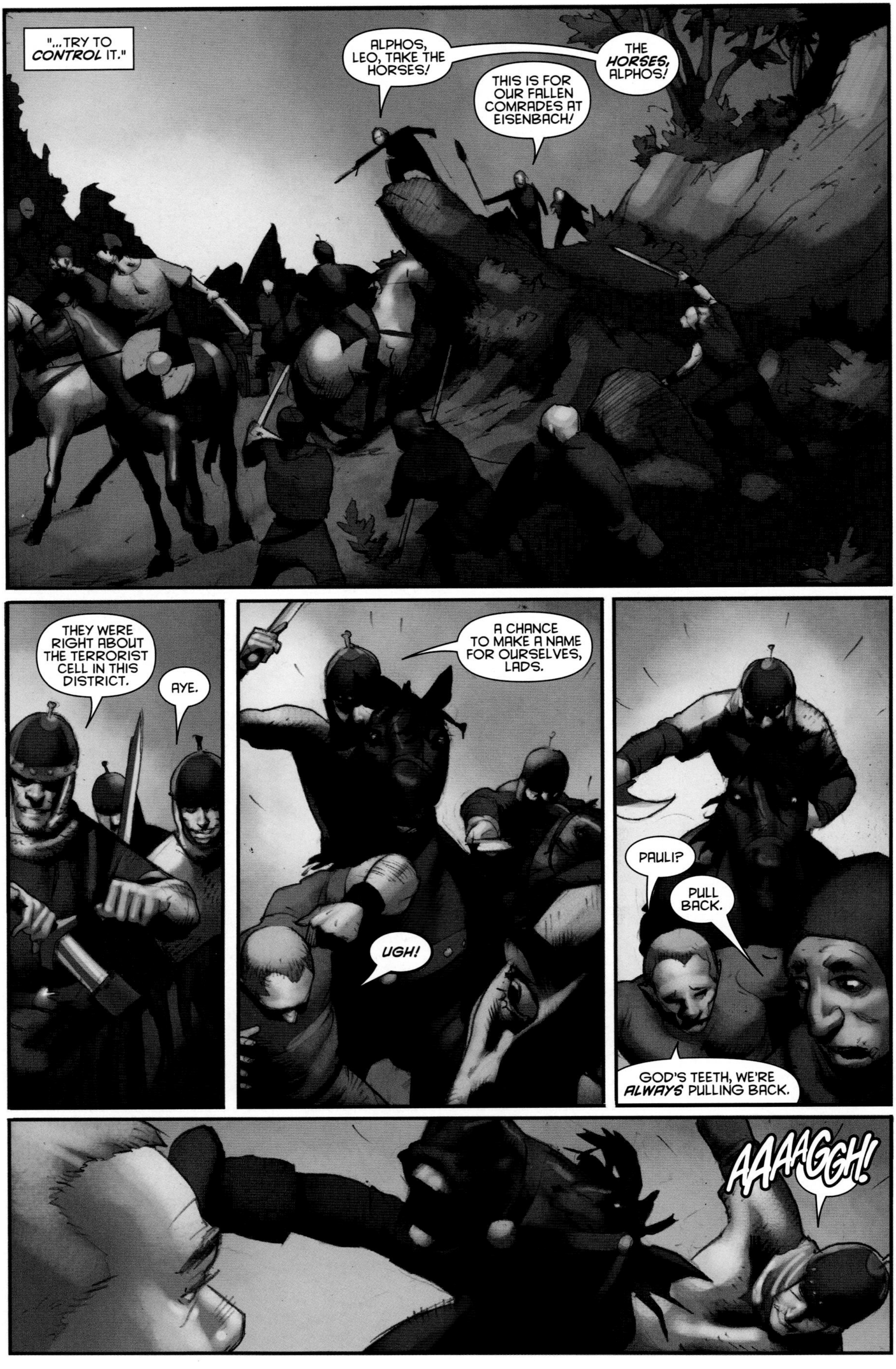
"...TRY TO *CONTROL* IT."
ALPHOS, LEO, TAKE THE HORSES!
THE *HORSES,* ALPHOS!
THIS IS FOR OUR FALLEN COMRADES AT EISENBACH!
THEY WERE RIGHT ABOUT THE TERRORIST CELL IN THIS DISTRICT.
AYE.
A CHANCE TO MAKE A NAME FOR OURSELVES, LADS.
UGH!
PAULI?
PULL BACK.
GOD'S TEETH, WE'RE *ALWAYS* PULLING BACK.
AAAAGGH!

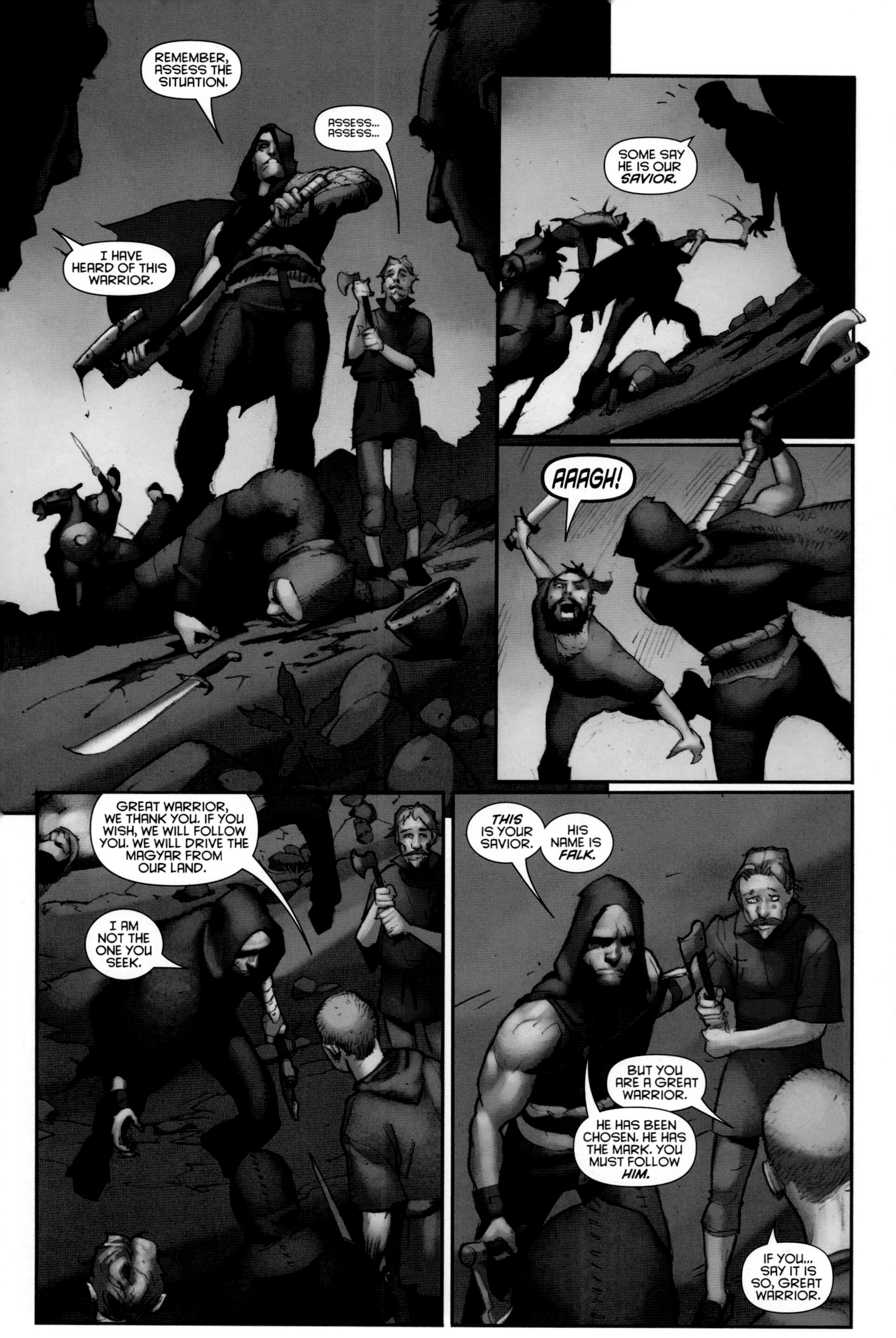
REMEMBER, ASSESS THE SITUATION.
ASSESS... ASSESS...
I HAVE HEARD OF THIS WARRIOR.
SOME SAY HE IS OUR SAVIOR.
AAAGH!
GREAT WARRIOR, WE THANK YOU. IF YOU WISH, WE WILL FOLLOW YOU. WE WILL DRIVE THE MAGYAR FROM OUR LAND.
I AM NOT THE ONE YOU SEEK.
THIS IS YOUR SAVIOR.
HIS NAME IS FALK.
BUT YOU ARE A GREAT WARRIOR.
HE HAS BEEN CHOSEN. HE HAS THE MARK. YOU MUST FOLLOW HIM.
IF YOU... SAY IT IS SO, GREAT WARRIOR.

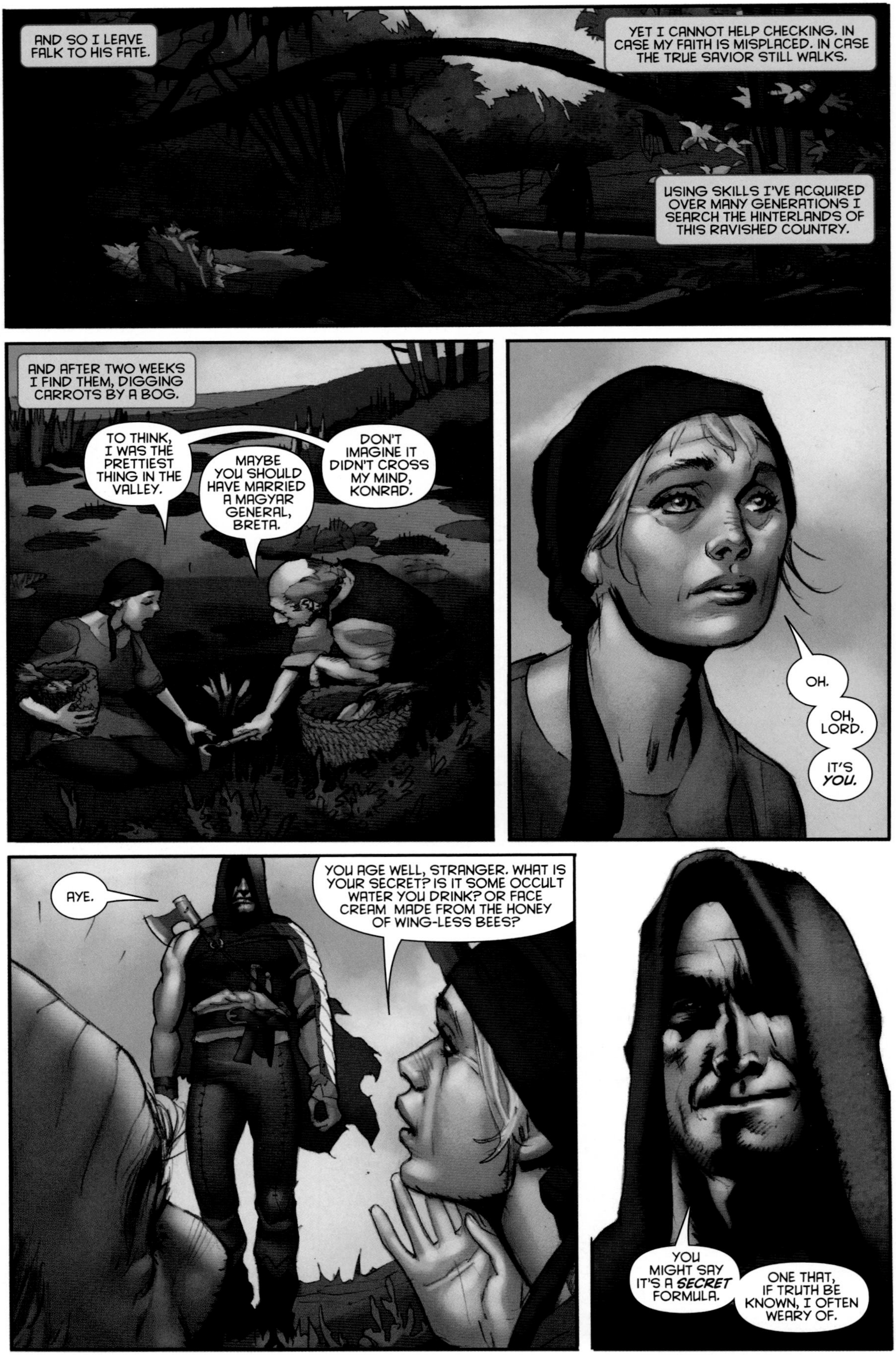
AND SO I LEAVE FALK TO HIS FATE.
YET I CANNOT HELP CHECKING. IN CASE MY FAITH IS MISPLACED. IN CASE THE TRUE SAVIOR STILL WALKS.
USING SKILLS I'VE ACQUIRED OVER MANY GENERATIONS I SEARCH THE HINTERLANDS OF THIS RAVISHED COUNTRY.
AND AFTER TWO WEEKS I FIND THEM, DIGGING CARROTS BY A BOG.
TO THINK, I WAS THE PRETTIEST THING IN THE VALLEY.
DON'T IMAGINE IT DIDN'T CROSS MY MIND, KONRAD.
MAYBE YOU SHOULD HAVE MARRIED A MAGYAR GENERAL, BRETA.
OH.
OH, LORD.
IT'S *YOU.*
AYE.
YOU AGE WELL, STRANGER. WHAT IS YOUR SECRET? IS IT SOME OCCULT WATER YOU DRINK? OR FACE CREAM MADE FROM THE HONEY OF WING-LESS BEES?
YOU MIGHT SAY IT'S A *SECRET* FORMULA.
ONE THAT, IF TRUTH BE KNOWN, I OFTEN WEARY OF.

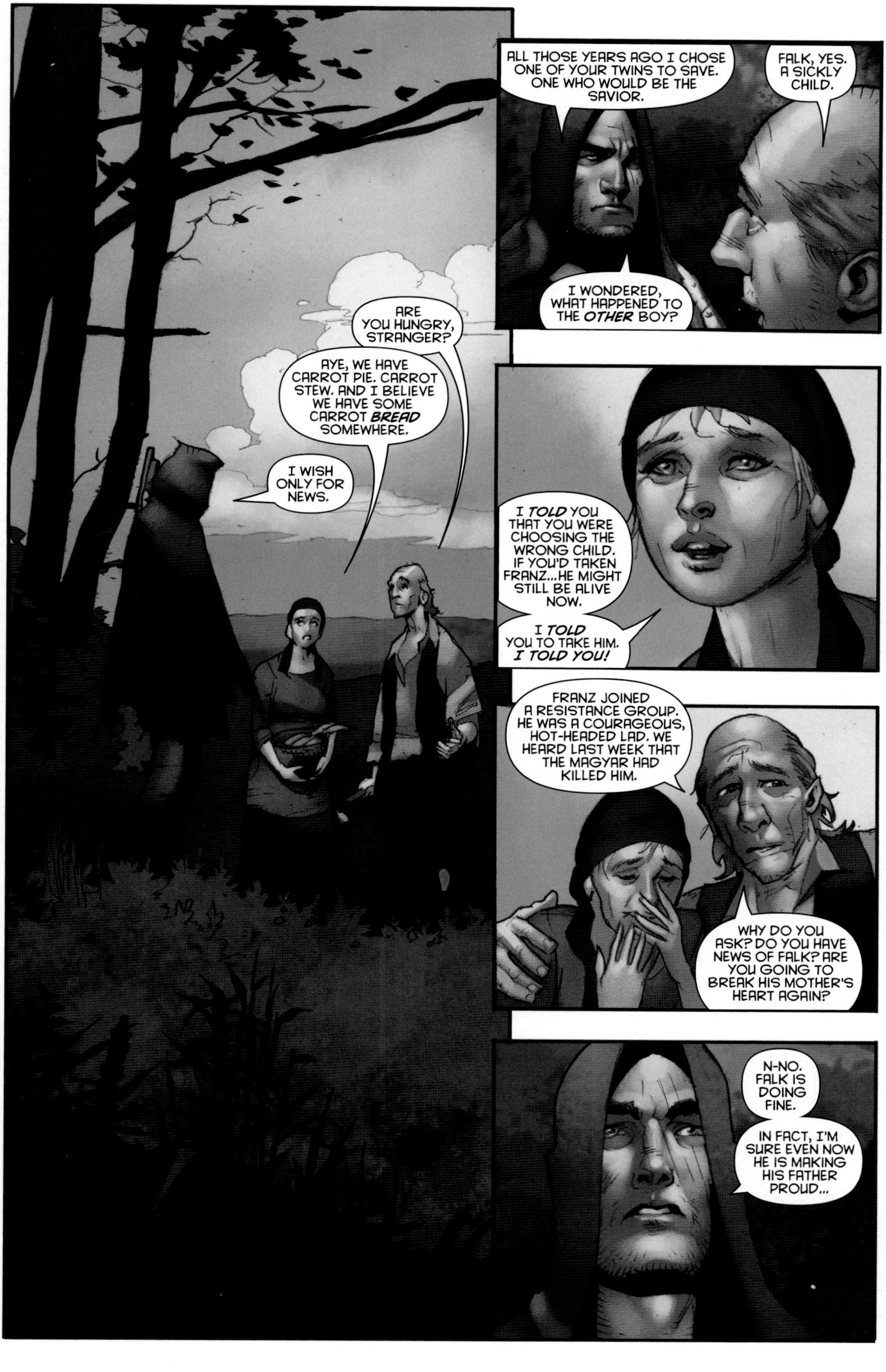
ARE YOU HUNGRY, STRANGER?
AYE, WE HAVE CARROT PIE. CARROT STEW. AND I BELIEVE WE HAVE SOME CARROT *BREAD* SOMEWHERE.
I WISH ONLY FOR NEWS.
ALL THOSE YEARS AGO I CHOSE ONE OF YOUR TWINS TO SAVE. ONE WHO WOULD BE THE SAVIOR.
FALK, YES. A SICKLY CHILD.
I WONDERED, WHAT HAPPENED TO THE *OTHER* BOY?
I *TOLD* YOU THAT YOU WERE CHOOSING THE WRONG CHILD. IF YOU'D TAKEN FRANZ...HE MIGHT STILL BE ALIVE NOW.
I *TOLD* YOU TO TAKE HIM. ***I TOLD YOU!***
FRANZ JOINED A RESISTANCE GROUP. HE WAS A COURAGEOUS, HOT-HEADED LAD. WE HEARD LAST WEEK THAT THE MAGYAR HAD KILLED HIM.
WHY DO YOU ASK? DO YOU HAVE NEWS OF FALK? ARE YOU GOING TO BREAK HIS MOTHER'S HEART AGAIN?
N-NO. FALK IS DOING FINE.
IN FACT, I'M SURE EVEN NOW HE IS MAKING HIS FATHER PROUD...

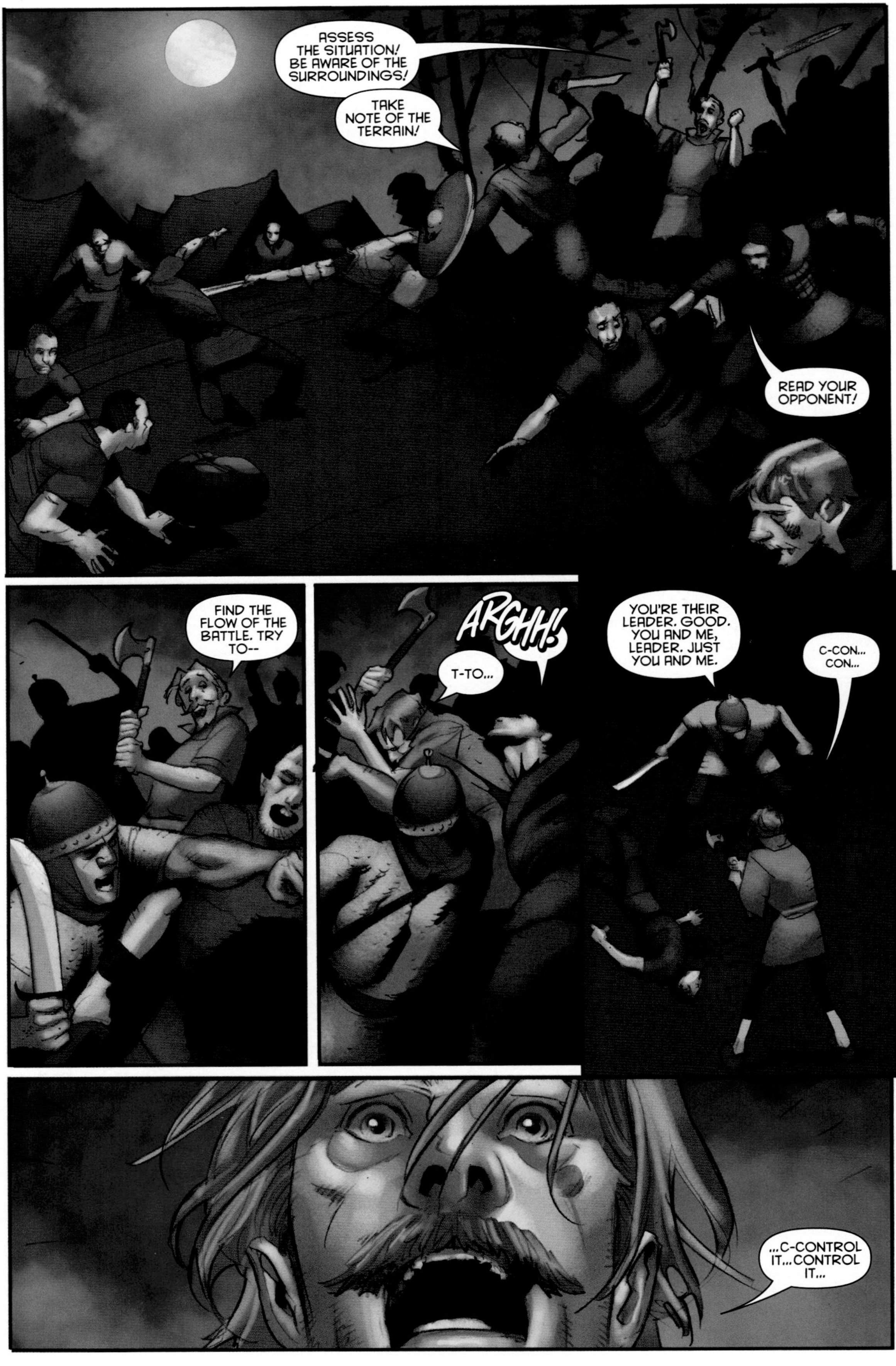
ASSESS THE SITUATION! BE AWARE OF THE SURROUNDINGS!
TAKE NOTE OF THE TERRAIN!
READ YOUR OPPONENT!
FIND THE FLOW OF THE BATTLE. TRY TO--
T-TO...
ARGHH!
YOU'RE THEIR LEADER. GOOD. YOU AND ME, LEADER. JUST YOU AND ME.
C-CON... CON...
...C-CONTROL IT...CONTROL IT...

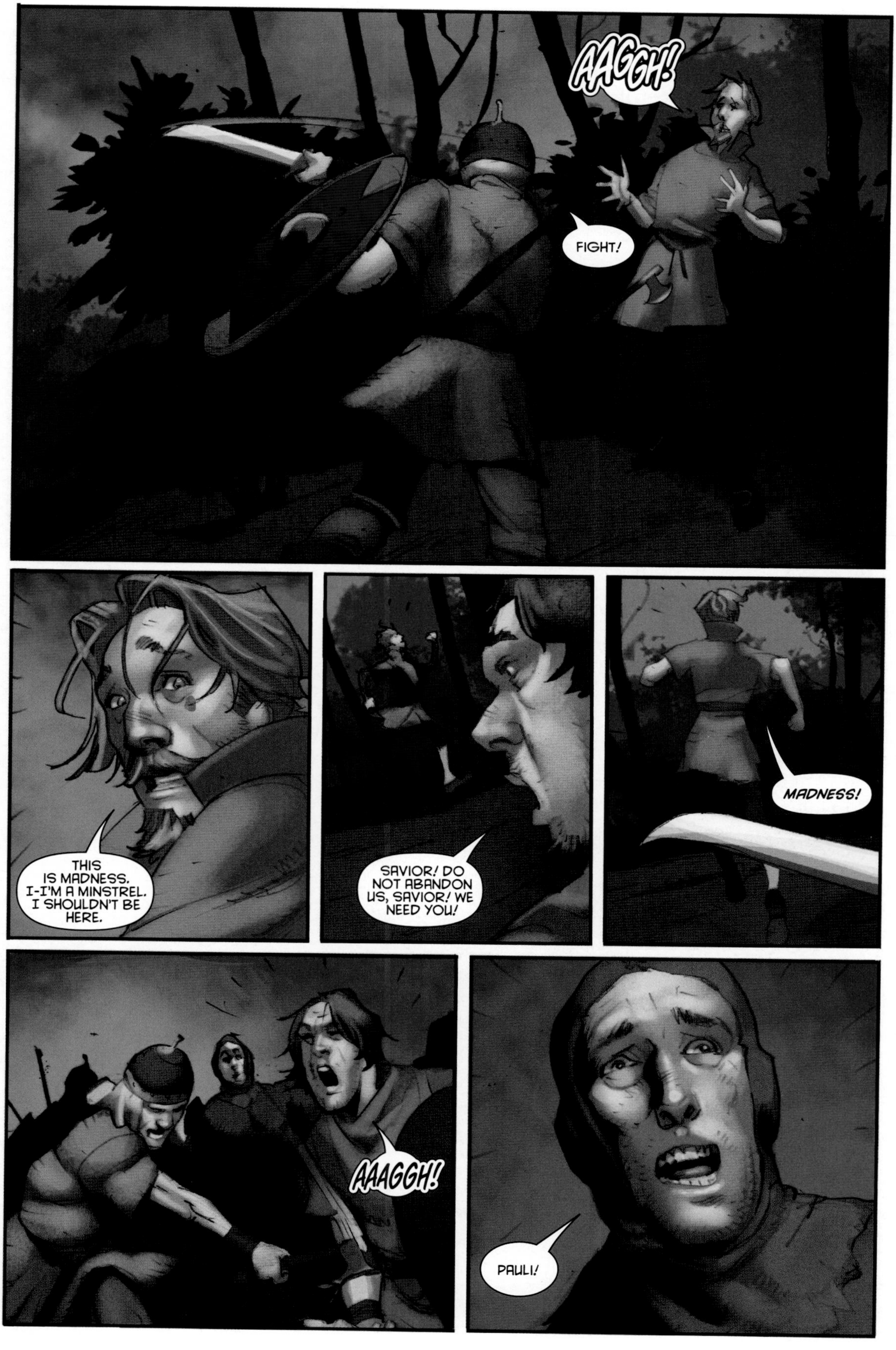
AAGGH!
FIGHT!
THIS IS MADNESS. I-I'M A MINSTREL. I SHOULDN'T BE HERE.
SAVIOR! DO NOT ABANDON US, SAVIOR! WE NEED YOU!
MADNESS!
AAAGGH!
PAULI!

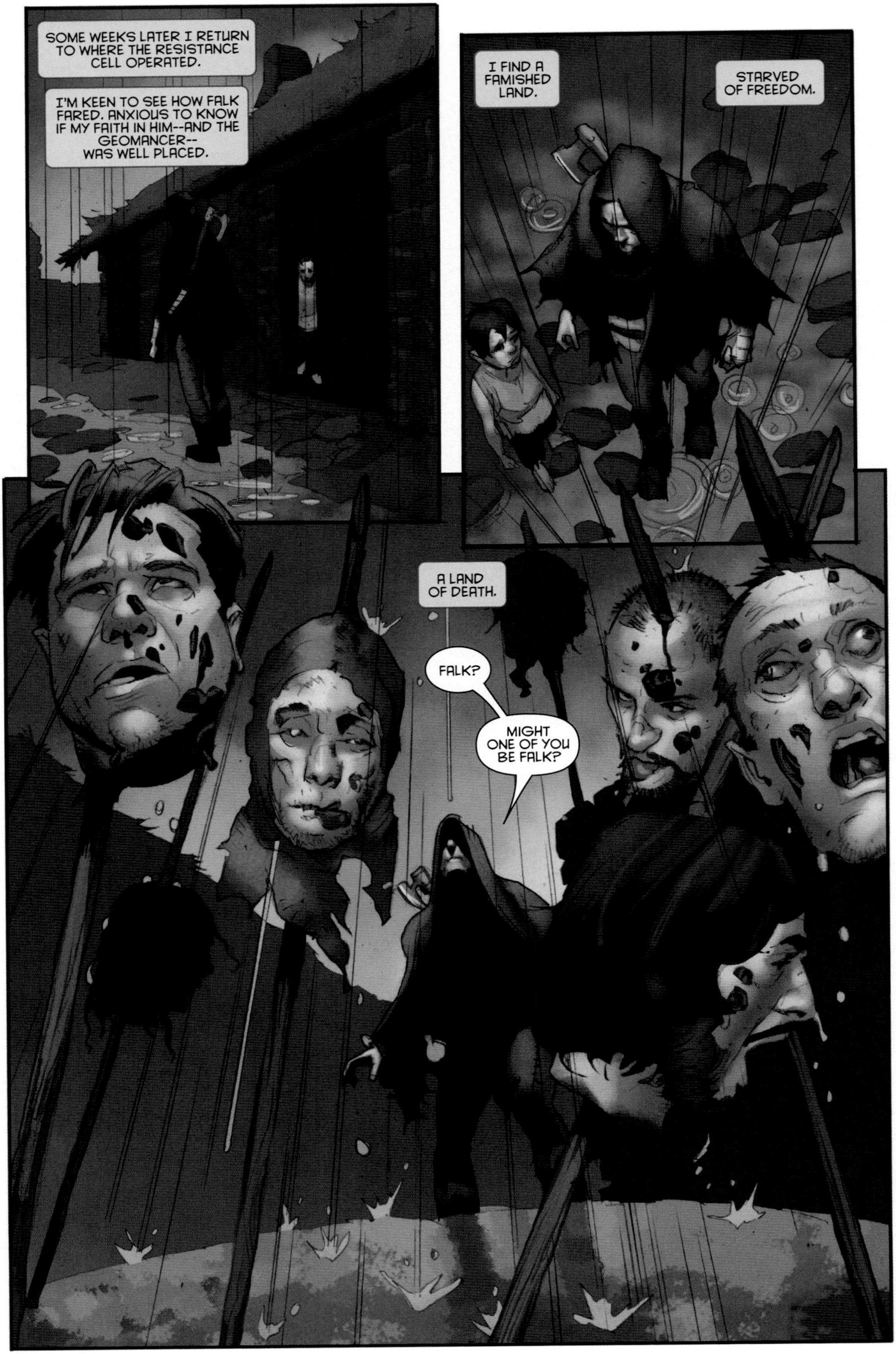
SOME WEEKS LATER I RETURN TO WHERE THE RESISTANCE CELL OPERATED.
I'M KEEN TO SEE HOW FALK FARED. ANXIOUS TO KNOW IF MY FAITH IN HIM--AND THE GEOMANCER--WAS WELL PLACED.
I FIND A FAMISHED LAND.
STARVED OF FREEDOM.
A LAND OF DEATH.
FALK?
MIGHT ONE OF YOU BE FALK?

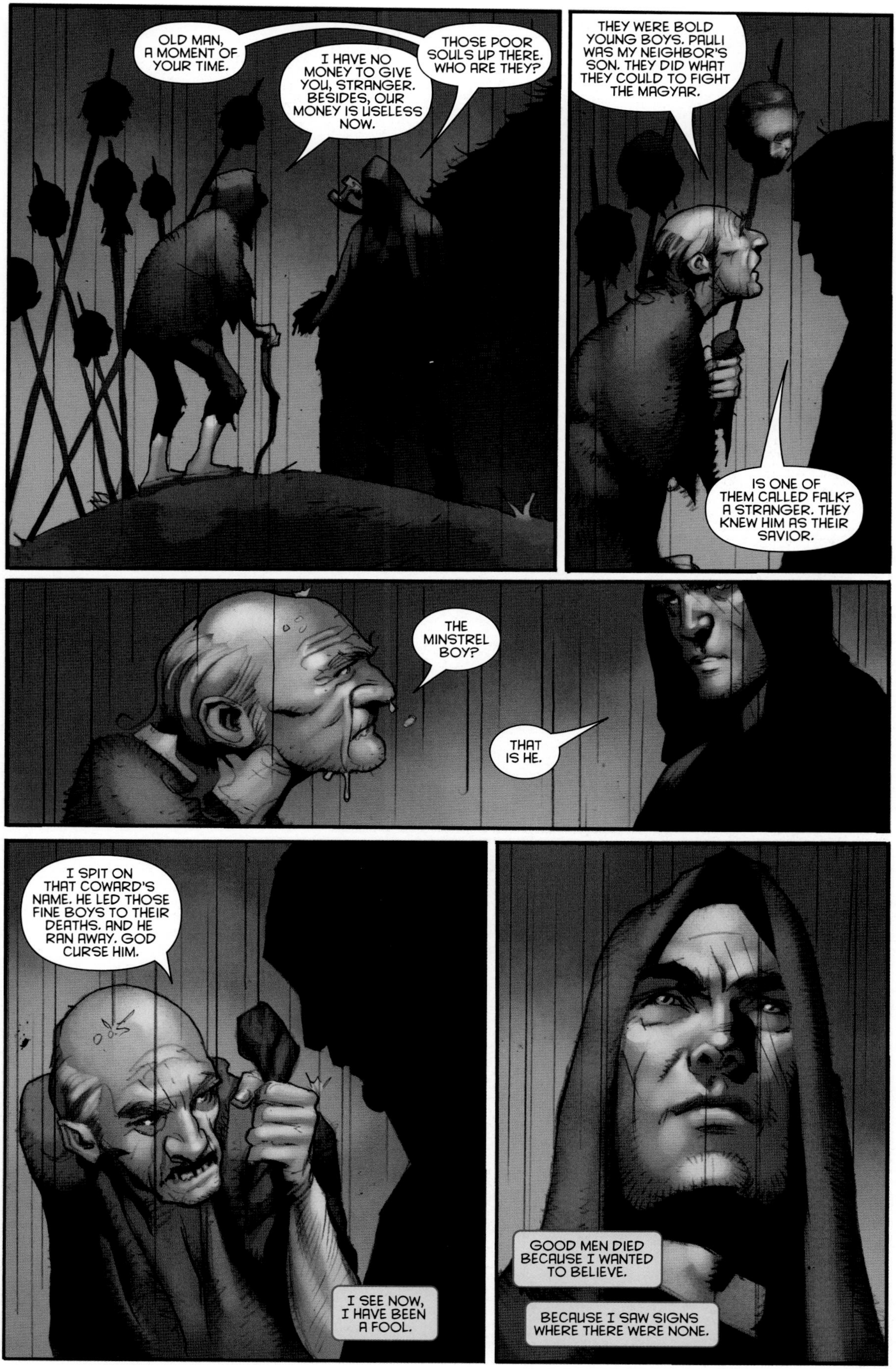
OLD MAN, A MOMENT OF YOUR TIME.
I HAVE NO MONEY TO GIVE YOU, STRANGER. BESIDES, OUR MONEY IS USELESS NOW.
THOSE POOR SOULS UP THERE. WHO ARE THEY?
THEY WERE BOLD YOUNG BOYS. PAULI WAS MY NEIGHBOR'S SON. THEY DID WHAT THEY COULD TO FIGHT THE MAGYAR.
IS ONE OF THEM CALLED FALK? A STRANGER. THEY KNEW HIM AS THEIR SAVIOR.
THE MINSTREL BOY?
THAT IS HE.
I SPIT ON THAT COWARD'S NAME. HE LED THOSE FINE BOYS TO THEIR DEATHS. AND HE RAN AWAY. GOD CURSE HIM.
I SEE NOW, I HAVE BEEN A FOOL.
GOOD MEN DIED BECAUSE I WANTED TO BELIEVE.
BECAUSE I SAW SIGNS WHERE THERE WERE NONE.

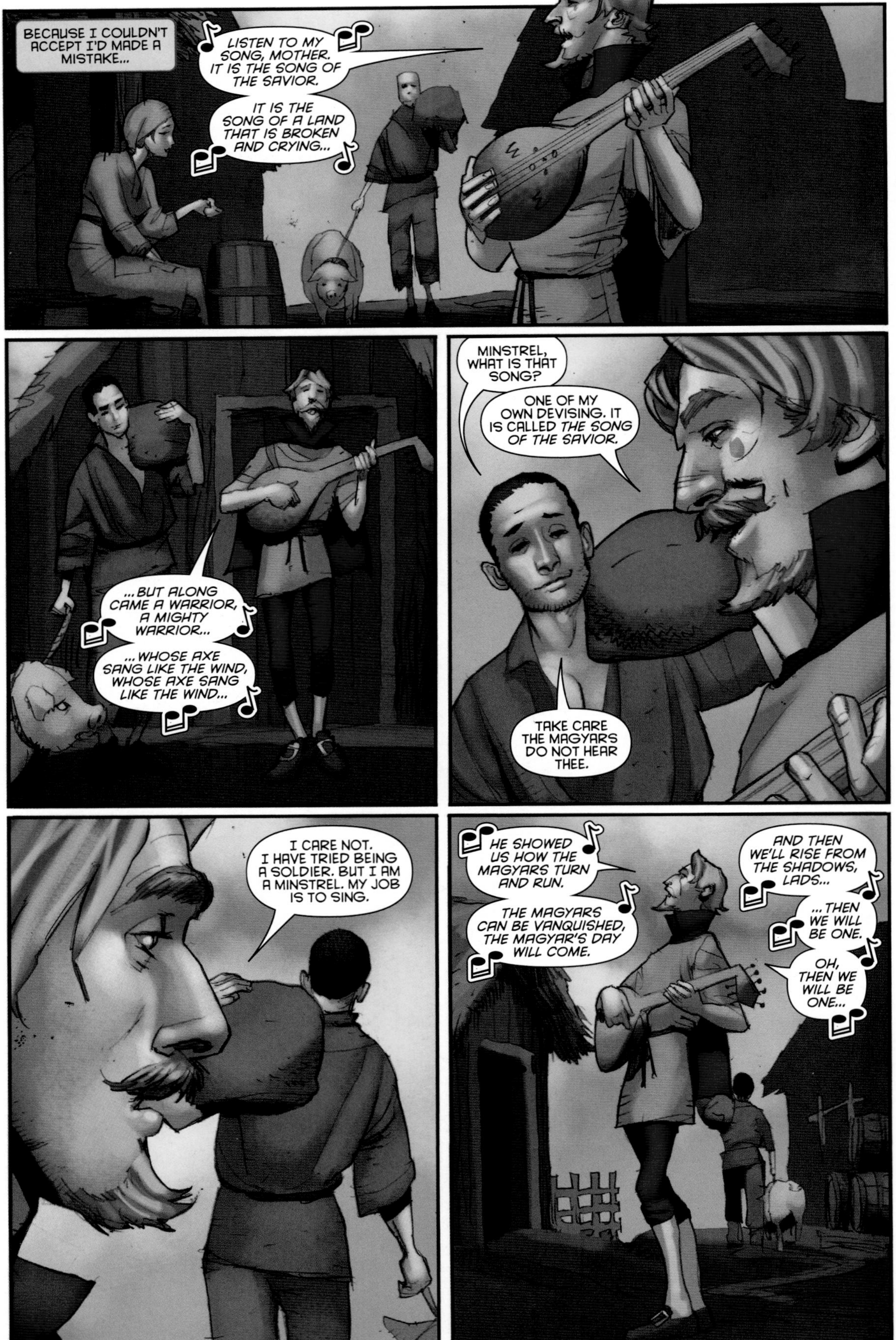
BECAUSE I COULDN'T ACCEPT I'D MADE A MISTAKE...
LISTEN TO MY SONG, MOTHER. IT IS THE SONG OF THE SAVIOR.
IT IS THE SONG OF A LAND THAT IS BROKEN AND CRYING...
...BUT ALONG CAME A WARRIOR, A MIGHTY WARRIOR...
...WHOSE AXE SANG LIKE THE WIND, WHOSE AXE SANG LIKE THE WIND...
MINSTREL, WHAT IS THAT SONG?
ONE OF MY OWN DEVISING. IT IS CALLED THE SONG OF THE SAVIOR.
TAKE CARE THE MAGYARS DO NOT HEAR THEE.
I CARE NOT. I HAVE TRIED BEING A SOLDIER. BUT I AM A MINSTREL. MY JOB IS TO SING.
HE SHOWED US HOW THE MAGYARS TURN AND RUN.
THE MAGYARS CAN BE VANQUISHED, THE MAGYAR'S DAY WILL COME.
AND THEN WE'LL RISE FROM THE SHADOWS, LADS...
...THEN WE WILL BE ONE.
OH, THEN WE WILL BE ONE...

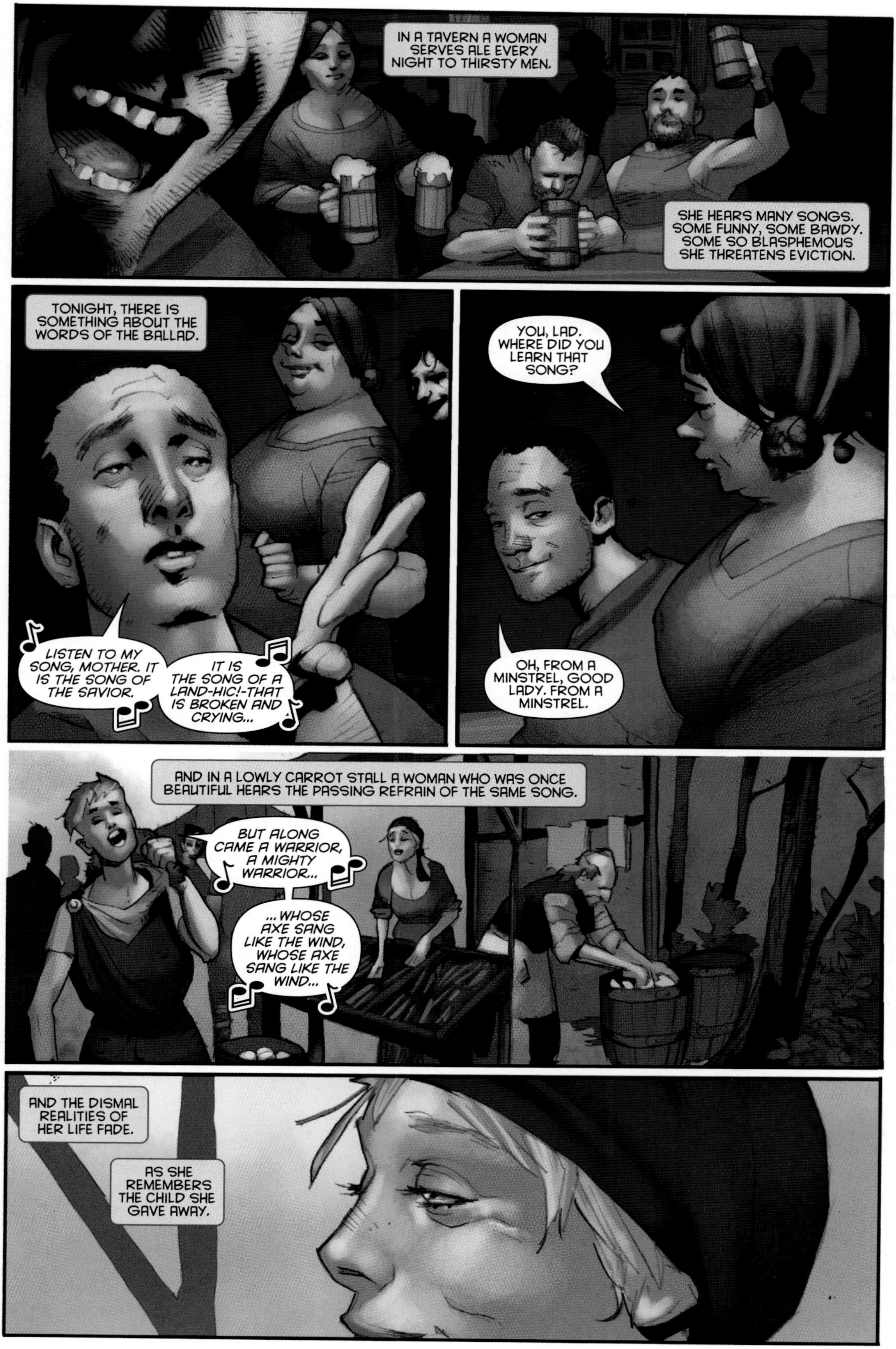
IN A TAVERN A WOMAN SERVES ALE EVERY NIGHT TO THIRSTY MEN.
SHE HEARS MANY SONGS. SOME FUNNY, SOME BAWDY. SOME SO BLASPHEMOUS SHE THREATENS EVICTION.
TONIGHT, THERE IS SOMETHING ABOUT THE WORDS OF THE BALLAD.
LISTEN TO MY SONG, MOTHER. IT IS THE SONG OF THE SAVIOR.
IT IS THE SONG OF A LAND-HIC!-THAT IS BROKEN AND CRYING...
YOU, LAD. WHERE DID YOU LEARN THAT SONG?
OH, FROM A MINSTREL, GOOD LADY. FROM A MINSTREL.
AND IN A LOWLY CARROT STALL A WOMAN WHO WAS ONCE BEAUTIFUL HEARS THE PASSING REFRAIN OF THE SAME SONG.
BUT ALONG CAME A WARRIOR, A MIGHTY WARRIOR...
...WHOSE AXE SANG LIKE THE WIND, WHOSE AXE SANG LIKE THE WIND...
AND THE DISMAL REALITIES OF HER LIFE FADE.
AS SHE REMEMBERS THE CHILD SHE GAVE AWAY.

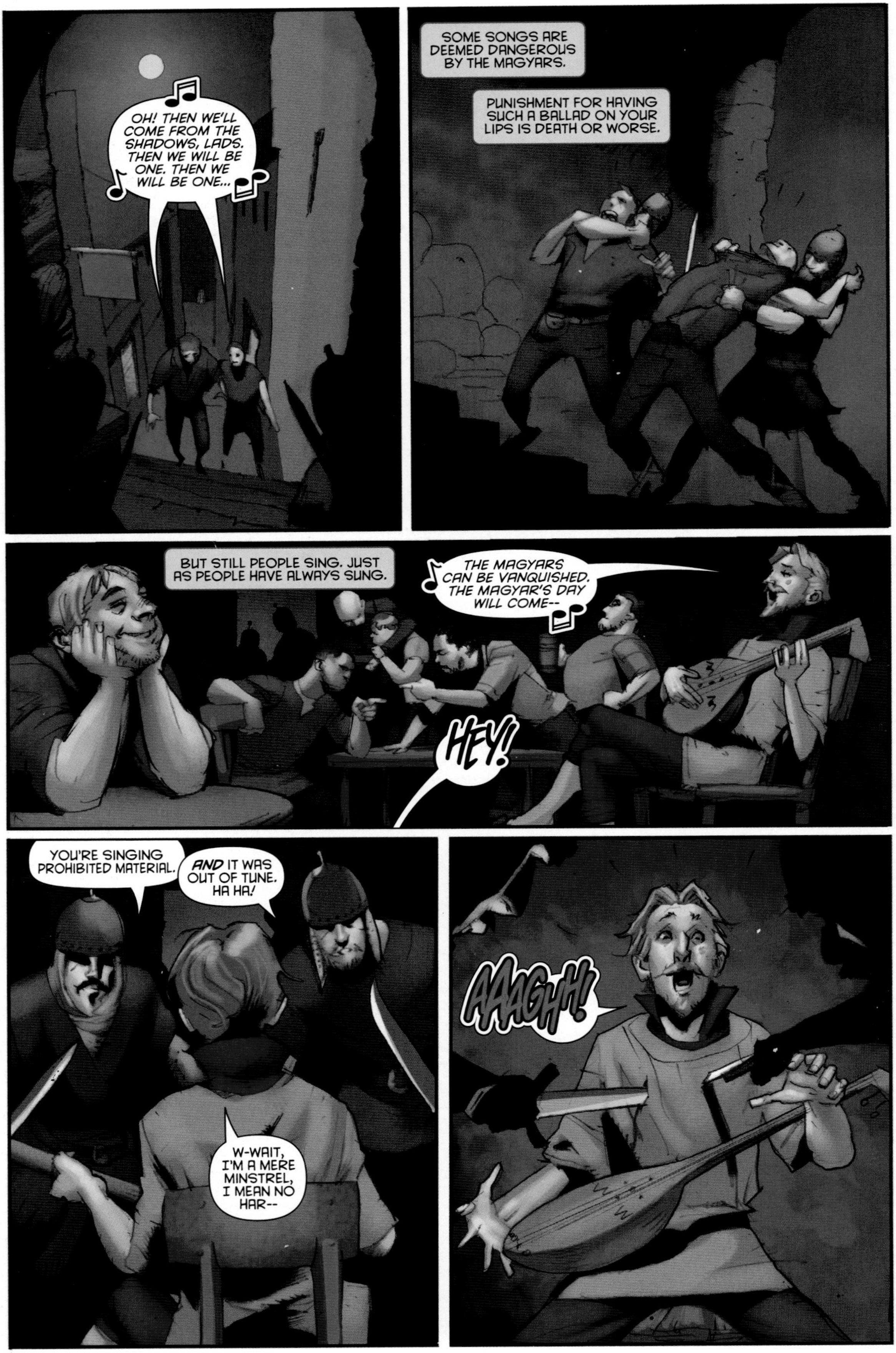
OH! THEN WE'LL COME FROM THE SHADOWS, LADS. THEN WE WILL BE ONE. THEN WE WILL BE ONE...
SOME SONGS ARE DEEMED DANGEROUS BY THE MAGYARS.
PUNISHMENT FOR HAVING SUCH A BALLAD ON YOUR LIPS IS DEATH OR WORSE.
BUT STILL PEOPLE SING. JUST AS PEOPLE HAVE ALWAYS SUNG.
THE MAGYARS CAN BE VANQUISHED. THE MAGYAR'S DAY WILL COME--
HEY!
YOU'RE SINGING PROHIBITED MATERIAL.
AND IT WAS OUT OF TUNE. HA HA!
W-WAIT, I'M A MERE MINSTREL, I MEAN NO HAR--
AAAGHH!

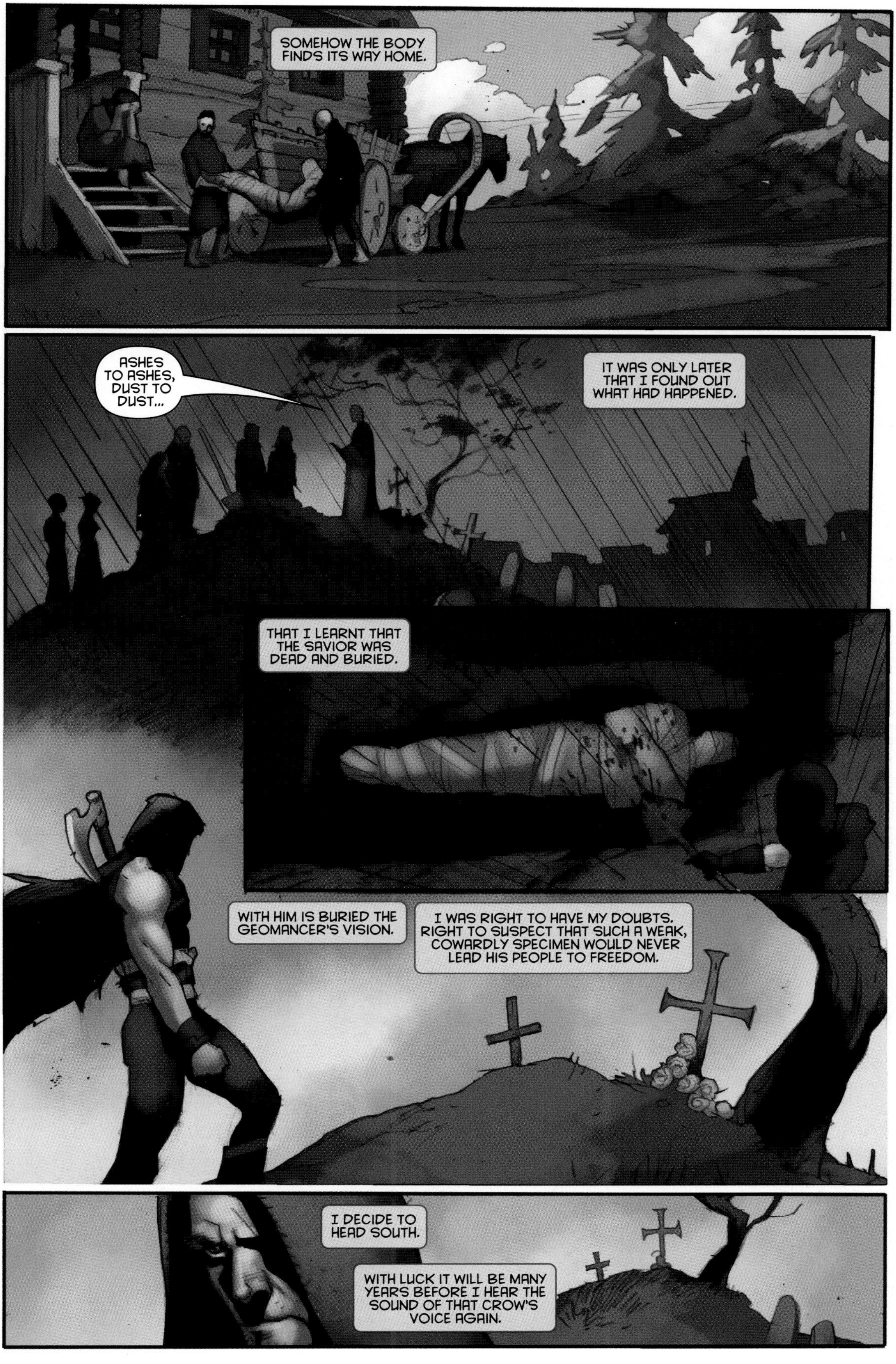
SOMEHOW THE BODY FINDS ITS WAY HOME.
ASHES TO ASHES, DUST TO DUST...
IT WAS ONLY LATER THAT I FOUND OUT WHAT HAD HAPPENED.
THAT I LEARNT THAT THE SAVIOR WAS DEAD AND BURIED.
WITH HIM IS BURIED THE GEOMANCER'S VISION.
I WAS RIGHT TO HAVE MY DOUBTS. RIGHT TO SUSPECT THAT SUCH A WEAK, COWARDLY SPECIMEN WOULD NEVER LEAD HIS PEOPLE TO FREEDOM.
I DECIDE TO HEAD SOUTH.
WITH LUCK IT WILL BE MANY YEARS BEFORE I HEAR THE SOUND OF THAT CROW'S VOICE AGAIN.

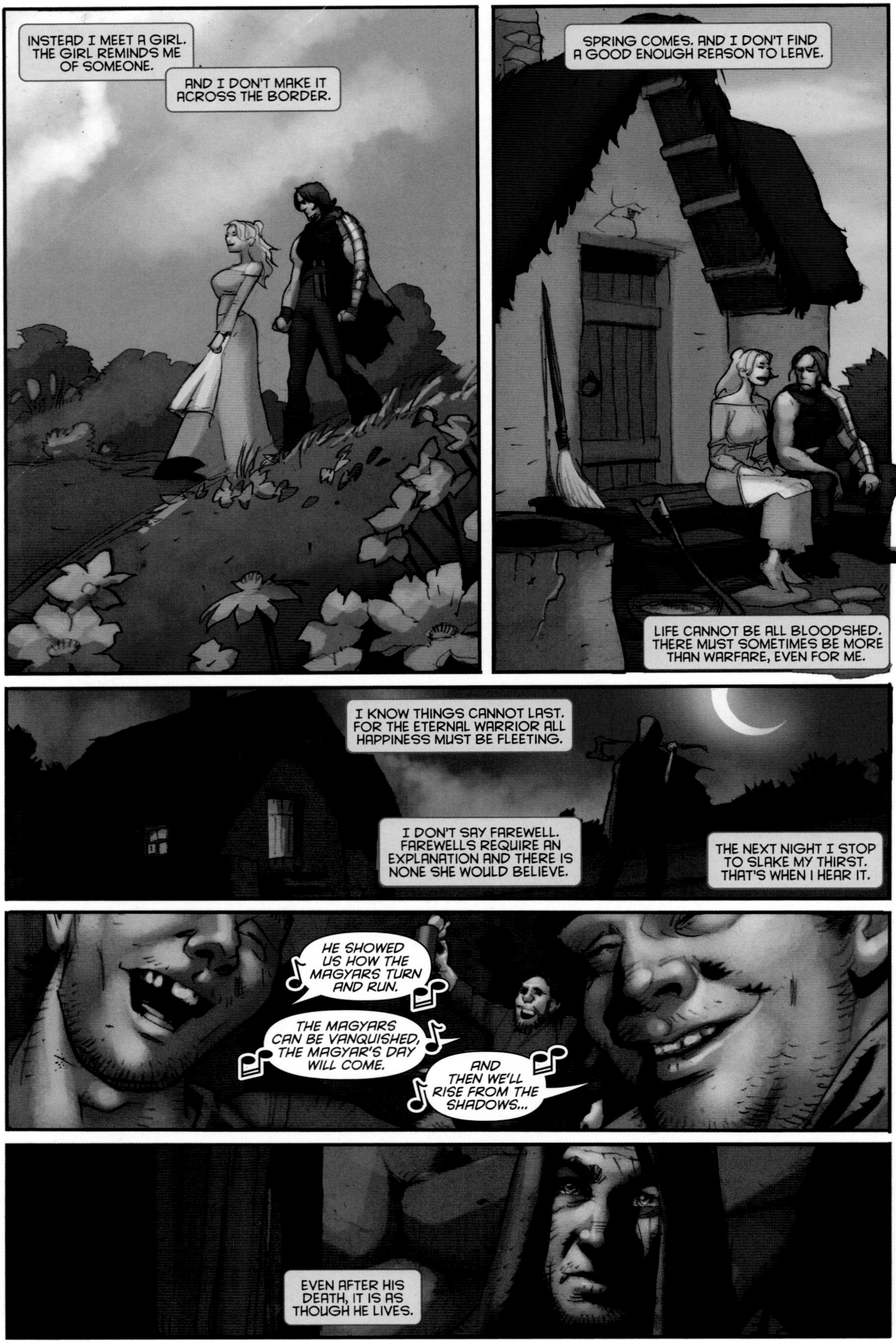
INSTEAD I MEET A GIRL. THE GIRL REMINDS ME OF SOMEONE.
AND I DON'T MAKE IT ACROSS THE BORDER.
SPRING COMES. AND I DON'T FIND A GOOD ENOUGH REASON TO LEAVE.
LIFE CANNOT BE ALL BLOODSHED. THERE MUST SOMETIMES BE MORE THAN WARFARE, EVEN FOR ME.
I KNOW THINGS CANNOT LAST. FOR THE ETERNAL WARRIOR ALL HAPPINESS MUST BE FLEETING.
I DON'T SAY FAREWELL. FAREWELLS REQUIRE AN EXPLANATION AND THERE IS NONE SHE WOULD BELIEVE.
THE NEXT NIGHT I STOP TO SLAKE MY THIRST. THAT'S WHEN I HEAR IT.
HE SHOWED US HOW THE MAGYARS TURN AND RUN.
THE MAGYARS CAN BE VANQUISHED, THE MAGYAR'S DAY WILL COME.
AND THEN WE'LL RISE FROM THE SHADOWS...
EVEN AFTER HIS DEATH, IT IS AS THOUGH HE LIVES.

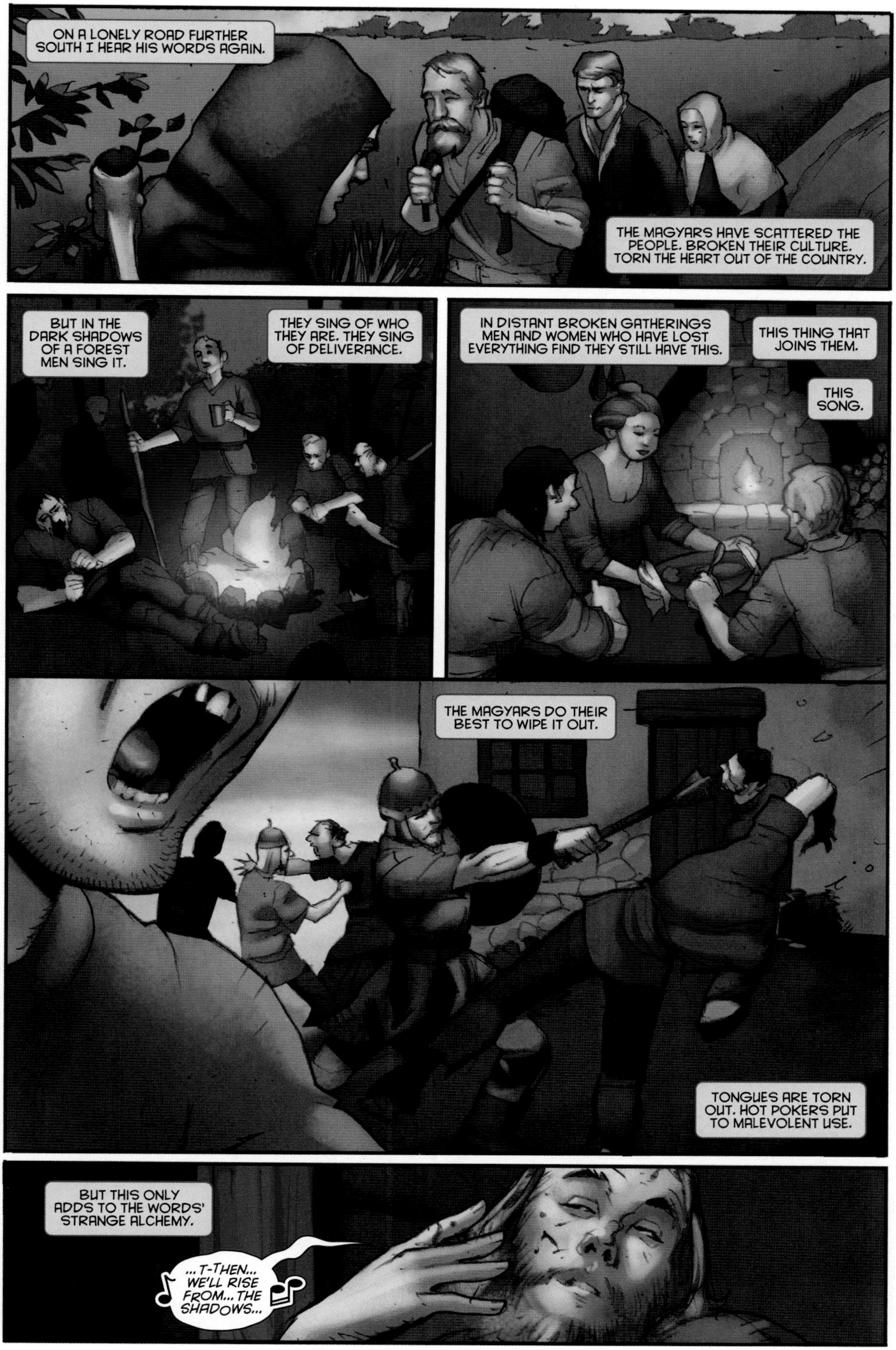
ON A LONELY ROAD FURTHER SOUTH I HEAR HIS WORDS AGAIN.
THE MAGYARS HAVE SCATTERED THE PEOPLE. BROKEN THEIR CULTURE. TORN THE HEART OUT OF THE COUNTRY.
BUT IN THE DARK SHADOWS OF A FOREST MEN SING IT.
THEY SING OF WHO THEY ARE. THEY SING OF DELIVERANCE.
IN DISTANT BROKEN GATHERINGS MEN AND WOMEN WHO HAVE LOST EVERYTHING FIND THEY STILL HAVE THIS.
THIS THING THAT JOINS THEM.
THIS SONG.
THE MAGYARS DO THEIR BEST TO WIPE IT OUT.
TONGUES ARE TORN OUT. HOT POKERS PUT TO MALEVOLENT USE.
BUT THIS ONLY ADDS TO THE WORDS' STRANGE ALCHEMY.
...T-THEN... WE'LL RISE FROM... THE SHADOWS...

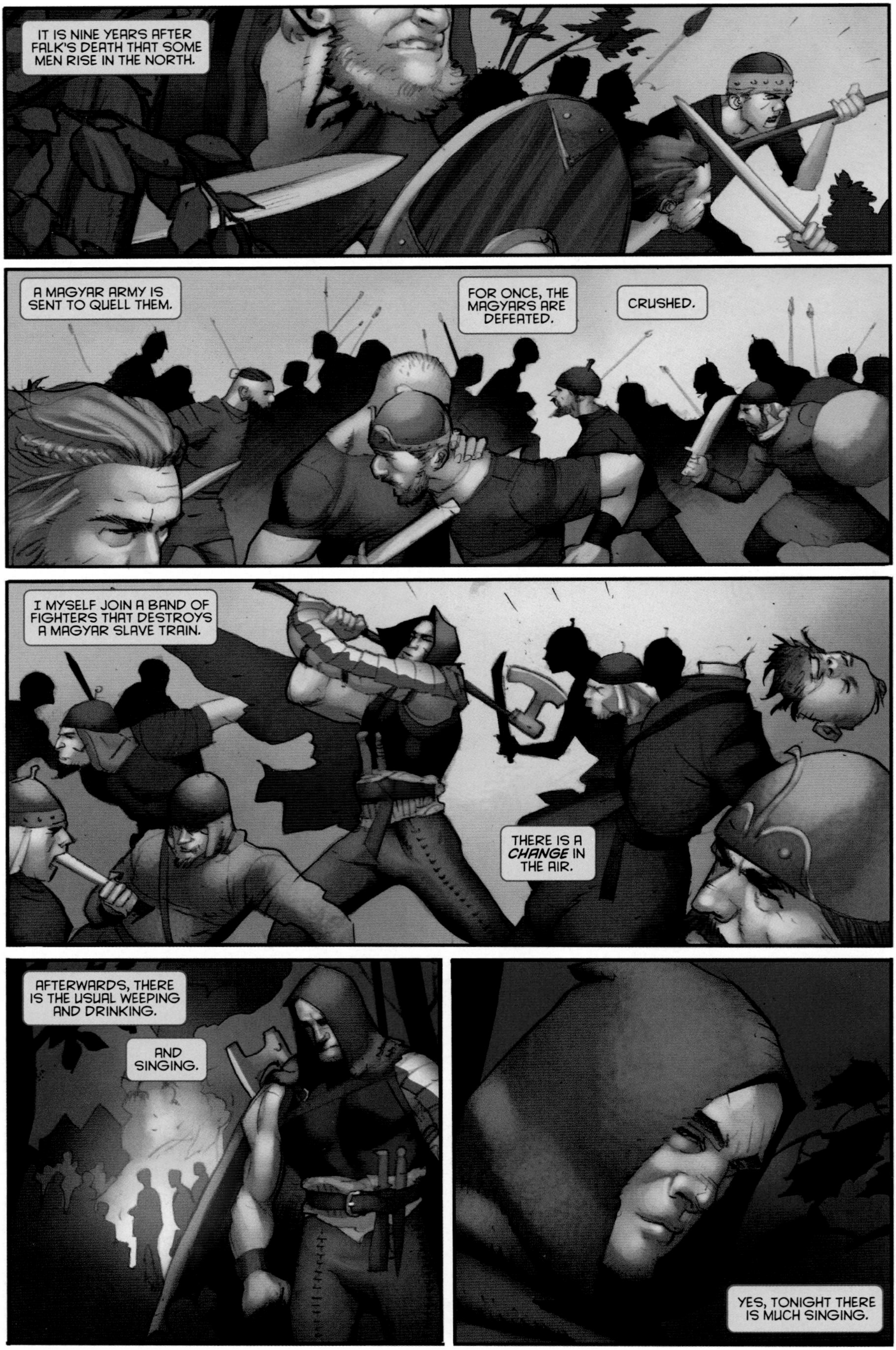
IT IS NINE YEARS AFTER FALK'S DEATH THAT SOME MEN RISE IN THE NORTH.
A MAGYAR ARMY IS SENT TO QUELL THEM.
FOR ONCE, THE MAGYARS ARE DEFEATED.
CRUSHED.
I MYSELF JOIN A BAND OF FIGHTERS THAT DESTROYS A MAGYAR SLAVE TRAIN.
THERE IS A *CHANGE* IN THE AIR.
AFTERWARDS, THERE IS THE USUAL WEEPING AND DRINKING.
AND SINGING.
YES, TONIGHT THERE IS MUCH SINGING.

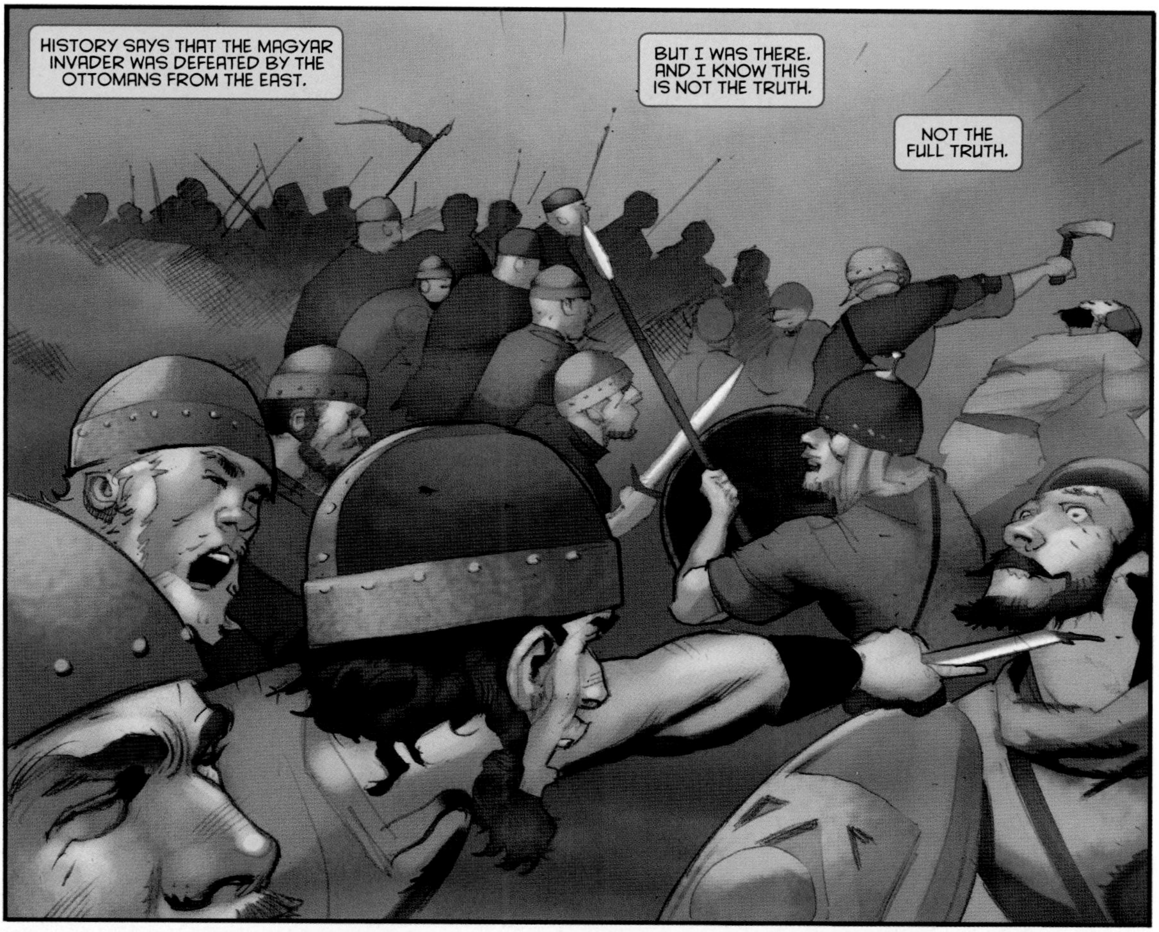
HISTORY SAYS THAT THE MAGYAR INVADER WAS DEFEATED BY THE OTTOMANS FROM THE EAST.
BUT I WAS THERE. AND I KNOW THIS IS NOT THE TRUTH.
NOT THE FULL TRUTH.

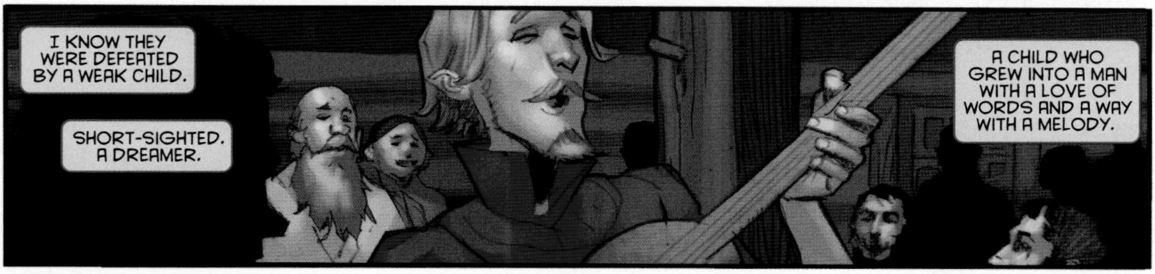
I KNOW THEY WERE DEFEATED BY A WEAK CHILD.
SHORT-SIGHTED. A DREAMER.
A CHILD WHO GREW INTO A MAN WITH A LOVE OF WORDS AND A WAY WITH A MELODY.

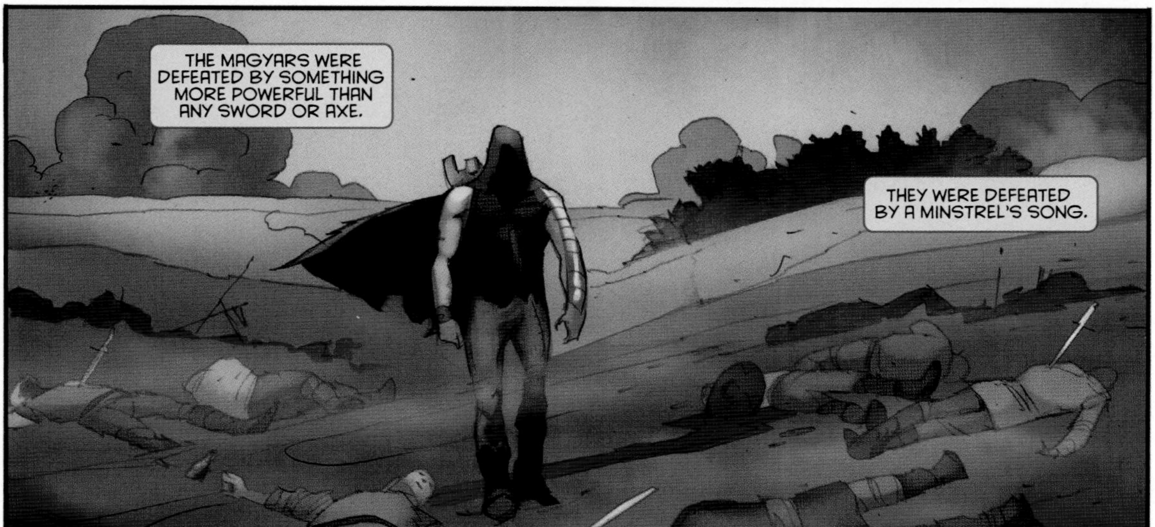
THE MAGYARS WERE DEFEATED BY SOMETHING MORE POWERFUL THAN ANY SWORD OR AXE.
THEY WERE DEFEATED BY A MINSTREL'S SONG.

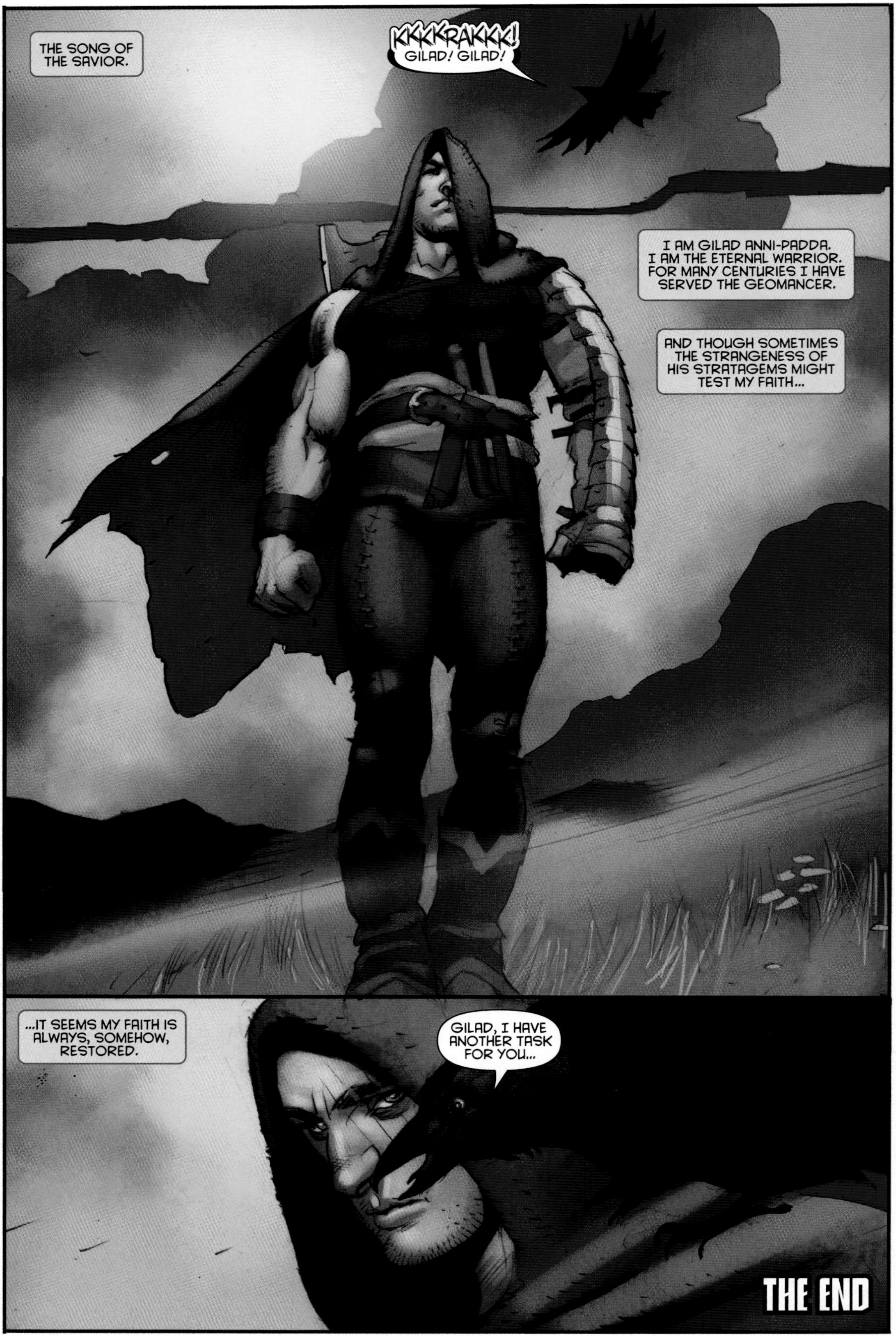
THE SONG OF THE SAVIOR.
KKKKRAKKK! GILAD! GILAD!
I AM GILAD ANNI-PADDA. I AM THE ETERNAL WARRIOR. FOR MANY CENTURIES I HAVE SERVED THE GEOMANCER.
AND THOUGH SOMETIMES THE STRANGENESS OF HIS STRATAGEMS MIGHT TEST MY FAITH...
...IT SEEMS MY FAITH IS ALWAYS, SOMEHOW, RESTORED.
GILAD, I HAVE ANOTHER TASK FOR YOU...
THE END

GALLERY

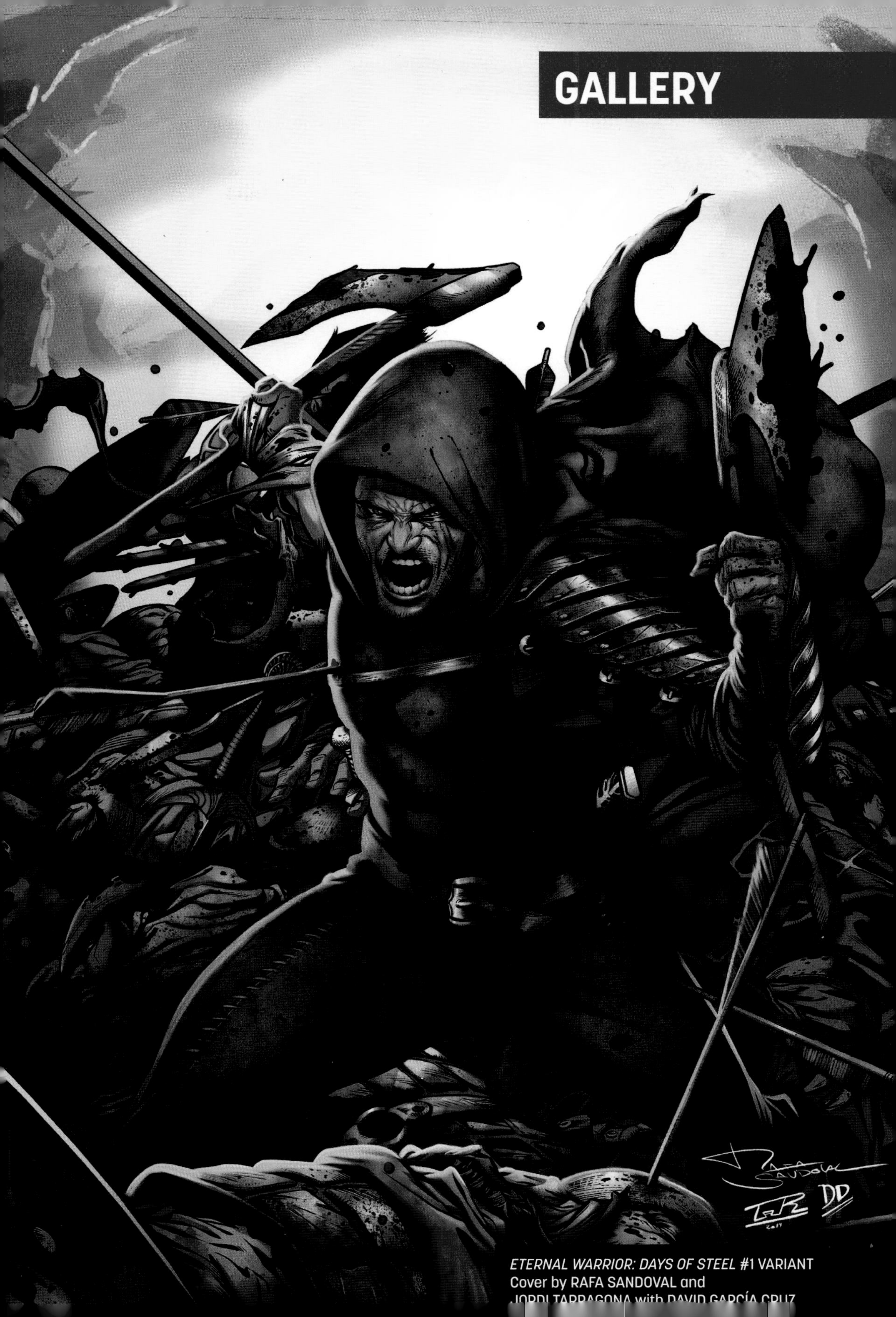

ETERNAL WARRIOR: DAYS OF STEEL #1 VARIANT
Cover by RAFA SANDOVAL and
JORDI TARRAGONA with DAVID GARCÍA CRUZ

ETERNAL WARRIOR: DAYS OF STEEL #1 VARIANT
Cover by CARY NORD (this page) with BRIAN REBER (facing)

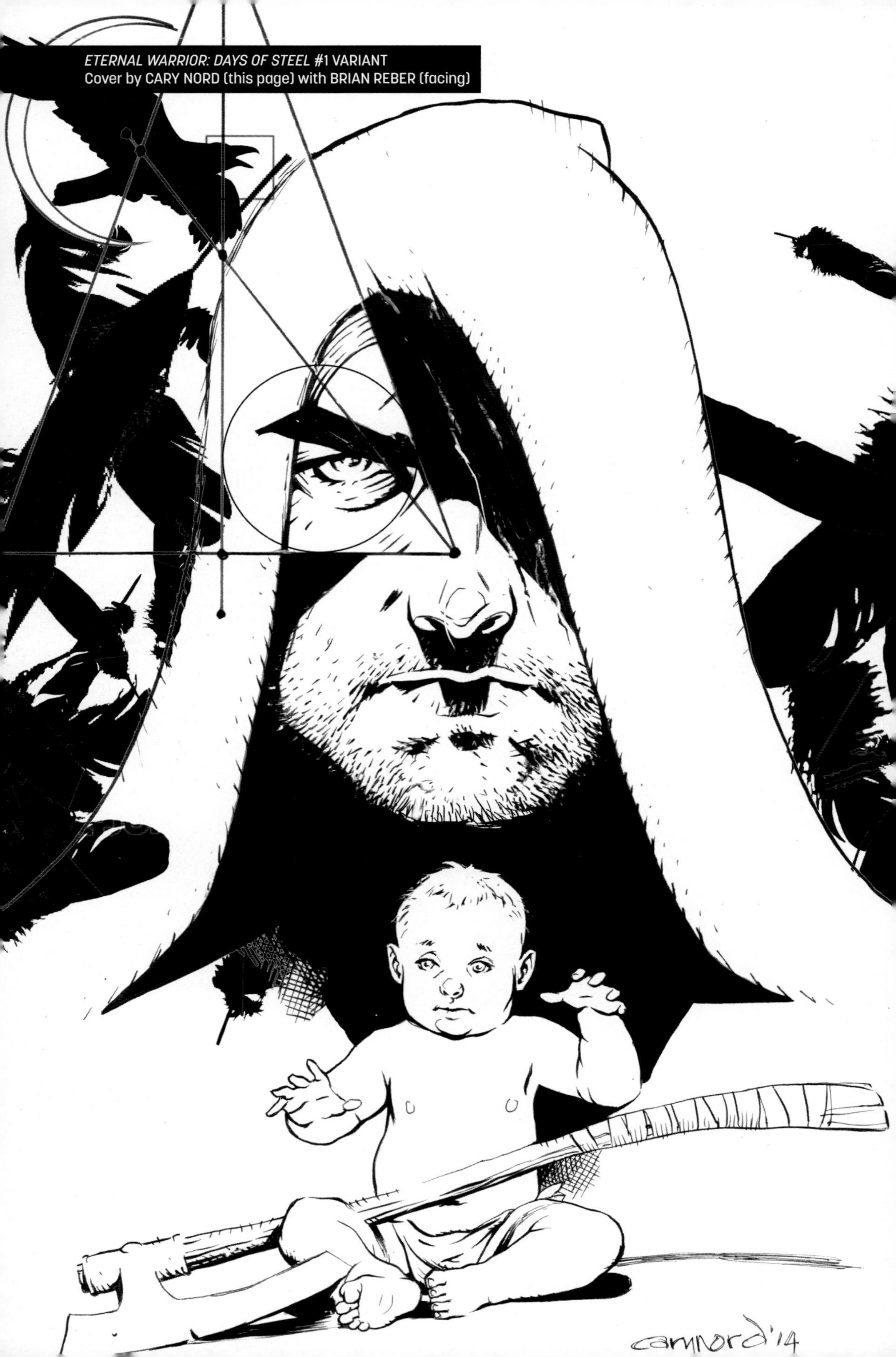
carynord'14

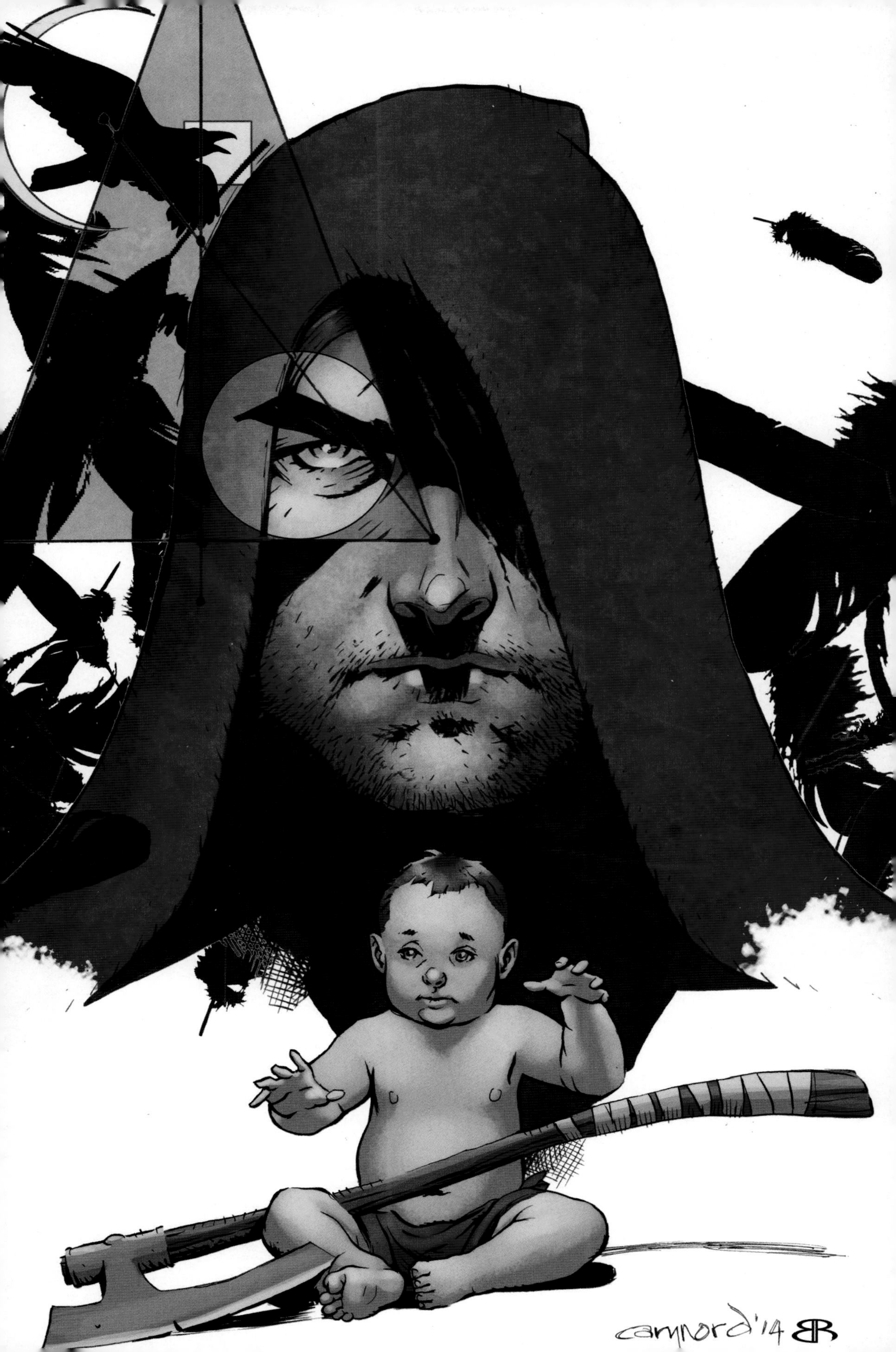
camnord'14

ETERNAL WARRIOR: DAYS OF STEEL #2 COVER
Art by LEWIS LAROSA

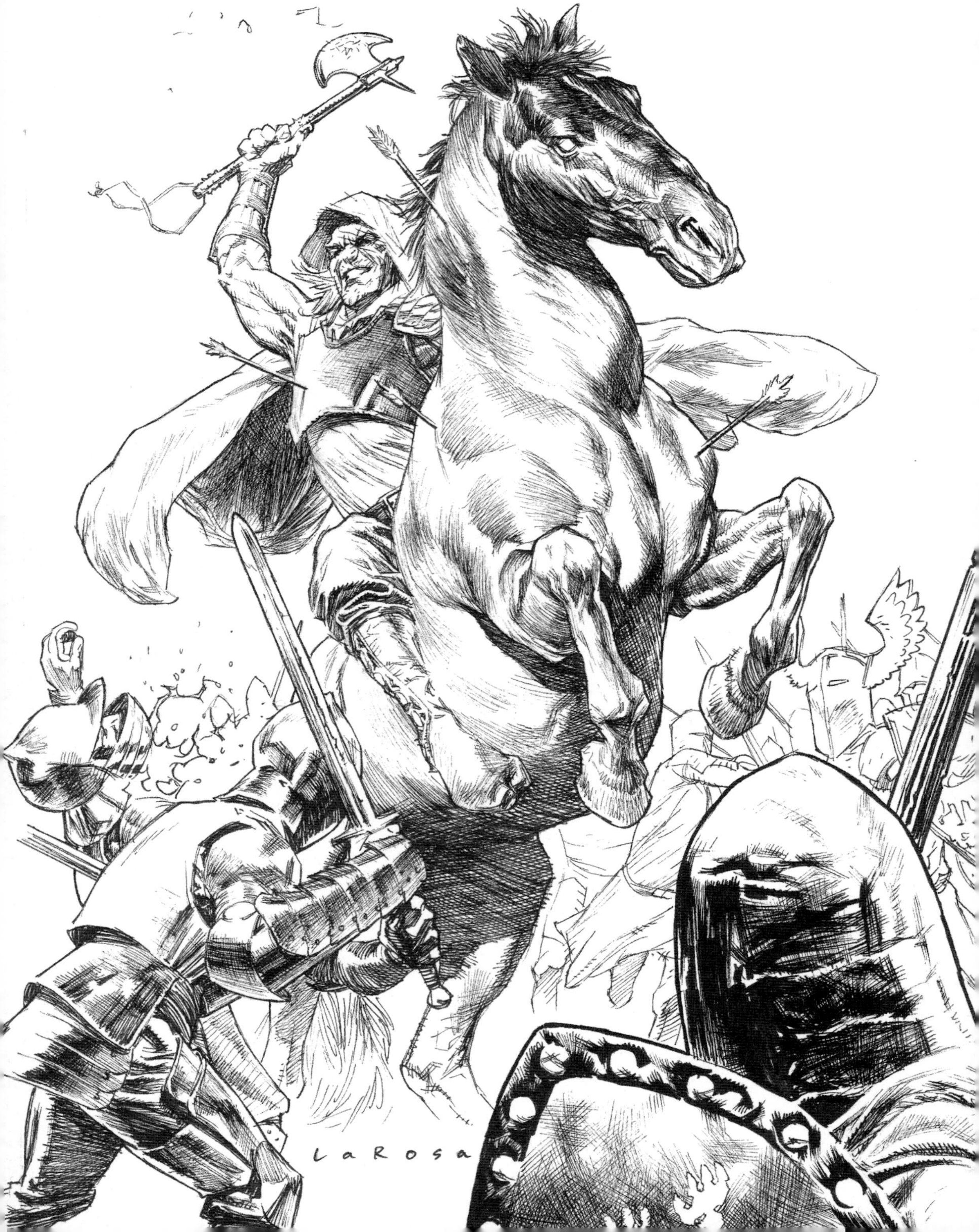
LaRosa

ETERNAL WARRIOR: DAYS OF STEEL #2 VARIANT
Cover by RAFAEL ALBUQUERQUE

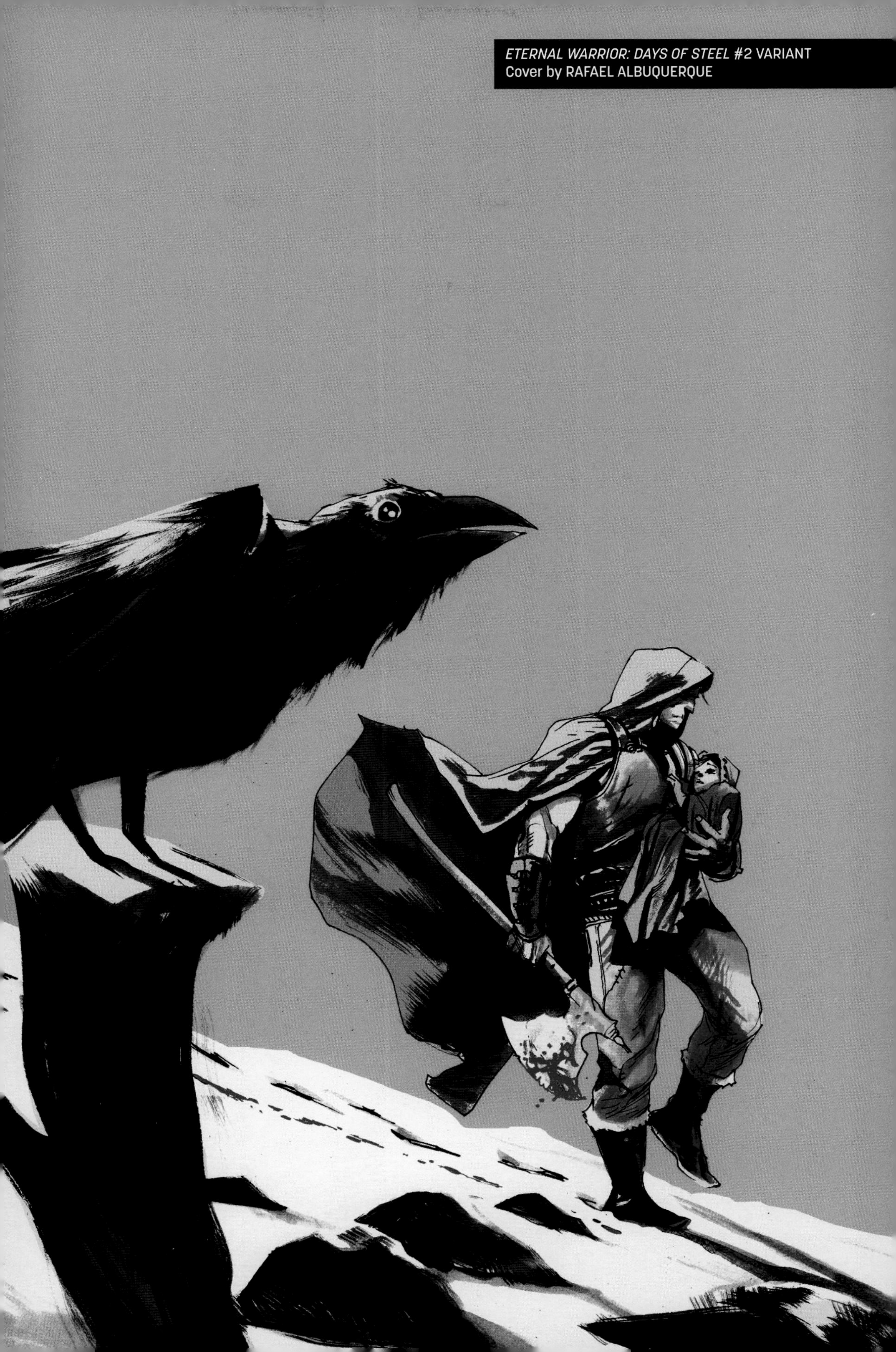

ETERNAL WARRIOR: DAYS OF STEEL #3 COVER
Art by TREVOR HAIRSINE

ETERNAL WARRIOR: DAYS OF STEEL #3 VARIANT
Cover by AL BARRIONUEVO (this page) with
DAVID BARON (facing)

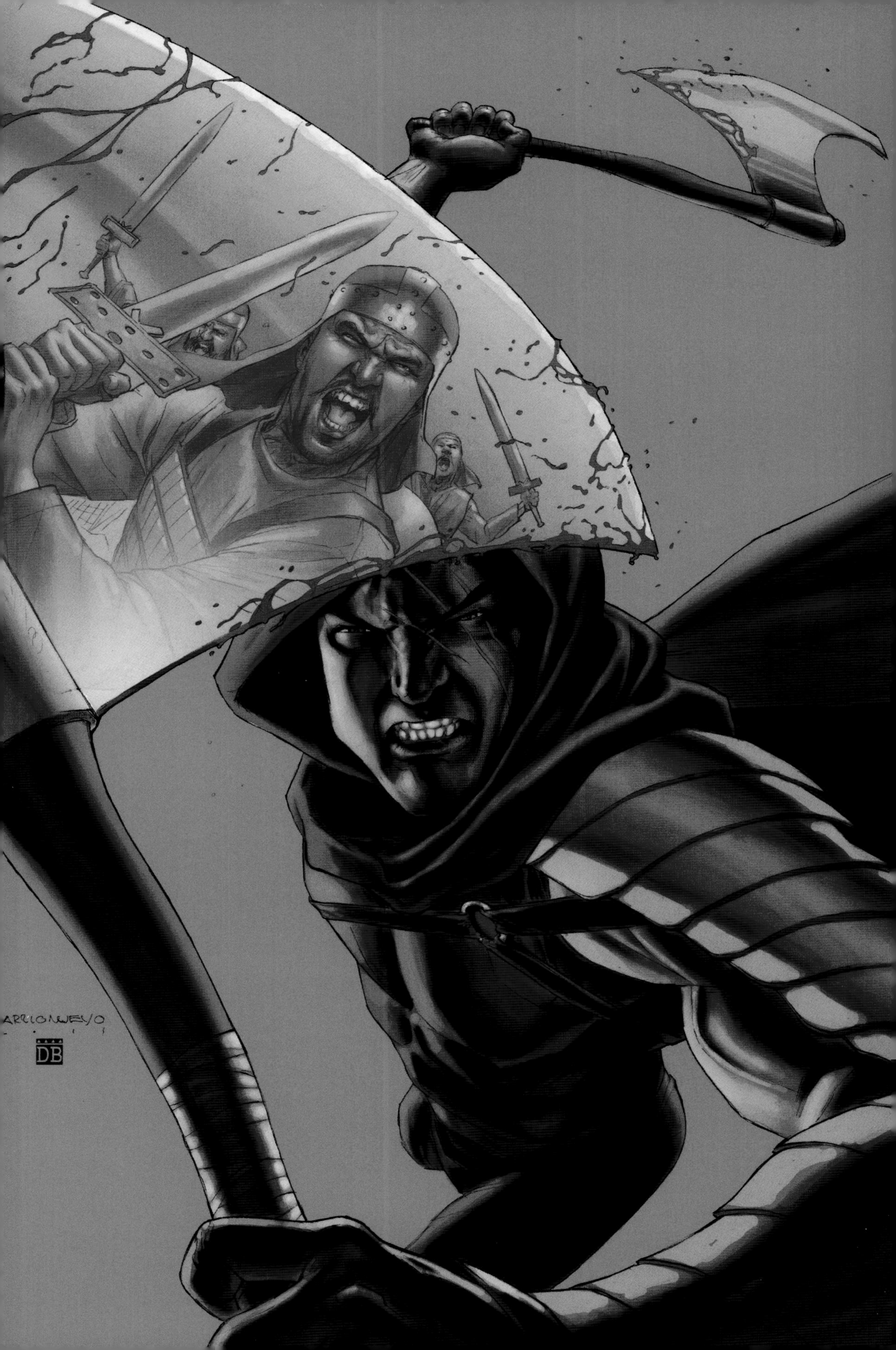

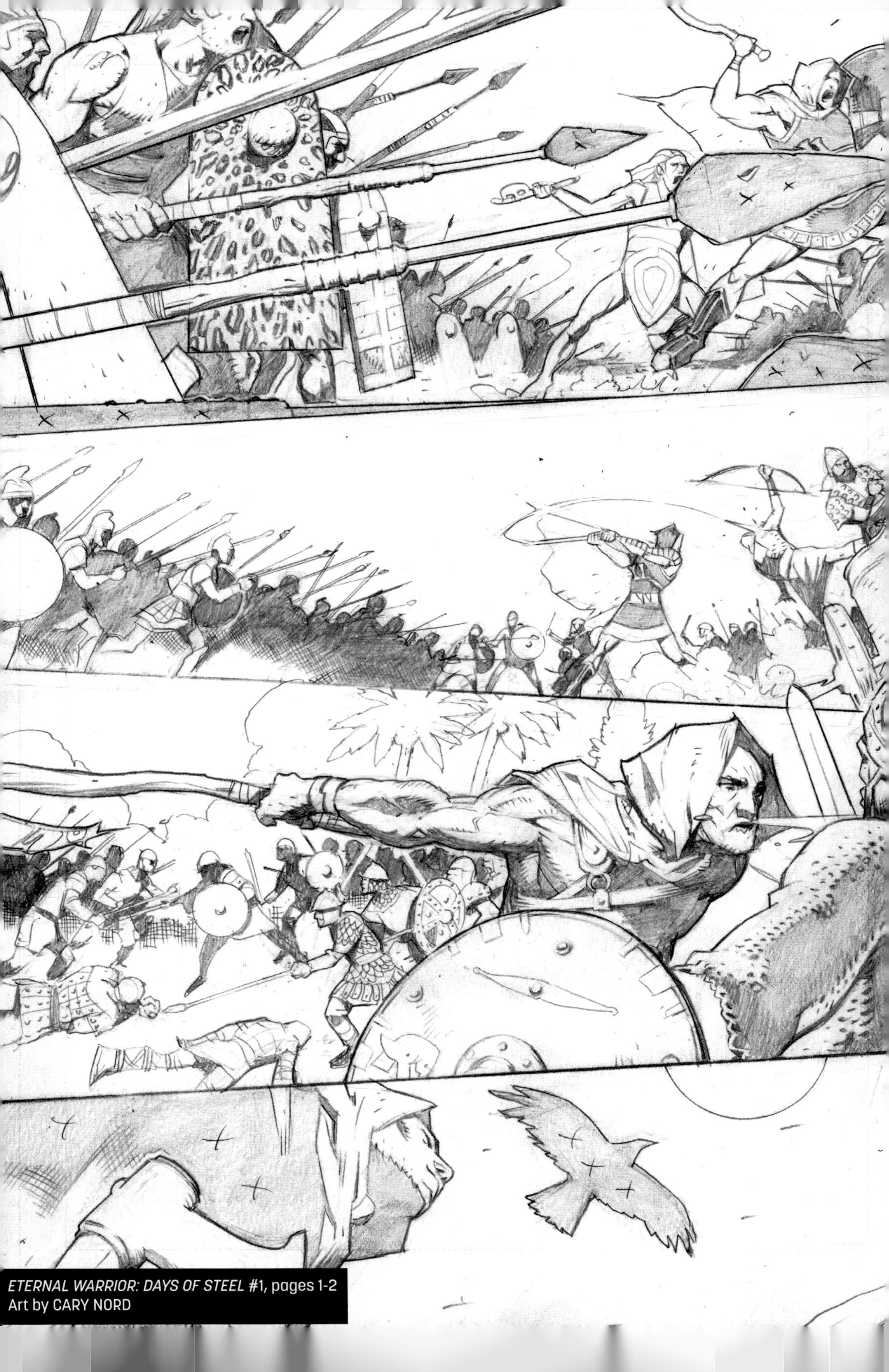

ETERNAL WARRIOR: DAYS OF STEEL #1, pages 1-2
Art by CARY NORD

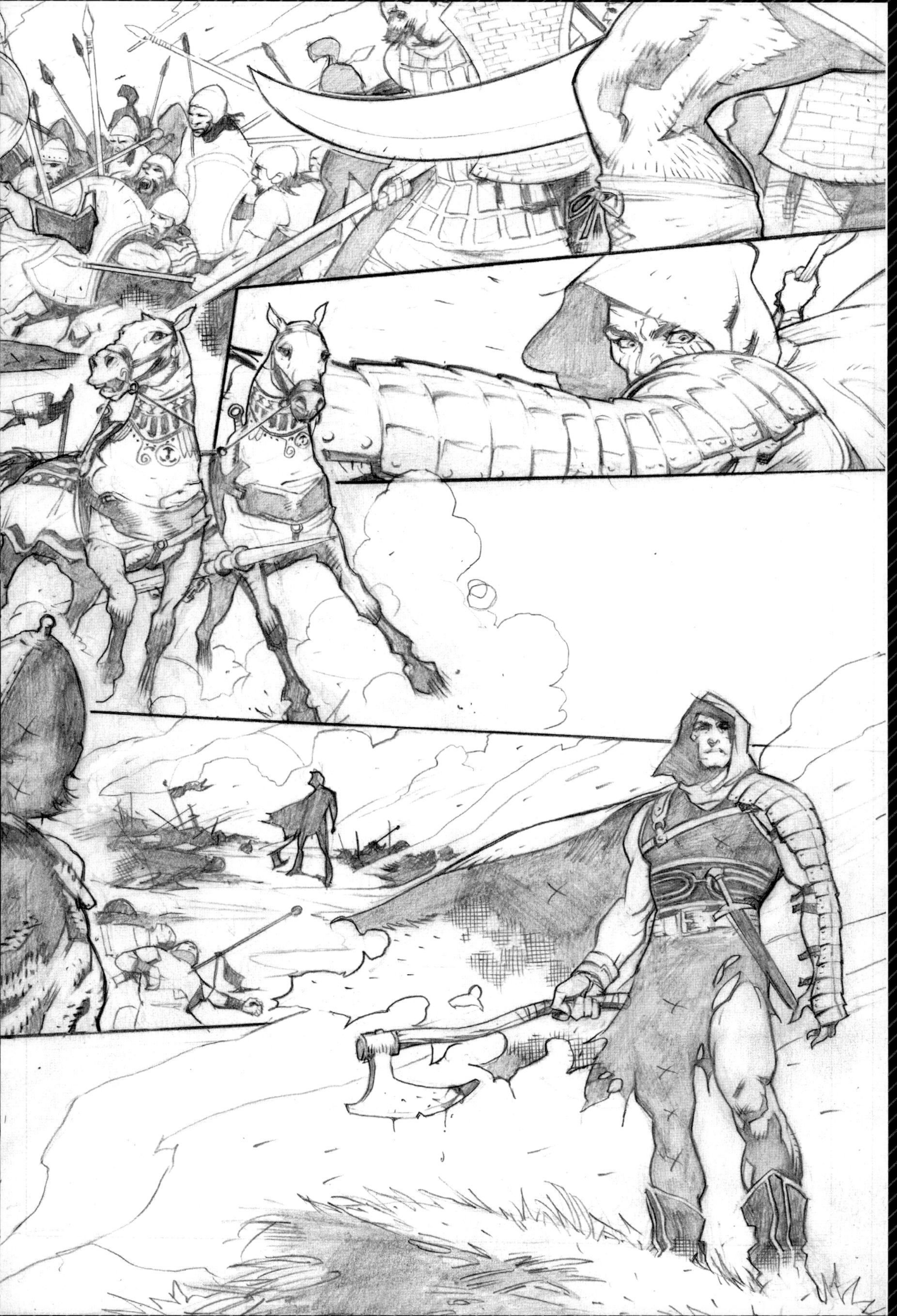

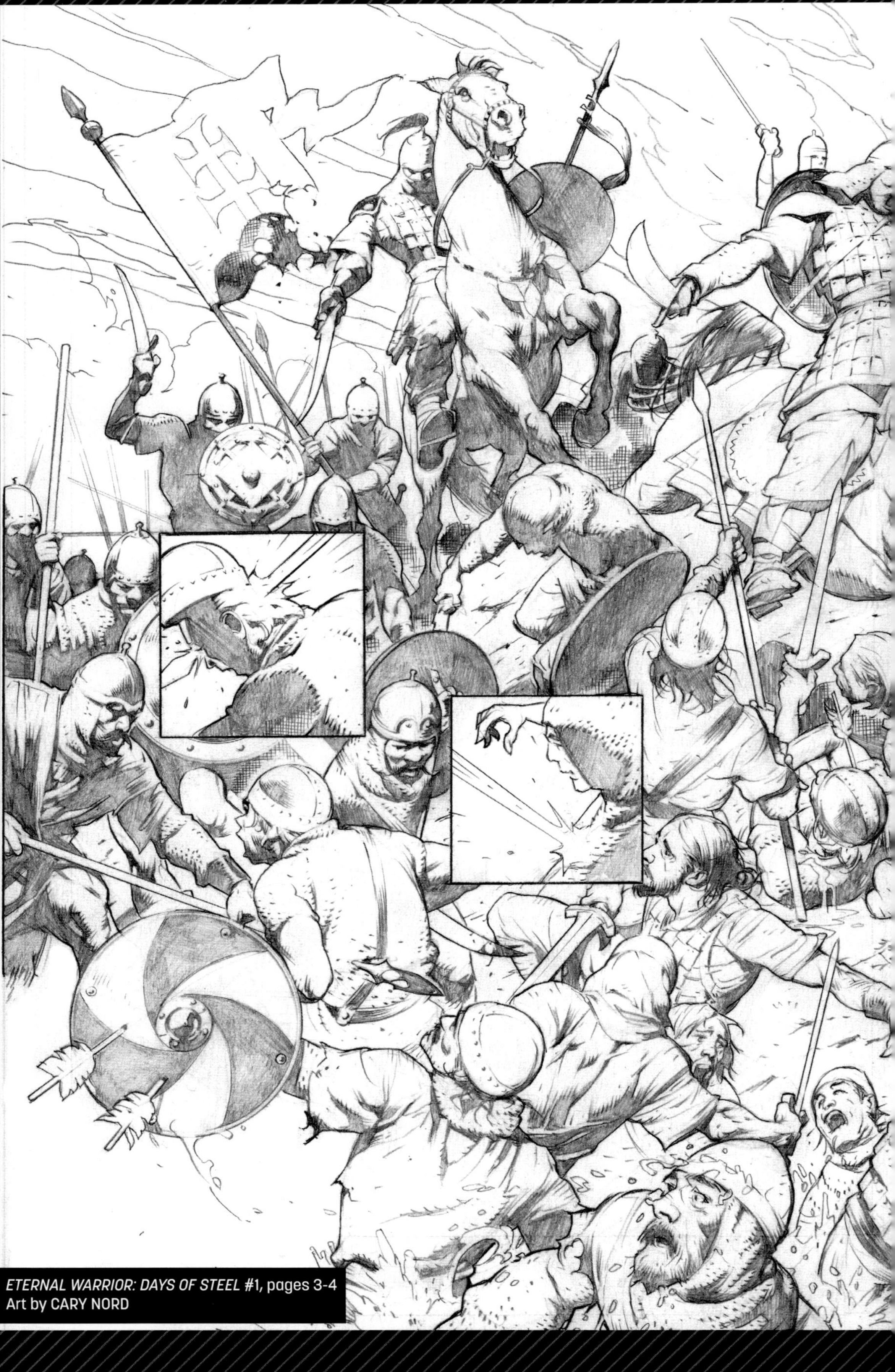

ETERNAL WARRIOR: DAYS OF STEEL #1, pages 3-4
Art by CARY NORD

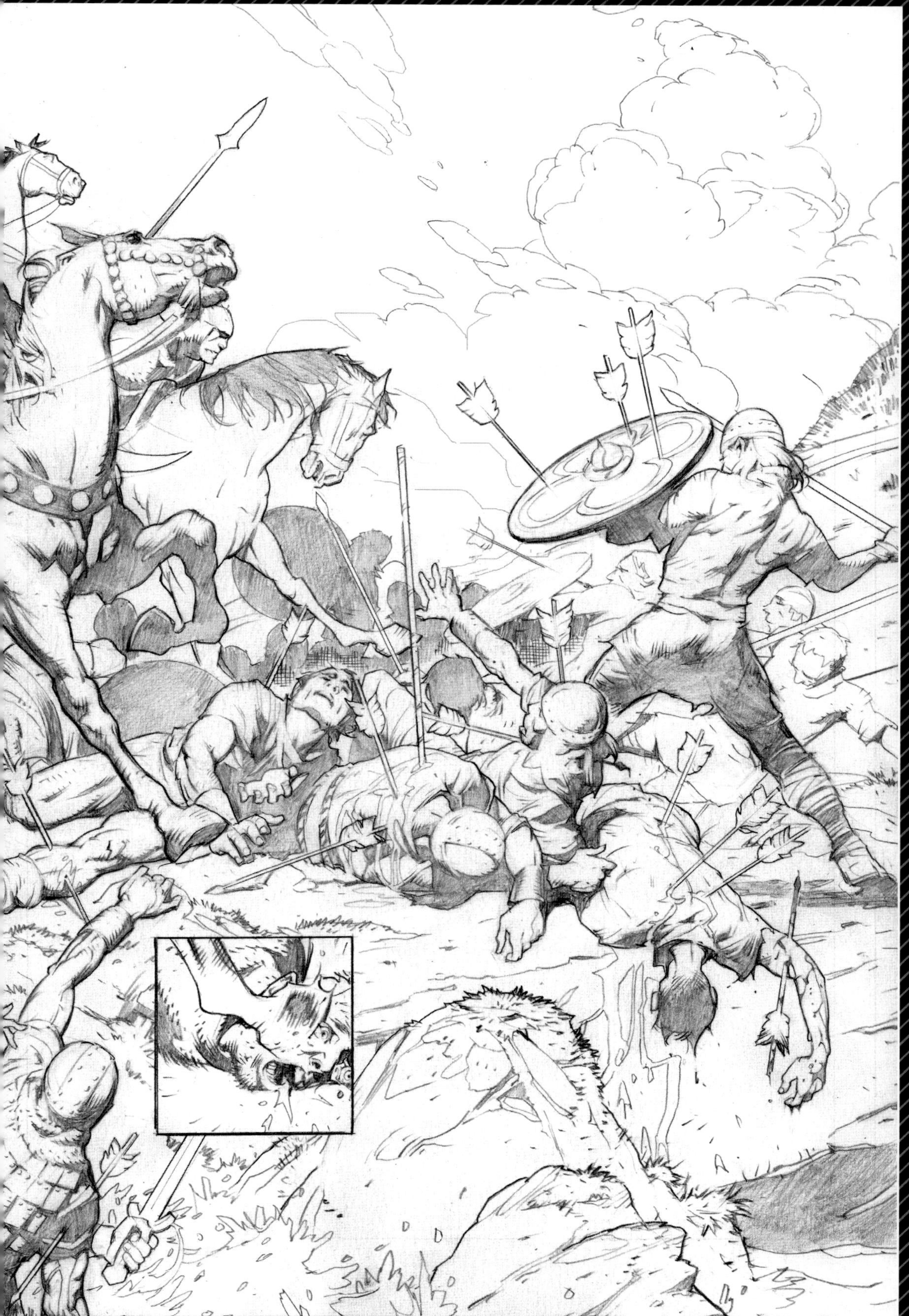

ETERNAL WARRIOR: DAYS OF STEEL #1, p. 5
Art by CARY NORD

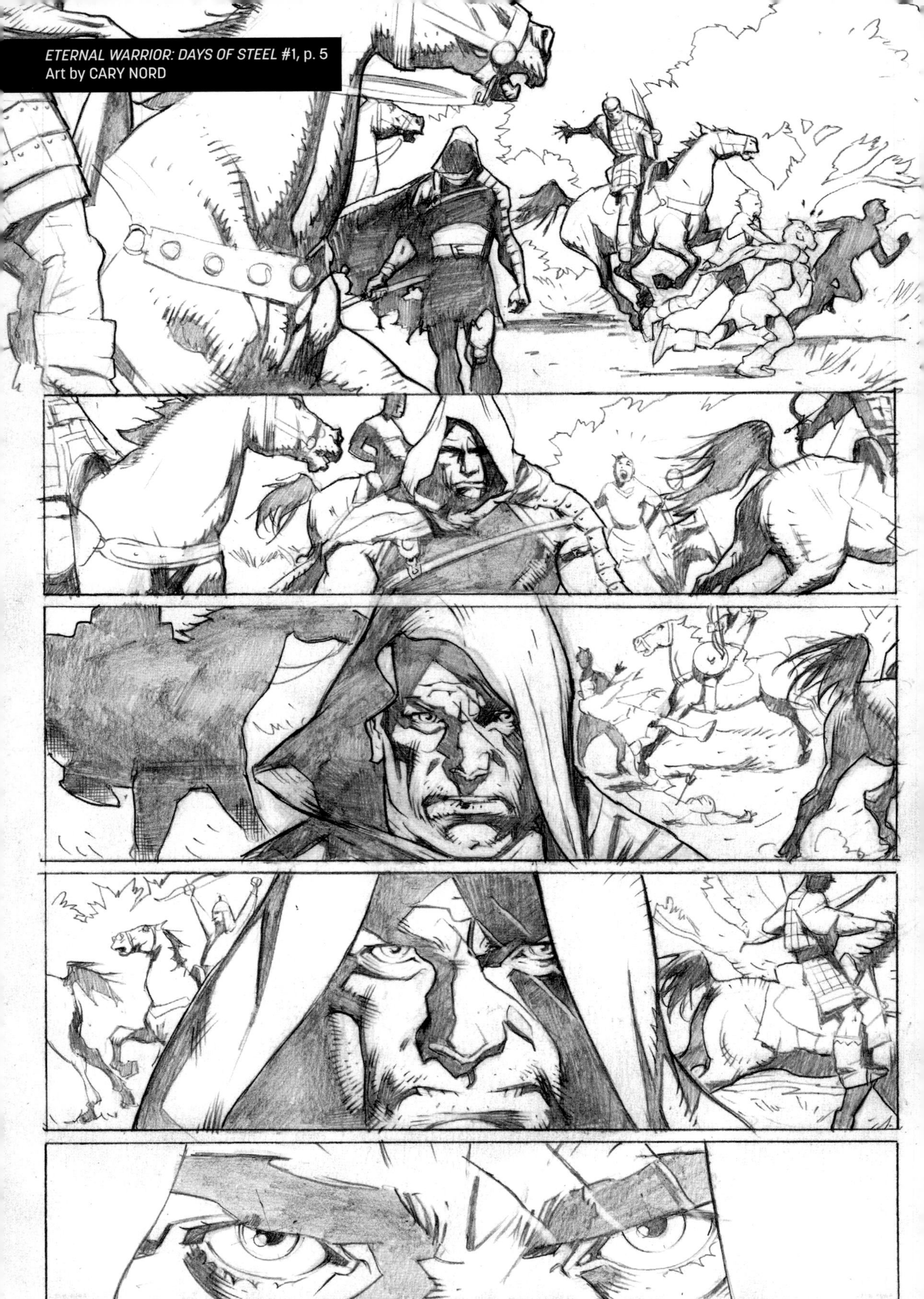

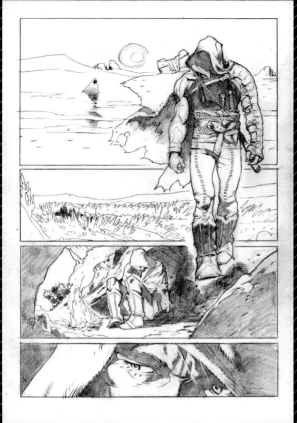

ETERNAL WARRIOR: DAYS OF STEEL #1, p. 8
Art by CARY NORD

ETERNAL WARRIOR: DAYS OF STEEL #1, p. 9
Art by CARY NORD

ETERNAL WARRIOR: DAYS OF STEEL #1, p. 20
Art by CARY NORD

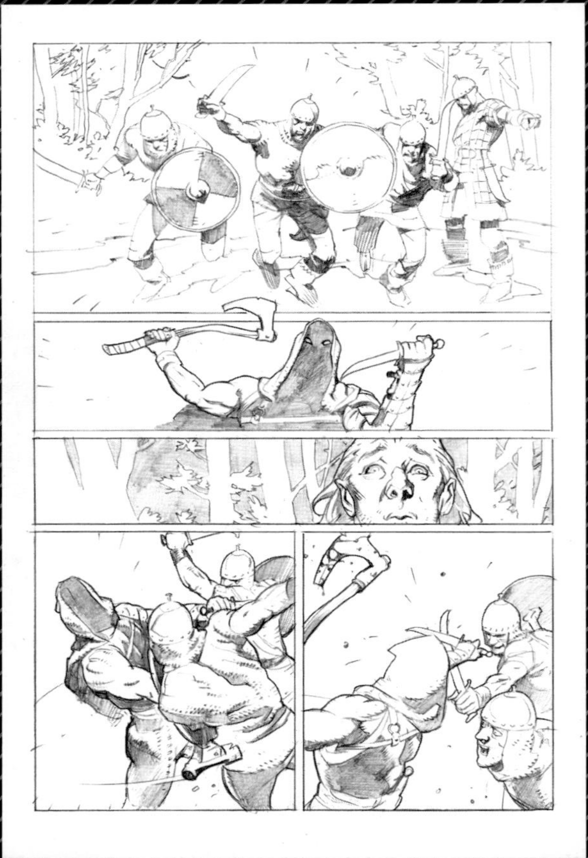

ETERNAL WARRIOR: DAYS OF STEEL #1, p. 21
Art by CARY NORD

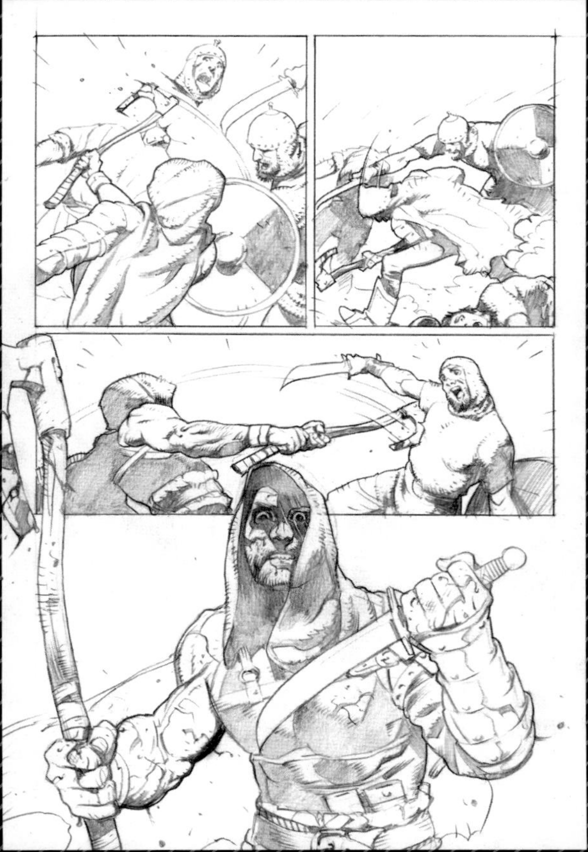

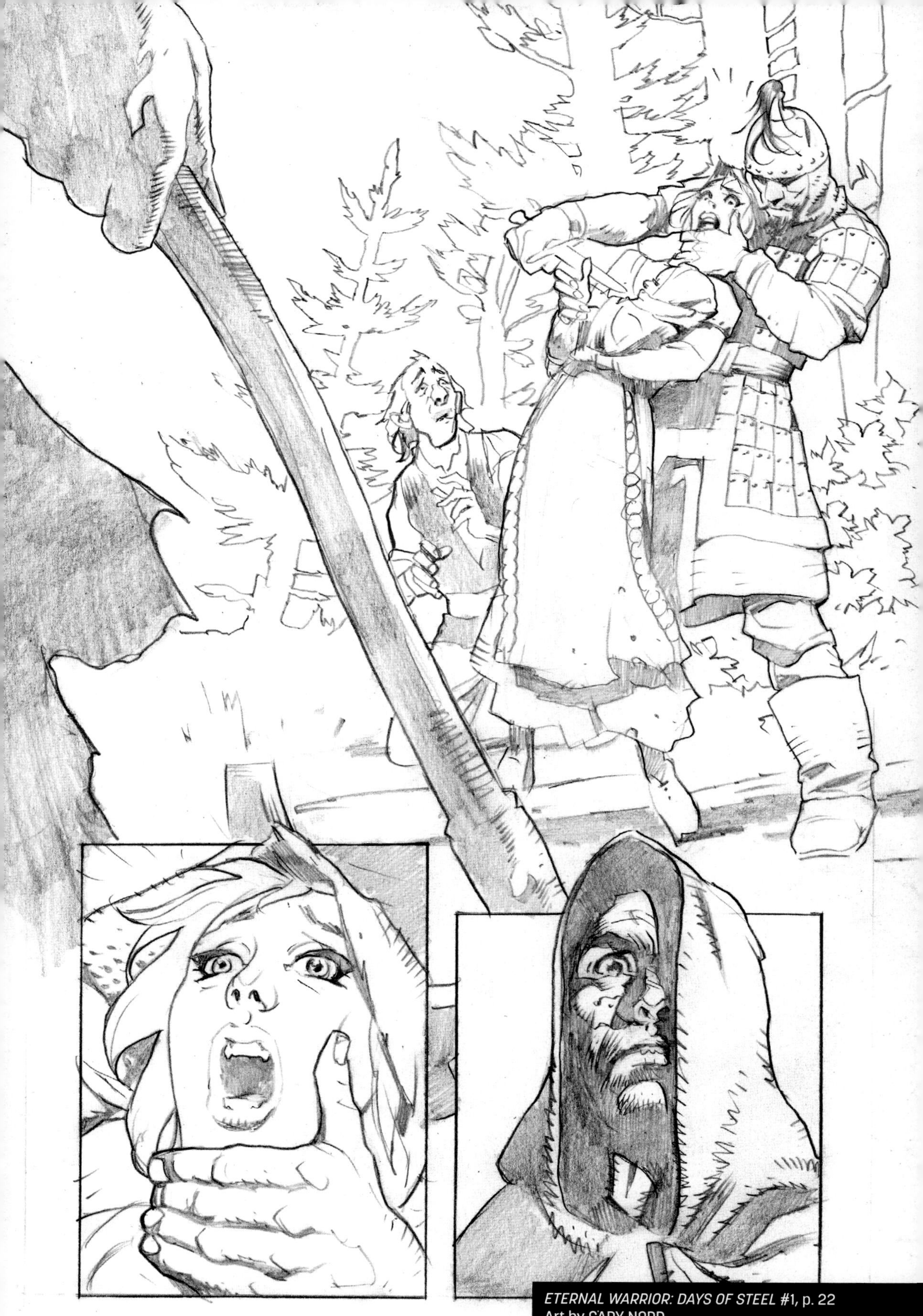

ETERNAL WARRIOR: DAYS OF STEEL #1, p. 22
Art by CARY NORD

ETERNAL WARRIOR: DAYS OF STEEL #2, p. 1
Art by CARY NORD

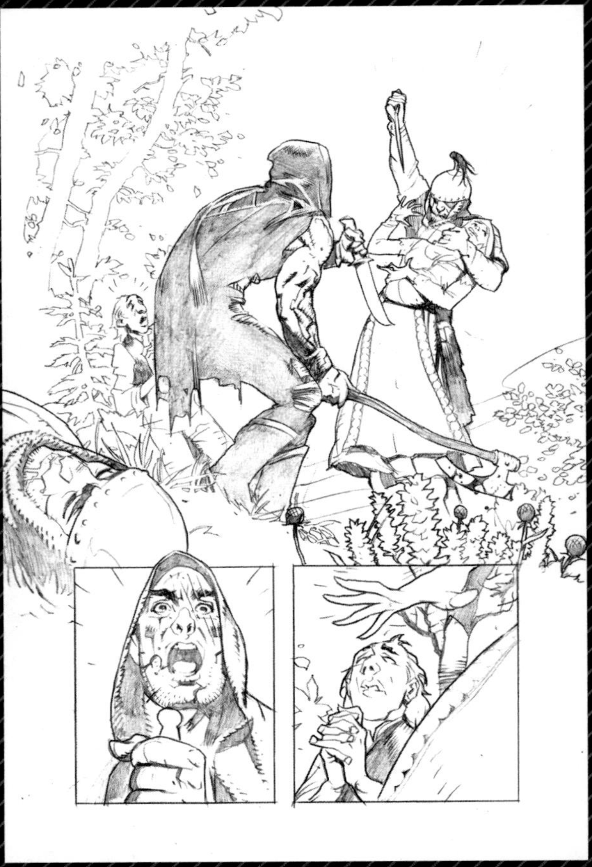

ETERNAL WARRIOR: DAYS OF STEEL #2, p. 2
Art by CARY NORD

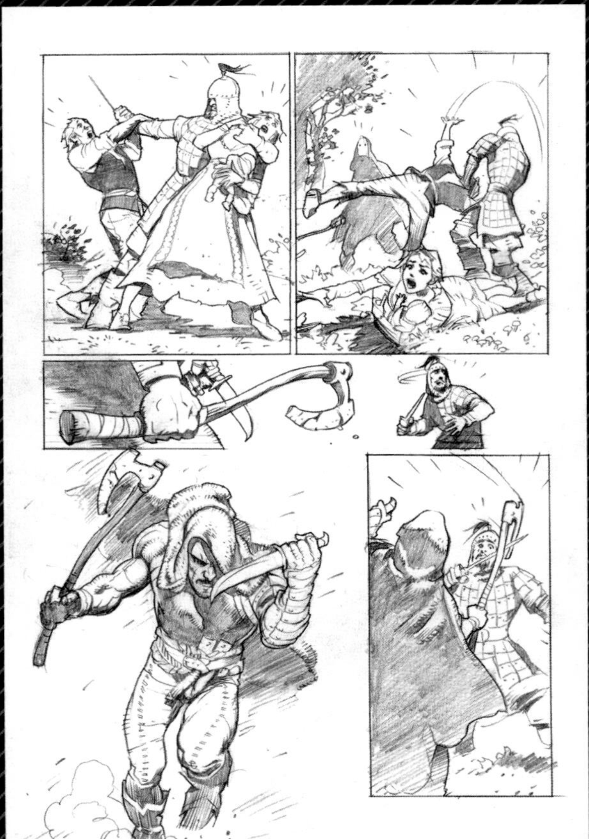

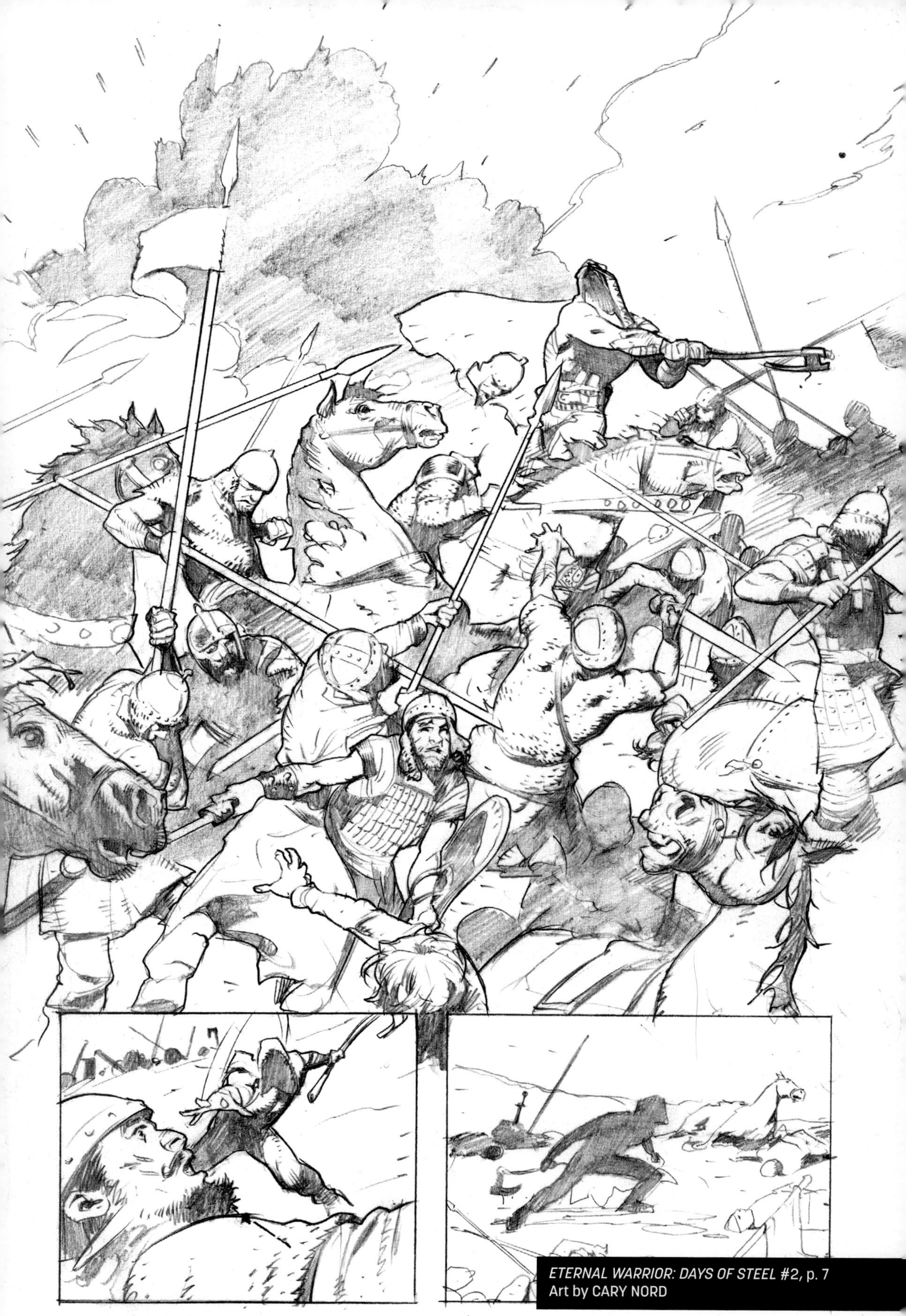

ETERNAL WARRIOR: DAYS OF STEEL #2, p. 7
Art by CARY NORD

ETERNAL WARRIOR: DAYS OF STEEL #2, p. 11
Art by CARY NORD

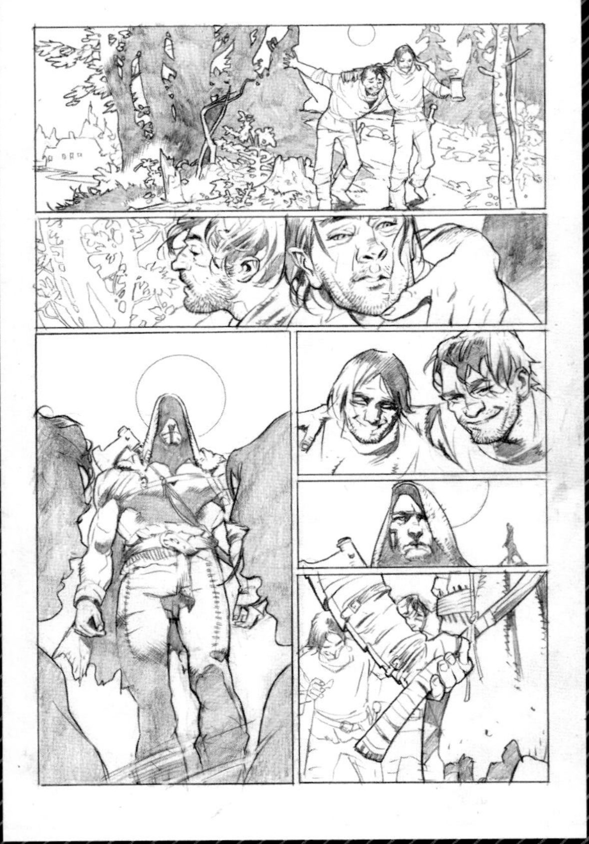

ETERNAL WARRIOR: DAYS OF STEEL #2, p. 12
Art by CARY NORD

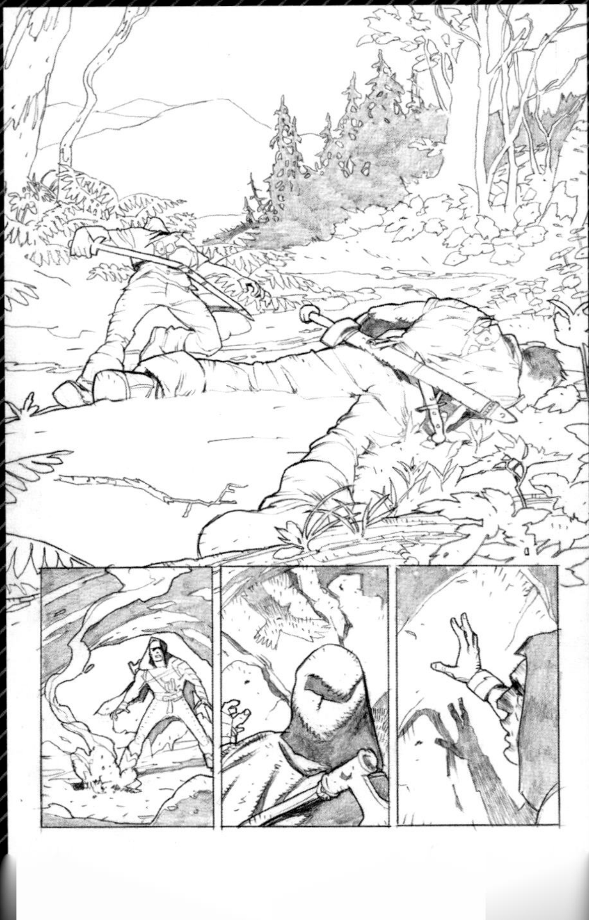

ETERNAL WARRIOR: DAYS OF STEEL #3, p. 3
Art by CARY NORD

ETERNAL WARRIOR: DAYS OF STEEL #3, p. 4
Art by CARY NORD

ETERNAL WARRIOR: DAYS OF STEEL #3, p. 7
Art by CARY NORD

ETERNAL WARRIOR: DAYS OF STEEL #3, p. 8
Art by CARY NORD

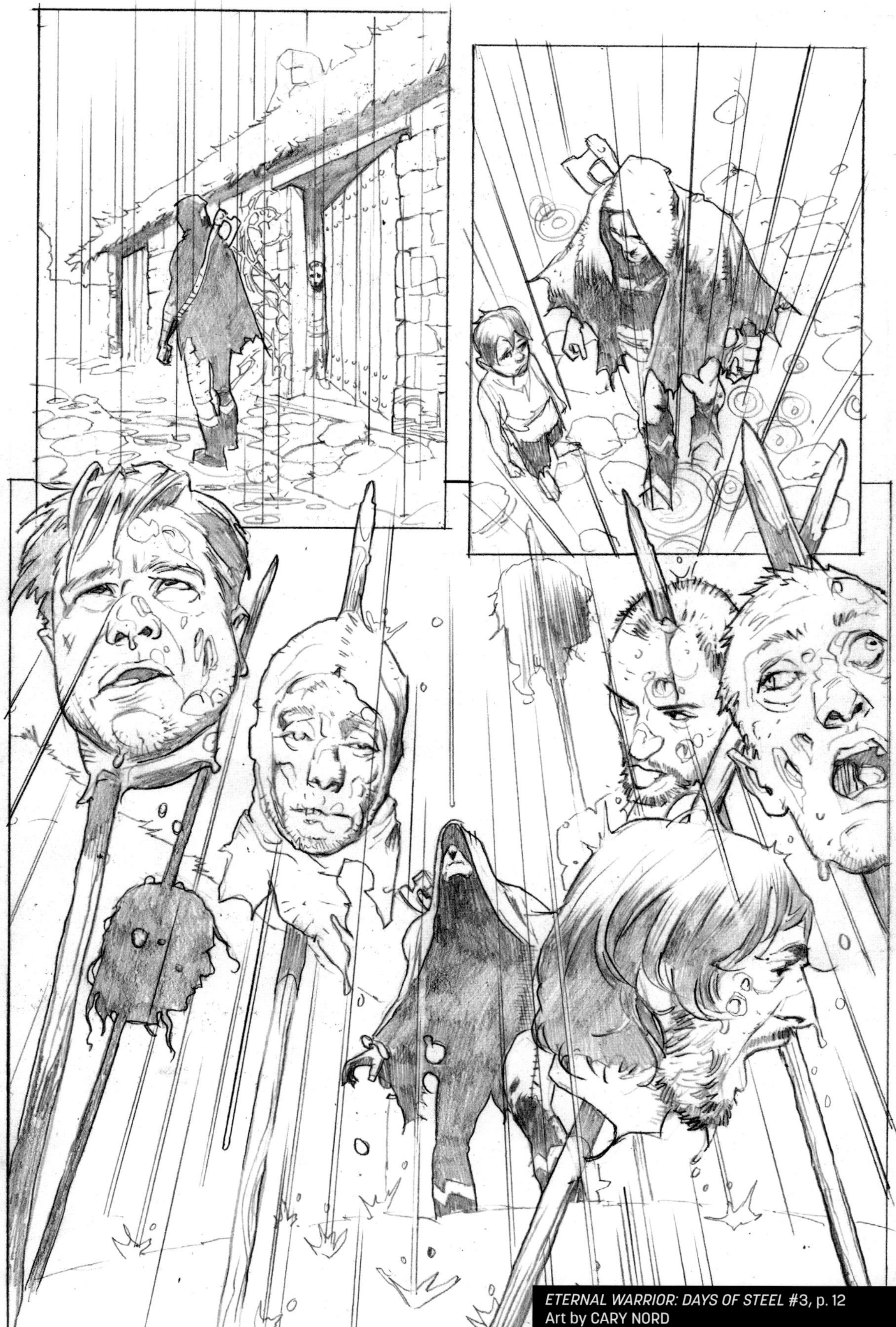

ETERNAL WARRIOR: DAYS OF STEEL #3, p. 12
Art by CARY NORD

EXPLORE THE VALIANT UNIVERSE

THE MICHELANGELO CODE
ARCHER & ARMSTRONG

SETTING THE WORLD ON FIRE
BLOODSHOT

OMEGA RISING
HARBINGER

BY THE SWORD
X-O MANOWAR

THE WORLD'S WORST SUPERHERO TEAM
QUANTUM AND WOODY!
KLANG.

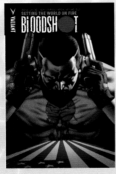

ARCHER & ARMSTRONG

Volume 1: The Michelangelo Code
ISBN: 9780979640988

Volume 2: Wrath of the Eternal Warrior
ISBN: 9781939346049

Volume 3: Far Faraway
ISBN: 9781939346148

Volume 4: Sect Civil War
ISBN: 9781939346254

Volume 5: Mission: Improbable
ISBN: 9781939346353

Volume 6: American Wasteland
ISBN: 9781939346421

Volume 7: The One Percent and Other Tales
ISBN: 9781939346537

ARMOR HUNTERS

Armor Hunters
ISBN: 9781939346452

Armor Hunters: Bloodshot
ISBN: 9781939346469

Armor Hunters: Harbinger
ISBN: 9781939346506

Unity Vol. 3: Armor Hunters
ISBN: 9781939346445

X-O Manowar Vol. 7: Armor Hunters
ISBN: 9781939346476

BLOODSHOT

Volume 1: Setting the World on Fire
ISBN: 9780979640964

Volume 2: The Rise and the Fall
ISBN: 9781939346032

Volume 3: Harbinger Wars
ISBN: 9781939346124

Volume 4: H.A.R.D. Corps
ISBN: 9781939346193

Volume 5: Get Some!
ISBN: 9781939346315

Volume 6: The Glitch and Other Tales
ISBN: 9781939346711

BLOODSHOT REBORN

Volume 1: Colorado
ISBN: 9781939346674

DEAD DROP

Dead Drop
ISBN: 9781939346858

THE DEATH-DEFYING DOCTOR MIRAGE

The Death-Defying Dr. Mirage
ISBN: 9781939346490

THE DELINQUENTS

The Delinquents
ISBN: 9781939346513

DIVINITY

DIVINITY
ISBN: 9781939346766

ETERNAL WARRIOR

Volume 1: Sword of the Wild
ISBN: 9781939346209

Volume 2: Eternal Emperor
ISBN: 9781939346292

Volume 3: Days of Steel
ISBN: 9781939346742

HARBINGER

Volume 1: Omega Rising
ISBN: 9780979640957

Volume 2: Renegades
ISBN: 9781939346025

Volume 3: Harbinger Wars
ISBN: 9781939346117

Volume 4: Perfect Day
ISBN: 9781939346155

Volume 5: Death of a Renegade
ISBN: 9781939346339

Volume 6: Omegas
ISBN: 9781939346384

HARBINGER WARS

Harbinger Wars
ISBN: 9781939346094

Bloodshot Vol. 3: Harbinger Wars
ISBN: 9781939346124

Harbinger Vol. 3: Harbinger Wars
ISBN: 9781939346117

EXPLORE THE VALIANT UNIVERSE

VALIANT
QUANTUM AND WOODY
BY PRIEST & BRIGHT
VOL 1: KLANG

VALIANT
BATTLE FOR NEW JAPAN
RAI

VALIANT
THE VALIANT

VALIANT
THE DEATH-DEFYING
DOCTOR MIRAGE

VALIANT
DIVINITY

IMPERIUM
インピリアム

/olume 1: Collecting Monsters
SBN: 9781939346759

NINJAK

/olume 1: Weaponeer
SBN: 9781939346667

QUANTUM AND WOODY!

/olume 1: The World's Worst Superhero Team
SBN: 9781939346186

/olume 2: In Security
SBN: 9781939346230

/olume 3: Crooked Pasts, Present Tense
SBN: 9781939346391

/olume 4: Quantum and Woody Must Die!
SBN: 9781939346629

QUANTUM AND WOODY BY PRIEST & BRIGHT

olume 1: Klang
SBN: 9781939346780

olume 2: Switch
SBN: 9781939346803

olume 3: And So...
SBN: 9781939346865

RAI

Volume 1: Welcome to New Japan
ISBN: 9781939346414

Volume 2: Battle for New Japan
ISBN: 9781939346612

Volume 3: The Orphan
ISBN: 9781939346841

SHADOWMAN

Volume 1: Birth Rites
ISBN: 9781939346001

Volume 2: Darque Reckoning
ISBN: 9781939346056

Volume 3: Deadside Blues
ISBN: 9781939346162

Volume 4: Fear, Blood, And Shadows
ISBN: 9781939346278

Volume 5: End Times
ISBN: 9781939346377

Ivar, Timewalker

Volume 1: Making History
ISBN: 9781939346636

UNITY

Volume 1: To Kill a King
ISBN: 9781939346261

Volume 2: Trapped by Webnet
ISBN: 9781939346346

Volume 3: Armor Hunters
ISBN: 9781939346445

UNITY (Continued)

Volume 4: The United
ISBN: 9781939346544

Volume 5: Homefront
ISBN: 9781939346797

THE VALIANT

The Valiant
ISBN: 9781939346605

VALIANT ZEROES AND ORIGINS

Valiant: Zeroes and Origins
ISBN: 9781939346582

X-O MANOWAR

Volume 1: By the Sword
ISBN: 9780979640940

Volume 2: Enter Ninjak
ISBN: 9780979640995

Volume 3: Planet Death
ISBN: 9781939346087

Volume 4: Homecoming
ISBN: 9781939346179

Volume 5: At War With Unity
ISBN: 9781939346247

Volume 6: Prelude to Armor Hunters
ISBN: 9781939346407

Volume 7: Armor Hunters
ISBN: 9781939346476

Volume 8: Enter: Armorines
ISBN: 9781939346551

Volume 9: Dead Hand
ISBN: 9781939346650

EXPLORE THE VALIANT UNIVERSE

VALIANT
HARBINGER
DELUXE EDITION 2

OMNIBUSES

Archer & Armstrong: The Complete Classic Omnibus
ISBN: 9781939346872
Collecting ARCHER & ARMSTRONG (1992) #0-26, ETERNAL WARRIOR (1992) #25 along with ARCHER & ARMSTRONG: THE FORMATION OF THE SECT.

Quantum and Woody: The Complete Classic Omnibus
ISBN: 9781939346360
Collecting QUANTUM AND WOODY (1997) #0, 1-21 and #32, THE GOAT: H.A.E.D.U.S. #1, and X-O MANOWAR (1996) #16

X-O Manowar Classic Omnibus Vol. 1
ISBN: 9781939346308
Collecting X-O MANOWAR (1992) #0-30, ARMORINES #0, X-O DATABASE #1, as well as material from SECRETS OF THE VALIANT UNIVERSE #1

DELUXE EDITIONS

Archer & Armstrong Deluxe Edition Book 1
ISBN: 9781939346223
Collecting ARCHER & ARMSTRONG #0-13

VALIANT
ARMOR HUNTERS
DELUXE EDITION

Armor Hunters Deluxe Edition
ISBN: 9781939346728
Collecting ARMOR HUNTERS #1-4, ARMOR HUNTERS: AFTERMATH #1, ARMOR HUNTERS: BLOODSHOT #1-3, ARMOR HUNTERS: HARBINGER #1-3, UNITY #8-11 and X-O MANOWAR #23-29

Bloodshot Deluxe Edition Book 1
ISBN: 9781939346216
Collecting BLOODSHOT #1-13

Harbinger Deluxe Edition Book 1
ISBN: 9781939346131
Collecting HARBINGER #0-14

Harbinger Deluxe Edition Book 2
ISBN: 9781939346773
Collecting HARBINGER #15-25, HARBINGER: OMEGAS #1-3, and HARBINGER: BLEEDING MONK #0

Harbinger Wars Deluxe Edition
ISBN: 9781939346322
Collecting HARBINGER WARS #1-4, HARBINGER #11-14, and BLOODSHOT #10-13

Quantum and Woody Deluxe Edition Book 1
ISBN: 9781939346681
Collecting QUANTUM AND WOODY #1-12 and QUANTUM AND WOODY: THE GOAT #0

Q2: The Return of Quantum and Woody Deluxe Edition
ISBN: 9781939346568
Collecting Q2: THE RETURN OF QUANTUM AND WOODY #1-5

VALIANT
JAMES ASMUS TOM FOWLER MING DOYLE
KANO JORDIE BELLAIRE DAVE LANPHEAR
QUANTUM AND WOODY!
DELUXE EDITION 1
MEH!

Shadowman Deluxe Edition Book 1
ISBN: 9781939346438
Collecting SHADOWMAN #0-10

Unity Deluxe Edition Book 1
ISBN: 9781939346575
Collecting UNITY #0-14

X-O Manowar Deluxe Edition Book 1
ISBN: 9781939346100
Collecting X-O MANOWAR #1-14

X-O Manowar Deluxe Edition Book 2
ISBN: 9781939346520
Collecting X-O MANOWAR #15-22, and UNITY #1-4

VALIANT
JIM SHOOTER | DAVID LAPHAM
CHILDREN OF THE EIGHTH DAY
HARBINGER
VALIANT MASTERS

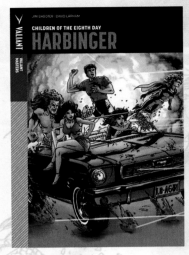

VALIANT MASTERS

Bloodshot Vol. 1 - Blood of the Machine
ISBN: 9780979640933

H.A.R.D. Corps Vol. 1 - Search and Destroy
ISBN: 9781939346285

Harbinger Vol. 1 - Children of the Eighth Day
ISBN: 9781939346483

Ninjak Vol. 1 - Black Water
ISBN: 9780979640971

Rai Vol. 1 - From Honor to Strength
ISBN: 9781939346070

Shadowman Vol. 1 - Spirits Within
ISBN: 9781939346018

VALIANT
KEVIN VANHOOK | DON PERLIN
BLOOD OF THE MACHINE
BLOODSHOT
VALIANT MASTERS

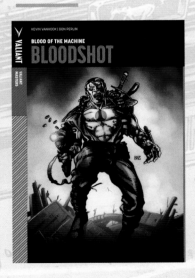

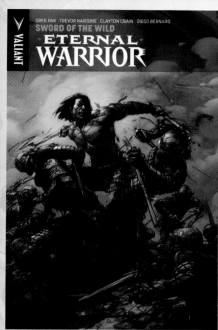

ETERNAL WARRIOR | READING ORDER

GREG PAK | TREVOR HAIRSINE | CLAYTON CRAIN | DIEGO BERNARD
SWORD OF THE WILD
ETERNAL WARRIOR
VALIANT

Eternal Warrior Vol. 1: Sword of the Wild

ARCHER & ARMSTRONG
GOOD LUCK WITH THAT!

Archer & Armstrong Vol. 2: Wrath of the Eternal Warrior **(OPTIONAL)**

TO KILL A KING
UNITY

Unity Vol. 1: To Kill a King **(OPTIONAL)**

ETERNAL EMPEROR
ETERNAL WARRIOR
VALIANT

Eternal Warrior Vol. 2: Eternal Emperor

"A stunning spectacle... Gorgeously rendered comic-book action..."
- The Onion/A.V. Club

"★★★★★... Action-packed, well-written, and overflowing with potential."
- Comic Vine

ETERNAL WARRIOR
DAYS OF STEEL
VALIANT

Eternal Warrior: Days of Steel

JEFF LEMIRE | MATT KINDT | PAOLO RIVERA | JOE RIVERA
THE VALIANT
VALIANT

The Valiant

ROBERT VENDITTI
ROBERT GILL
DOUG BRAITHWAITE
BOOK OF DEATH
VALIANT

Book of Death

Take up the blade and venture into battle with the Earth's undying protector!

From master storytellers
GREG PAK, PETER MILLIGAN, TREVOR HAIRSINE, CARY NORD, and more!

VALIANT®

THE VALIANT®

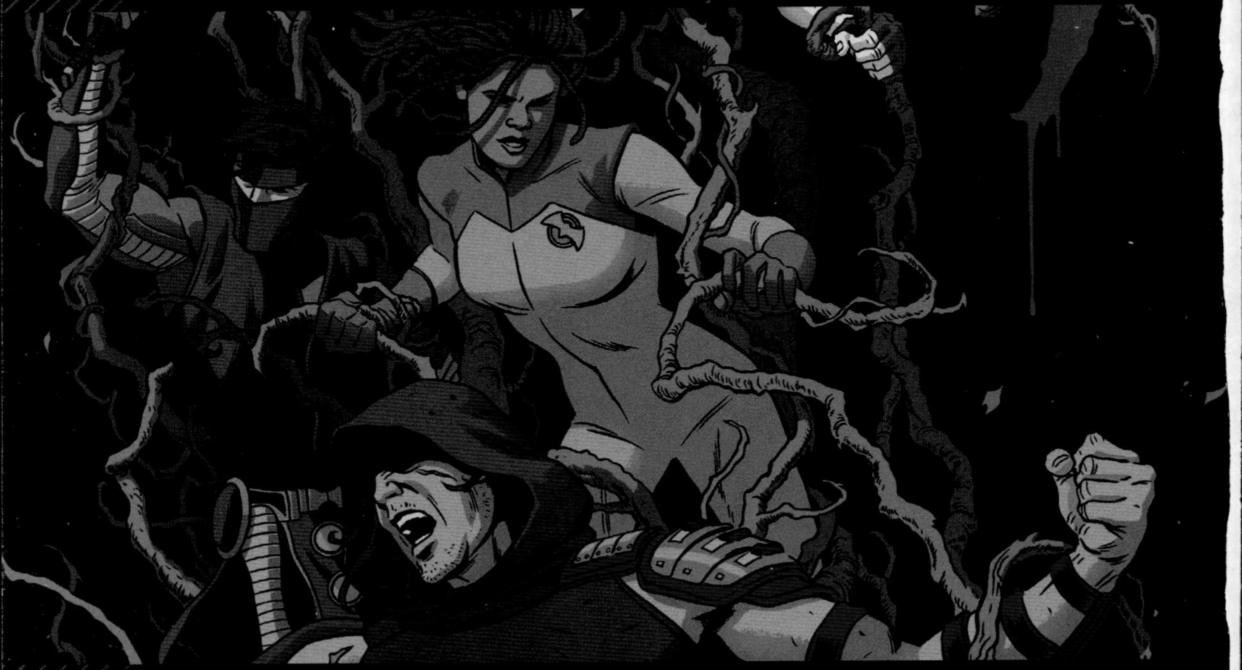

A BATTLE TEN MILLENNIA IN THE MAKING IS ABOUT TO BEGIN...

The Eternal Warrior has protected the Earth for more than 10,000 years. A master of countless weapons and long forgotten martial arts, he is guided by the Geomancers – those who speak for the Earth. During his long watch, the Eternal Warrior has failed three times. Each time, the Geomancer was killed... and a new dark age for humanity began. Each time, he was unable to stop The Immortal Enemy – a monstrous force of nature. A civilization killer. A horror that appears differently each time it arrives... and whose seemingly only purpose is to bring disorder and darkness to the world. Now, the time has come for The Immortal Enemy to return once more. But, this time, the Eternal Warrior will be ready. This time, he has a force greater than any single warrior. This time, he has... THE VALIANT.

Presenting the complete sold-out epic from New York Times best-selling writers Jeff Lemire (BLOODSHOT REBORN, *All-New Hawkeye*) & Matt Kindt (RAI, *Mind MGMT*) and Eisner Award-winning artist Paolo Rivera (*Daredevil*), discover why Valiant is one of the most critically acclaimed publishers in comics today with an all-star introduction to a visionary cast of heroes and villains from across the Valiant Universe.

Collecting THE VALIANT #1-4.

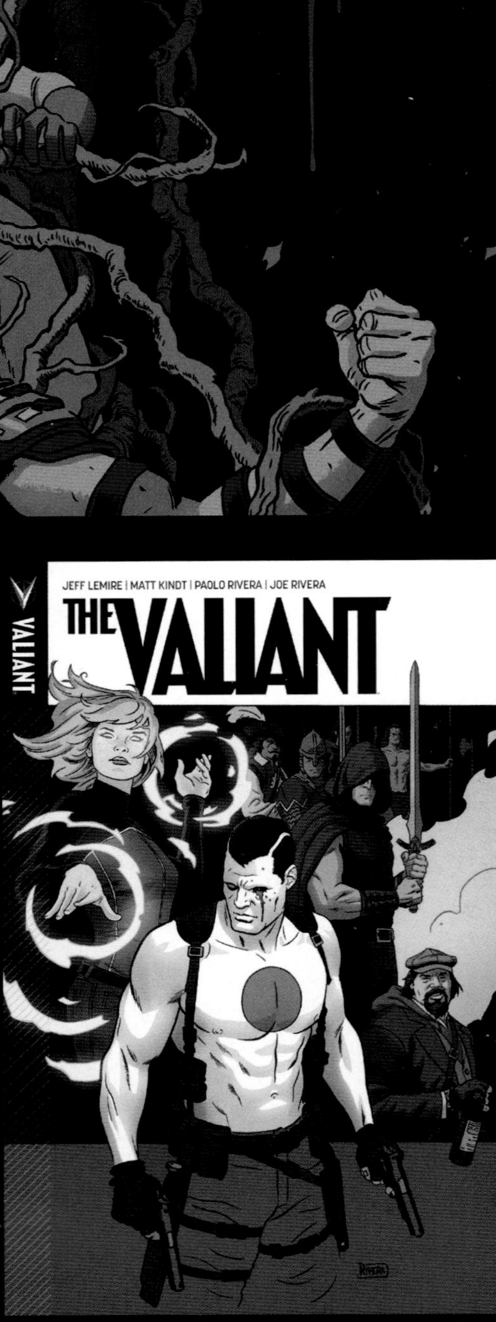

VALIANT
JEFF LEMIRE | MATT KINDT | PAOLO RIVERA | JOE RIVERA
THE VALIANT

TRADE PAPERBACK
ISBN: 978-1-939346-60-5